Strategies for Recognizing and Eliminating Gender Bias

for Healthcare Leaders

Grace E. Terrell, MD, MMM, CPE, FACP, FACPE

American Association for
PHYSICIAN
LEADERSHIP

AAPL books are available at special quantity discounts to use as premiums and sales
promotions, or for use in corporate training programs. For more information, please
write to Special Sales at journal@physicianleaders.org

This publication is designed to provide general information and is sold with the
understanding that neither the author nor the publisher is engaged in rendering legal,
accounting, ethical, or clinical advice. If legal or other expert advice is required, the
services of a competent professional person should be sought.

13   8 7 6 5 4 3 2 1

Copyedited, typeset, indexed, and printed in the United States of America

PUBLISHER
Nancy Collins

PRODUCTION MANAGER
Jennifer Weiss

DESIGN & LAYOUT
Carter Publishing Studio

COPYEDITOR
Patricia George

This book is dedicated to Robyn Lynn Terrell Garrison, who is well on her way on her own healthcare leadership journey.

ACKNOWLEDGMENTS

Over the course of my career, I have learned so much from so many that has contributed to my thinking in writing this book about gender issues in healthcare leadership that any attempt to comprehensively acknowledge them all is *a priori* fraught with peril. Nonetheless, some should be called out. Thank you to all the strong female healthcare leaders I have directly worked with over the course of my professional career, including Glenda Billings, Karen Cannon, Katie Henry, Anne Hill, Phillina Lai, Danielle Mahaffy, Kelly Reed, Jennifer Rucci, Elisabeth Stambaugh, Cindy Susienka, and Eldora Terrell. I am grateful for the life lessons taught to me by my mother, Anna Emerson, aunts Becky Pollock, Ruth DeCroce, and Jean Ludington, sisters Melody Emerson and Pam Zich, daughters Katy Garrison and Robyn Naron, not to mention scores of cousins, in-laws, grandparents, and a granddaughter. I am honored that four women healthcare leaders whom I greatly admire, permitted me to interview them and publish their stories in this book. Jennifer Bepple, Katie Henry, Sharon McLaughlin, and Mary Jo Williamson: your willingness to share your experiences with those who read this book is a priceless gift to me. Thank you, Nancy Collins and the AAPL team for having confidence to now publish a fourth book with me. Finally, I must acknowledge the profound influence the late Weldon Thornton has had on my life, including introducing me to writing of Carl Jung in a yearlong course on the Great Books at UNC Chapel Hill forty two years ago. For my ten classmates back then who are re-exploring these books 40+ years later with me, just "Wow!"

TABLE OF CONTENTS

ABOUT THE AUTHOR

Grace E. Terrell, MD, MMM, is a national thought leader in healthcare innovation and delivery system reform, and a serial entrepreneur in population health outcomes driven through patient care model design, clinical and information integration, and value-based payment models. She is also a practicing general internist. She is chief product officer of IKS Health, an international healthcare company designing simple solutions for the complex problems in healthcare. She has served as CEO of several companies, including Eventus WholeHealth, LLC, a company focused on providing holistic care to medically vulnerable adults, and Cornerstone Healthcare, one of the first medical groups to make the "move to value" by lowering the cost of care and improving its quality for the sickest, most vulnerable patients. She is the founding CEO of CHESS, a population health management company, and the former CEO of Envision Genomics, a company focused on the integration of precision medicine technology into population health frameworks for patients with rare and undiagnosed diseases.

Dr. Terrell has served as vice chair of the U.S. Department of Health and Human Services' Physician-Focused Payment Model Technical Advisory Committee, the chair of the board of the AMGA, is a founding member of the Oliver Wyman Health Innovation Center, and the co-author of *Value-Based Care and Payment Models* and *Reframing Contemporary Physician Leadership: We Started as Heroes.*

She is currently executive in residence at Duke University School of Medicine's MMCi Program, a member of the board of trustees for Guilford College, and a senior advisor for Oliver Wyman management consulting firm.

INTRODUCTION

Why is it that I have been the only woman in the board room so many times in my 30-year career? I have held four chief executive officer roles, served as chair of the board of two organizations, and participated in leadership roles in federal healthcare policy, consulting, and healthcare industry innovation. In most of those roles, the majority of people in the other leadership positions were men. In the third decade of the 21st century the fact that I am a woman in the C-suite and board room should not be remarkable, but unfortunately it frequently is.

I wrote this book to explore why so few women have had the experience of holding executive leadership positions and, I hope, to provide some insight into how we can change the persistent problem of gender inequality in healthcare leadership. I have drawn on my personal experiences, but also those of other women healthcare leaders, four whom I profile in the book.

Looking back in time at women in leadership roles in powerful patriarchal societies who were exceptions in their historical contexts, I wanted to identify traits and behaviors that explain their exceptionalism, but I also attempted to defy the constraints that make exceptionalism the only pathway to female empowerment. Although I have drawn liberally from the wells of both feminist historians and traditional critical thinkers, I have also explored the topic through the quantitative social research underway currently, whose post-pandemic iteration is demonstrating the damage gender discrimination plays in health inequity worldwide.

Many readers may find this to be a strange book because of its juxtaposition of personal anecdotes, copiously footnoted data points, feminist Jungian psychology, and extensive quotations from all over the intellectual landscape. Gender inequality is one of humankind's most wicked problems to solve, so, from that point of view, I feel no shame in how I have drawn on the writings of great thinkers with whom I have engaged, whether they are currently out of fashion or not.

You will see what I am alluding to by the end of chapter one, where you will go on a whirlwind journey of statistical and quantitative information on the state of gender leadership variance, with reference to analyses of scores of social scientists, before ending with Jungian psychology as a reference point for understanding the complex patriarchal building codes that have left us with glass ceilings and sticky floors.

The book will just get weirder from there, but if you stick with me, by the final chapter, we will have set up nicely some tactics for repairing the structural damage caused by the wicked problem.

One potential critique of this book may be that its focus on the unique problems of women in healthcare leadership does not take into account the perspective of non-binary gendered voices, nor adequately elaborate the more complex discriminatory challenges faced by non-white people in healthcare professions.

As a white, *cis*-gendered woman (contemporary identity phrasing I am still getting used to), I have written through the limited lens of my own experience. When data are available, however, I have tried to supply information in the text that differentiates the experiences of other groups of people who are impacted by discriminatory biases and barriers to leadership. Diversity, equity, and inclusion should be very robustly designed into our cultural and organizational objectives. By starting with misogyny, a discriminatory practice that spans all cultures and historical timeframes, I hope my approach can be useful in that broader DEI design process.

I want to make it clear up front that this book is not written from the perspective that the behaviors and experiences that I personally have lived should be a roadmap for others to follow. Rather, I believe women from all types of backgrounds and experiences should have ample opportunity to fill leadership roles in healthcare; understanding why and how that does not happen are crucial steps in remedying the situation.

When half of the world's population is excluded from full participation in leadership, power, and influence, everybody suffers. We simply do not have the time nor the luxury to settle for patriarchy any more. In a world facing ecological destruction from climate change, nuclear annihilation from ongoing worldwide wars and conflict, unprecedented mass killings from gun violence, and the assault on women's rights across cultures, we need the hearts and minds of women involved in solving these problems equally with men.

As a healthcare professional, I will address this through the lens of healthcare leadership inequality, because that is the space I know best. But the tactics I lay out in chapter eight can be cross disciplinary, and I challenge all of us to move from the constrictions of nouns to the power of verbs; actions, not archetypes, are what will yield us full agency.

PART I

Is Google Image the Collective Unconscious?

Take any search engine on any given day and plug in the word "leader" and notice how many of the images are of men, particularly white men.

(Google image/leader/accessed 6/4/2022)

CHAPTER ONE

Glass Ceilings, Sticky Floors, Chilly Rooms

Discrimination, whether intentional or unintentional, hurts everybody, not just those who are directly impacted by it. Women constitute most of the world's poorest people and the number of women living in rural poverty has increase by 50% since 1975. Women work two-thirds of the world's working hours and produce half of the world's food, yet they earn only 10% of the world's income and own less than 1% of the world's property.[1]

Gender discrimination affects not just the women themselves, but their children, families, and communities as well. Gender bias reduces productivity and innovation and narrows the potential for society to tap the greatest possible talent pool. It leads to less communal wealth and more narrowed approaches to creatively solving important social issues.

We are into the third decade of the 21st century, yet the headlines describing the gap in pay between women and men, the scarcity of women who reach the highest levels of leadership in organizations both large and small, and the disproportionate share of elected and appointed governmental positions held by men continues ceaselessly.

Comparing the median salary between men and women in 2021, women earned 82 cents for every dollar earned by men, according to an annual compensation survey by Payscale.[2] Even when the so-called "uncontrolled" raw numbers that consider other factors such as education, experience, locations, and industry, the gender wage gap still exists and is compounded over time.[3]

Although women earn the majority of college degrees and make up half the work force, the number of women who attain top leadership positions in industry remains shockingly low. In 2021, women led 167 of the top 3,000 companies in the United States, less than 6%.[4] As of September 2021, there were only 26 women serving as heads of state and/or government in 24 countries. Only 21% of government ministers were women and only

14 countries had 50% or more women cabinet members. Only 25% of all national parliamentarians are women. At the current rate, gender equality in the highest positions of power will not be reached for another 130 years.[5]

In the healthcare delivery system, women have fared no better. In 2021, Medscape's annual physician compensation survey showed men earn 27% more than women among primary care physicians, and male specialists earn 33% more. Women make up a greater percentage of primary care physicians, comprising only 33% of specialists, and make up a smaller percentage of the highest paid specialties. Women make up less than one-fifth of physicians in the highest-paying specialties: plastic surgery, orthopedics, cardiology, and urology.

On average, women physicians spend about 10% less time seeing patients than men, but this does not make up for the disproportionate decrease in compensation. Male physicians earn more than women in every age range with the wage gap in the middle age ranges widening over the past several years.[6]

Healthcare organizations are worse than other industries in promoting women to the highest leadership roles measured by the percentage of women who comprise the workforce. Women make up more than 65% of the hospital workforce, compared to 46% of the financial industry workforce and 26% of the technology industry workforce. But despite constituting the larger share of the healthcare workforce, women remain under-represented in leadership roles and it takes women longer to get to top positions. Women account for only a third of executive teams and just 13% of chief executive officers in the healthcare industry. It takes women on average three to five years longer to reach the chief executive officer position.[7]

The leadership gap in healthcare is a worldwide problem. Women comprise almost 70% of health and social care workers globally, nearly 90% of the nursing and midwifery workforce, yet hold only around 25% of leadership roles in healthcare.

The World Health Organization 2019 landmark report "Delivered by Women, Led by Men: A Gender and Equity Analysis of the Global Health and Social Workforce" examined specific factors contributing to the leadership gender gap: occupational segregation, bias, discrimination, harassment (including sexual harassment), and gender pay gap. Women comprise 91% of long-term care workers in OECD countries, 90% of nurses, but only 31% of ministers of health, 28% of deans of top public health and medical schools, 27% of executive heads and board chairs of global health organizations, 23%

of world health assembly heads of delegations, and 7.5% of Fortune 500 healthcare CEOs.[8]

Since the onset of the COVID-19 pandemic, the profound impact on women in the healthcare workforce has widened the leadership gap. Women have provided much of the healthcare in the pandemic but have not been represented with equity in decision-making. For example, 85% of 115 national COVID task forces had majority male membership.[9]

Although women have made heroic contributions across the healthcare sectors during the pandemic, their expertise has not been equally presented in the media. One study found that only one woman was quoted in the media as an expert on the pandemic for every three male experts.[10]

Despite contributions in vaccine development, health policymaking, and healthcare delivery, women have been underrepresented in the pandemic narrative. Only 12 out of 193 countries had a woman as head of government during the pandemic; these 12 countries had fewer COVID-19 deaths per capita, fewer days with confirmed deaths, lower peak in daily deaths per capital, and lower excess mortality. By June 2020, deaths from COVID-19 were six times lower in countries led by women.[11]

Women leaders spoke more frequently about the impact at the local level or on individuals and social welfare services to cushion financial shocks, whereas male leaders used war metaphors and aggressive language more often than women.[12] Because women comprise a high percentage of patient-facing healthcare workers, most healthcare workers infected with the COVID-19 virus have been women, and women have been victim to most of the COVID-associated attacks on healthcare workers.[13]

The inequality of unpaid work at home has worsened during the pandemic, such that many frontline female healthcare workers have struggled with managing parental responsibilities around school closures during quarantine with increased shift demands at hospitals and long-term care facilities. A recent McKinsey survey indicated that 22% of nurses plan to leave their current position providing direct patient care within the next year, due to increasing demands placed on healthcare workers, creating both a physical strain on those working on the frontlines and a psychological strain from those losing patients, coworkers, and loved ones.[14]

The pandemic's impact on inequalities has not been experienced just by lower-paid female healthcare workers. Frank and colleagues reported in *JAMA* network in November 2021 a cohort study of 276 working physicians who were parents during the pandemic. "Mothers were more likely than fathers to be responsible for childcare or schooling and household tasks, to work primarily from home, to reduce their work hours, and to experience work-to-family conflict, family-to-work conflict, and depressive and anxiety symptoms. A difference in depressive symptoms was observed among physician parents during the Covid-19 pandemic that was not present before the pandemic."[15]

SIXTY YEARS OF NON-DISCRIMINATION LAWS

There have been substantial efforts over the course of modern history to combat pay discrimination based upon gender bias. It has been nearly 60 years since the United States passed the Equal Pay Act of 1963, and Title VII of the Civil Rights Act of 1964 specifically prohibiting pay discrimination based upon gender:

EQUAL PAY ACT

SEC. 206. *[Section 6]*

(d) Prohibition of sex discrimination

(1) No employer having employees subject to any provisions of this section shall discriminate, within any establishment in which such employees are employed, between employees on the basis of sex by paying wages to employees in such establishment at a rate less than the rate at which he pays wages to employees of the opposite sex in such establishment for equal work on jobs the performance of which requires equal skill, effort, and responsibility, and which are performed under similar working conditions, except where such payment is made pursuant to (i) a seniority system; (ii) a merit system; (iii) a system which measures earnings by quantity or quality of production; or (iv) a differential based on any other factor other than sex: *Provided*, That an employer who is paying a wage rate differential in violation of this subsection shall not, in order to comply with the provisions of this subsection, reduce the wage rate of any employee.[16]

CIVIL RIGHTS ACT

SEC. 2000e-2. *[Section 703]*

(a) Employer practices

It shall be an unlawful employment practice for an employer -

(1) to fail or refuse to hire or to discharge any individual, or otherwise to discriminate against any individual with respect to his compensation, terms, conditions, or privileges of employment, because of such individual's race, color, religion, sex, or national origin; or

(2) to limit, segregate, or classify his employees or applicants for employment in any way which would deprive or tend to deprive any individual of employment

opportunities or otherwise adversely affect his status as an employee, because of such individual's race, color, religion, sex, or national origin.[17]

The Convention on the Elimination on All Forms of Discrimination Against Women set out, in legally binding form, internationally accepted principles on the rights of women more than 30 years ago and has been ratified by 186 sovereign states. Article 15 (1) of CEDAW explicitly provides that states that have ratified the convention shall accord to women equality with men and Article 2 commits states to "take all appropriate measures, including legislation, to modify or abolish existing laws, regulations, customs and practices which constitute discrimination against women."[18]

Unfortunately, having laws in place to prevent discrimination is not equivalent to having no discrimination. Still symbolically recognized across the world is Equal Pay Day, the date representing how far into a new year the average median women must work (in addition to their earnings last year) in order to have earned what the average median man had earned the entire previous year. It differs from year to year, but in 2022 in the United States it was March 15. For Asian-American women it was March 5. For African and Black American women it was August 22. For Native American women it was September 23. For Latinas it was November 20.

WE'VE BUILT ONE BIG UGLY BUILDING

So why haven't all the legislative efforts worked? An analysis from the European Organisation for Economic Co-operation and Development (OECD) attributes pay discrepancy to *"glass ceilings"* and *"sticky floors."* **Glass ceilings** refer to obstacles that stand in the way of women advancing their careers, while **sticky floors** are disadvantages women consistently face when they are starting their careers or are preparing to retire. The OECD concludes about 60% of a gender pay gap is the result of a glass ceiling while 40% comes from a sticky floor.[19]

In some circumstances, women may be more likely to look for jobs that have non-wage benefits, such as a shorter commute, due to family responsibilities that more greatly fall on women. Women have a greater number of career disruptions, such as motherhood, where women tend to take more parental leave than men. They tend to dominate careers that pay less than male-dominated fields, sometimes due to societal or cultural norms and pressures, such as indirectly dissuading girls from entering STEM-related careers. But even in fields where women dominate the market, wage differences exist between men and women as well as advancement to leadership positions.

The **glass escalator** refers to the way men are put on a fast track to advancement when entering primarily female-dominated professions.[20] Male nurses earn higher wages and have faster attainment of leadership positions in the United States and six other countries where it has been studied.

According to Caren Goldberg, PhD, a professor of management who has studied the glass escalator effect, "Men that enter female-dominated professions tend to be promoted at faster rates than women in those professions. When you look at senior management, you tend to see men disproportionately represented. So, while there may be less than 5% of all nurses who are male, you see a much larger percentage than 5% in senior-level positions like hospital administrators.... Research indicated that stereotypes about what a prototypical man is matched with stereotypes about what a prototypical manager is. Because of the stereotype matching, men more readily fulfill our notions of what a manager should look like. And when you are in a female-dominated profession, there are fewer people that have the ability to match it."[21]

Metaphors for Structural Barriers in Gender Discrimination	
Broken Rung	Structural barriers women face in climbing the career ladder such as inadequate information about competencies and skill sets required to advance; lack of access to mentors, sponsors, and role models; and lack of policies, practices, and processes that ensure all employees have equal opportunity to participate in early promotions.
Chilly Climate	Subtle ways women are treated differently at work that have a cumulative effect by dampening women's self-esteem, confidence, aspirations, and participation.
Concrete Floor	The minimum number or proportion of women necessary for a cabinet or board of directors to be perceived as legitimate.
Frozen Middle	Phenomenon where women's progress up the corporate ladder slows in the ranks of middle management.
Glass Ceiling	An invisible barrier that prevents women from rising beyond a certain level in a hierarchy.
Glass Cliff	The phenomenon of women in leadership roles being likelier than men to achieve leadership roles during periods of crisis and downturn, when the risk of failure is highest.
Glass Door	A barrier to initial hiring, where a job appears to be open to everyone but in fact is closed to women.
Glass Escalator	A phenomenon wherein men who join fields previously dominated by women, such as nursing and teaching, are promoted and given more opportunities compared to the women, as if the men were taking escalators and the women were taking the stairs.

(table continues)

Metaphors for Structural Barriers in Gender Discrimination	
Glass Wall	The phenomenon in which women may have a barrier to horizontal transfer in a corporation.
Labyrinth	Phenomenon that even with a glass ceiling shattered, female leaders do not encounter a single absolute barrier at a specific high level but face a complex set of obstacles that form a challenging labyrinth.
Leaky Pipes	The phenomenon where women and girls disappear in the pipeline for certain types of high-status and high-paid careers dominated by men, such as STEM-based professions.
Mommy Track	Work arrangement for women in the workforce that facilitates motherhood, but at the same time usually provides fewer opportunities for career advancement.
Sticky Floors	The pattern whereby women are less likely to start to climb the job ladder compared to men.

An analysis by the Association of American Medical Colleges in October 2021 confirmed that even at the highest positions of academic medicine, salary disparities among U.S. physicians demonstrate a persistent gender pay gap.[22] AAMC's assessment demonstrates that female academic physicians, regardless of racial or ethnic group, earn less than men of every racial and ethnic group. Exploring the reasons for these persistent patterns, scholars point to a phenomenon called "second-generation gender bias," which they describe as "not overt, like the sexism that was common before Title VII of the Civil Rights Act of 1964 and Title IX of the Education Amendments of 1972. Instead, it involves prejudices that are embedded in unconscious beliefs about what leaders look like, how men and women should behave, and how women's work is assigned and valued in our professional institutions and society."[23]

So, nearly 60 years after the passage of federal laws prohibiting discrimination based upon gender and 30 years after the international adoption of CEDAW, data indicate it will take more than 200 years to achieve gender parity in the highest paid surgical specialty in the United States[24] and more than 100 years to reach gender parity in political representation and executive management.[25]

Moreover, the global pandemic has reversed progress on gender equality. The World Economic Forum's annual global gender parity gap evaluates global progress in achieving equality between men and women. The WEF's 2021 Global Gender Gap report concluded that gender equality in four key dimensions — economic participation and opportunity, educational attainment, health and survival, and political empowerment — is currently 68% closed, down half a percentage point from the previous year.[26] Women have been disproportionately impacted by the coronavirus pandemic. They comprise 70% of healthcare workers, which increased their exposure and stress during 2020. Due to their greater representation in lower-paying jobs, they have a higher unemployment rate than men, and domestic violence rates climbed significantly during the pandemic.[27]

STEREOTYPES, PROTOTYPES, AND SECOND-GENERATION GENDER BIAS

Most of the literature evaluating gender parity attributes these data to conscious or unconscious bias based upon *stereotypes* or *prototypes*. Ibarra, Ely, and Kolb's seminal article in *Harvard Business Review* on how gender bias impacts the ability to rise to leadership positions asserts that *second-generation gender bias* presumes a lack of discriminatory intent but is "embedded in *stereotypes* and organizational practices that can be hard to detect."[28]

In these models of study, gender bias is based upon generalized beliefs about a particular category of people. For example, psychologist Margaret Neale, a negotiations professor at Stanford Graduate School of Business, notes that female CEOs of moderate size to large organizations have no problem negotiating on behalf of their company but have a very difficult time asking their board of directors for a raise on their own behalf. "As a woman, it is unacceptable for me to be greedy on my own, but it's completely acceptable for me to negotiate for someone else, because that is a caretaking thing, a communal thing."[29] Thus, a stereotype that women are natural caregivers and should be selfless constrains even these powerful female executives from advocating for themselves.

Stereotype threat is a concept based on the research done by social psychologist and Columbia University provost Claude M. Steele and colleagues that exposes how pervasive stereotypes can actually influence behavior and performance and perpetuate themselves. Individuals live with an awareness of negative stereotypes about their identity group, which often undermines their efforts to move beyond it. Steele and his colleagues demonstrated that merely being reminded of one's identity group in situations where that identity is built on stereotypes of inadequate performance can contribute to underperformance, such as situations where women are told they are taking a difficult mathematics test after being reminded that they are women and women typically perform worse than men on such tests.

Steele asserts that "despite the strong sense we have of ourselves as autonomous individuals, evidence consistently shows that contingencies tied to our social identities do make a difference in shaping our lives, from the way we perform in certain situations to the careers and friends we choose."[30] He indicates that a second dimension of reality is that "identity threats based upon stereotypes to damage to our functioning and play an important role in some of society's most important social problems, including racism social class, and gender achievement gaps that persistently plague and distort our society to the equally persistent intergroup tensions that often trouble our social relations."[31]

Steele focuses his research on the insight that these threats impair a broad range of human functioning by allocating mental resources and precise patterns of brain activation that simply take a toll on human beings as they interact with others in our society. He found that there are "feasible things that can be done to reduce these threats in schools and classrooms that can dramatically reduce the racial and gender achievement gaps that so discouragingly characterize our society."

ARCHETYPES BEFORE STEREOTYPES

From my point of view, the work that Steele and others have done understanding stereotypes is important and insightful, but I believe there is something more inscrutable underlying this quagmire. Deep cultural *archetypes* exist and continue to influence our social structures and impact our efforts to counter gender discrimination. These archetypes have been part of patriarchal culture for millennia.

An archetype is defined as a pattern or model of which all things of the same type are representations and copies. Stereotypes are oversimplified and generalized character traits. As recurring symbols and motifs across cultures, archetypes represent universal patterns of human nature. The tenacity of gender discrimination can be explained by the cultural and historical archetypes we experience as part of the patriarchal societies in which much of the world's human race resides.

Human beings have developed stories about what an individual's identity means based on cultural building blocks that have existed for centuries. These archetypes show up over and over in patterned story motifs that repeat from generation to generation. As we are beginning to emerge from a 5,000-year period of human history built on patriarchal restrictions on induvial human freedom, understanding how these archetypes still echo through the lives of women and men on a daily basis can help us understand the solutions we must construct that limit discrimination in all its forms.

Although often dismissed by contemporary psychologists for being outdated and biased, the early 20th century psychologist C.G. Jung developed a theory of psychology founded on the concept of archetypes, which I believe can provide insights into what types of barriers women still face in taking on leadership roles. Jung asserted that archetypes are inherited ideas of modes of thought that are derived from the experiences of the human race and are present in the unconscious of the individual:[32]

> Since the earliest times, the inborn manner of action has been called instinct and for this manner of psychic apprehension of the object I have proposed the term *archetype*. This term embraces the same idea as is contained in 'primordial image'....The archetype is a symbolical formula, which always begins to function whenever there are not conscious ideas present....These archetypes, whose innermost nature is inaccessible to experience, represent the precipitate of psychic functioning of the whole ancestral line...[33]

Jung's archetypes are a kind of psychic counterpart of instinct, of innate unspecific knowledge, derived from the sum of human history, which prefigures and directs conscious behavior.[34]

Jung's ideas have been criticized significantly for the implication that these unconscious ideas are preconfigured in nature and because they lack necessary scientific confirmation, making them more a presumed foundational truth akin to a religious or mystic belief than scientific theory.[35] But if you push beyond these legitimate criticisms around heritability, the underlying idea of a prototypal model upon which we define our experience and make decisions, it is useful.

The concept of primordial patterns was first conceived by Plato 2,500 years ago; he developed the concept of "forms" or "ideas." Plato's theory is that there are timeless, unchangeable absolute "ideas" that are the non-physical essences of all things. His student Aristotle's critique is built on the rejection of an independently existing world of forms outside of physical reality.

Jung is more Platonic than Aristotelian. Jung's contribution is his insight that these deep patterns (archetypes) exist independently of any current event. He perceived them to "exert influence both across all domains of experience and throughout the stages of each individual's development." He asserted they can be "deduced through the development of storytelling over tens of thousands of years, indicating repeating patterns of individual and group experience, behaviors, and effects across the planet, apparently displaying common themes."[36]

Gender discrimination can be interpreted as built on the classic archetypal ways men and women are perceived, which continues to impact women's opportunities through the subconscious biases that such archetypes engender.

Jung asserted a "collective unconscious" exists that is part of the unconscious mind which is derived from ancestral memory and experience and is common to all humankind, as distinct from the individual's unconscious. His focus on its heritability has been greatly criticized due to its scientific unprovability and mystic undertones. But the Jungian concept of the "collective unconscious" does not come across as so strange if you search for key words like "leader" and "hero" on contemporary search engines such as Google Image.

Nearly every image displayed for "leader" on any day I search shows picture after picture of men, usually white, often carrying a stick or wearing a tie. The same goes for "boss." The same goes for "hero" ... and "doctor" ... and "surgeon" ... and "manager." Google's algorithm is built on heuristics that can be thought of as our collective unconscious, although perhaps not so unconscious anymore. In the age of the world wide web, the collective unconscious does not have to be inherited in a genetic sense. It is, however, something we have inherited in a cultural sense. And in the Google version of the collective unconscious, the leadership archetypes are not gender neutral. Gender bias is not deliberately built into Google's algorithms or those of any other search engine. Rather, the material that search engines mine, and now artificial intelligence machines train on, is based on the collective information sources our patriarchal culture has produced.

Some feminist critics of Jung's archetype theory have focused on the archetypes as being reductionistic and providing a stereotyped view of femininity and masculinity.[37] From their feminist perspectives, archetypes are not inherited images; they are part of the tendency to structure experience in certain ways and have been influenced historically by the patriarchal culture in which they are manifest. As Demaris S. Weir discerned, "Women caught in seemingly isolated individual struggles are acting out the culture-wide struggle of all women to realize their full humanity (one that includes, for example, a strong intellect) in a society which devalues them and offers no complete vision of their possibilities of empowerment."[38]

My perspective is that the reductionistic nature of the archetypes explains much of the unconscious bias that impacts women. By understanding them, and learning how they impact decision-making, we can perhaps develop tools to counteract their negative consequences and, if we choose, exploit their positive consequences.

The main archetypes that are characterized as "feminine" are not typically perceived as embodying leadership. Consider the female archetypes: mother, daughter, sister, grandmother, witch, bitch, and whore. The positive, safe ones are all contextualized within family roles, in the home. The other archetypes, all decidedly pejorative, are external to the home.

This is not the case for male archetypes. True, familial archetypes exist for men, too: father, brother, grandfather, son. But consider the broader range of non-domestic archetypes: hero, villain, trickster, explorer, magician, creator, to name a few. Within the social context of work, culture, and governance, the relative paucity of female archetypal constructs constrains the representative heuristics by which many decisions are subconsciously made. Consider how Ibarra and colleagues analyze the barriers to women rising to leadership positions:

> People become leaders by internalizing a leadership identity and developing a sense of purpose.... Integrating leadership into one's core identity is particularly challenging for women, who must establish credibility in a culture that is deeply conflicted about whether, when, and how they should exercise authority. Practices that equate leadership with behaviors considered more common in men suggest that women are simply not cut out to be leaders.[39]

"Exercising authority" is constrained for women within the traditional feminine archetypes:

> In most cultures masculinity and leadership are closely linked: The ideal leader, like the ideal man, is decisive, assertive, and independent. In contrast, women are expected to be nice, caretaking, and unselfish. The mismatch between conventionally feminine qualities and the qualities thought necessary for leadership puts female leaders in a double bind. Numerous studies have shown that women who excel in traditionally male domains are viewed as competent but less likable than their male counterparts. Behaviors that suggest self-confidence or assertiveness in men often appear arrogant or abrasive in women. Meanwhile, women in positions of authority who enact a conventionally feminine style may be liked but are not respected. They are deemed too emotional to make tough decisions and too soft to be strong leaders.[40]

What can we do about this double bind? I believe the answer is to explore deeply these traditional archetypes in which women are often subconsciously perceived and identify when and how they impact women in healthcare leadership.

I am an existentialist. I believe the freedom to choose, develop, and actualize our place in the world depends on understanding the underlying constructs in which our choices are made. The tension between the ability to "internalize a leadership identity" and the underlying subconscious archetypes that influence the way we perceive the world and are perceived by others is essential to understand if we are to solve the gender double bind. The tension between archetypal boundaries and existential choices has defined the internal dialogue I have used in understanding how to develop meaning in my own career, and the story of my leadership path may be useful for other women creating their own path.

This book is based on insights I have acquired from my own atypical leadership journey. I have learned how to identify patterns of dialogue and interactions in which I perceive the underlying biases inherent in the archetypes are at play. Sometimes, I have been able to choose when and how to manipulate these archetypes to keep them from being a trap.

Just as they have been since before human beings could write, stories and storytelling are still crucial parts of what it means to be human. Human beings draw upon the archetypal storylines we have all learned in our cultures to explain what events in our lives mean. Unfortunately, we often limit the creative possibilities of these stories by failing to recognize the constraints inherent in the pure archetypal forms.

Although Aristotle himself was certainly not an advocate for gender equality (in fact, he really was not convinced women were fully human), the creativity of Aristotelian philosophy is embracing the variance of the real, not ideal world. When we rigidly stick to unconscious archetype structures to manage our lives and cultures, we all lose. But if we are able to identify the constraints of these structures, we have the opportunity to free ourselves from them.

Gender discriminatory attitudes deeply entrenched in societies have enormous negative impact on the well-being of women. A 2022 Commonwealth Fund analysis of 10 high-income countries demonstrated that the United States does the poorest job of serving the healthcare needs of women compared to any other high-income nation. Women in the United States have the highest rates of avoidable death compared to women in other high-income countries; they are less like to have a regular doctor and more likely to report problems paying medical bills.

Women of reproductive age in the United States have among the highest rates of multiple chronic conditions and the highest rate of mental health needs. They spend more out of pocket on healthcare than women in other high-income countries and are the most likely to skip or delay needed care because of costs. They have the highest maternal mortality rate and are among the highest group with unmet mental health needs.[41] Shamefully, a woman in American today is 50% more likely than her own mother to die in childbirth.[42] For black and brown women, these statistics are exponentially, horrifyingly worse.

Women leaders can make a difference in improving the health status of women and their families. We need to crack the nut of gender bias, discrimination, and sometimes outright persecution by understanding its origins and engineering its demise. In healthcare, the place to start is in the empowerment of women as leaders at every level of our organizations and, most especially, the C-suites. Patriarchy just isn't a good look anymore. It hurts all of us.

The Leaky Pipeline: Corporate Gender Representation 2016

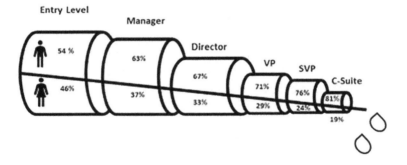

CHAPTER TWO

Archetypes as Psychic Prisons

The system of patriarchy is a historic construct; it has a beginning; it will have an end. Its time seems to have nearly run its course – it no longer serves the needs of men or women and in its inextricable link to militarism, hierarchy, and racism it threatens the very existence of life on earth.... A feminist world-view will enable women and men to free their minds from patriarchal thought and practice and at last to build a world free of dominance and hierarchy, a world that is truly human.[43]

— Gerda Lerner

COGNITIVE BIAS

I happen to have a perfect grandchild. She is my first. She is six months old. She is absolutely beautiful. As far as I know, there has never before been a child as perfect as she on the planet. Now, if you ask her mom and dad, they might mention a few fussy spells now and then, a desire to be held all hours of the night and day, and an occasional messy diaper. If you meet them, you should ignore these observations. She is perfect. You have my word.

All of us have cognitive biases, which are the systematic errors in thinking that occur when we are processing and interpreting information in the world around us. As human beings, we have certain tools at our disposal to allow us to make sense of the world. These tools include storytelling, pattern recognition, emotional intelligence, instinctual behaviors, introspection, observations, abductive reasoning, among many others. As members of families, communities, cultures, and societies, we interact with one another to give meaning to our collective experiences.

The processes we use as individual human beings in our sensemaking are prone to error through cognitive biases, which are the habitual mistakes we make in our intuitional and reasoning thinking processes. Having cognitive biases does not mean you are deliberately discriminating. But due to our chronic lack of awareness of their impact on our behaviors and actions, cognitive biases can create processes and environments that are set up to be inherently discriminatory.

John Manoogian III and Buster Benson created a conceptual map of every type of cognitive bias known to date and placed them in a diagram divided into four conundrums: *there's too much information, there's not enough meaning, there's not enough time and resources, and there's not enough memory in our brains.*[44] Their four conundrums are further divided into 20 categories, and deeper into 188 specific types of biases. The 20 categories are:

1. We notice things primed in memory or repeated often.
2. Bizarre, funny, visually striking, or anthropomorphic things stick out more than non-bizarre/unfunny things.
3. We notice when something has changed.
4. We are drawn to details that confirm our own existing beliefs.
5. We notice flaws in others more easily than we notice flaws in ourselves.
6. We tend to find stories and patterns even when looking at sparse data.
7. We fill in characteristics from stereotypes, generalities, and prior histories.
8. We imagine things and people we're familiar with or fond of as better.
9. We simplify probabilities and numbers to make them easier to think about.
10. We think we know what other people are thinking.
11. We project our current mindset onto the past and future.
12. To act, we must be confident we can make an impact and feel what we do is important.
13. To stay focused, we favor the immediate, relatable thing in front of us.
14. To get things done, we tend to complete things we've invested time and energy in.
15. To avoid mistakes, we aim to preserve autonomy and group status and avoid irreversible decisions.
16. We favor simple-looking options and complete information over complex, ambiguous options.
17. We edit and reinforce some memories after the fact.
18. We discard specifics for form generalities.
19. We reduce events and lists to their key elements.
20. We store memories differently based on how they were experienced.

I fully admit that, with respect to my thinking about my grandchild, I may be suffering a bit from bias number 8: *We imagine things and people we're familiar with or fond of as better.* I have no trouble admitting I am biased when it comes to my perfect little granddaughter. I see all of her actions and traits in a positive light and fiercely defend against any who might have an alternative point of view. As she grows up and encounters other people in the world, my granddaughter is likely to find not everyone has her grandmother's perspective, and developing her own identity will be impacted by many other people who simply do not share her grandmother's bias.

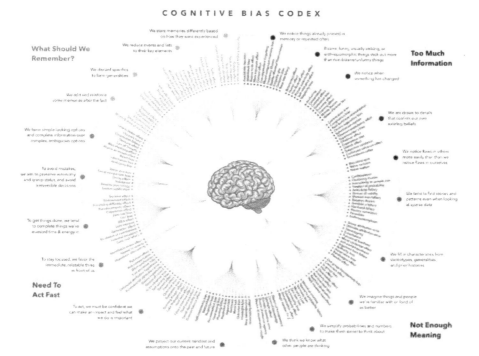

COGNITIVE BIAS CODEX

As a female child, my granddaughter will experience cognitive biases from everyone she interacts with that are based on their own understanding of who and what she represents. Her gender will cue cognitive sensemaking processes that have been developed through thousands of years of human culture. The patterned stories embedded in our cultures are built on archetypes whose origins reach back farther than written history, and can be seen in oral traditions from around the world and cultural artifacts that pre-date historical civilizations. The archetypes form the building blocks upon which some of the cognitive biases take hold. Consider these, for example:

> We notice things primed in memory or repeated often (like stories of heroes and damsels in distress).
>
> We notice when something has changed (like when a stock hero character is the "wrong" gender).
>
> We fill in characteristics from stereotypes, generalities, and prior histories (like women are excellent caregivers, men are natural leaders).
>
> We are drawn to details that confirm our own beliefs (like how men and women should look and behave).

We tend to find stories and patterns even when looking at sparse data (like interpreting a women's actions as being because she is a mother).

We favor simple-looking options and complete information over complex, ambiguous options (like rigid roles pre-defined in patriarchal societies).

Understanding how archetypes form the building blocks of many of our cognitive biases can help us overcome their constraints by equipping us with the ability to recognize when they may be limiting our ability to think and create more broadly.

THE ARCHETYPES

The important life work of Carl Jung was to identify the centrality of the archetypes to human psychology. Jung's description of the archetypes is fluid, and he changed and elaborated upon them throughout his career. Drawing upon the philosophies of Immanuel Kant (categories), Plato (ideas), and Schopenhauer (prototypes), he described the archetypes as "the introspectively recognizable form of *a priori* psychic orderedness."[45]

Jung had great interest in the distinction between the masculine (*animus*) and feminine (*anima)* and much of his structural analysis of archetypes approaches his categories with a gender-infused point of view. Subsequent Jungian thinkers have developed categories of female and male archetypes based on interpreting his work within the context of his animus/anima categorical distinctions.

One categorization group is built on seven female archetypes: the Lover, the Innocent Maiden, the Nurturing Mother, the Queen, the Huntress, the Wise Woman, and the Mystic.[46] Seven parallel masculine archetypes are the Hero, the Mentor, the Threshold Guardian, the Herald, the Shadow, the Trickster, and the Shapeshifter.[47] Another categorization is constructed around five archetypes, ostensibly gender-neutral, but most often being perceived as masculine in contemporary culture: the Hero, the Mentor, the Everyone, the Innocent, the Villain. Another version differentiates 12 archetypes, the vast majority seen as masculine: the Ruler, the Creator, the Sage, the Innocent, the Explorer, the Rebel, the Hero, the Wizard, the Jester, the Regular Guy/ Gal, the Lover, and the Caregiver.

Take a moment to use a search engine such as Google Image to search for "archetypes." In my experience, of the images of the 12 archetypes described, the only searches that bring up images of women are searches for the Innocent, the Sage, the Lover, and the Care Giver.

Feminist archetype critics have noted that Jung failed to see the possibility of certain archetypes as being pertinent to people of either gender altogether. For example, Carol Pearson's *The Hero Within: Six Archetypes We Live By* pushed back against Jung's assumption that the Warrior archetype is necessarily masculine.[48] Jung ignored women when considering male-dominated archetypes like the Hero or Warrior, refusing to acknowledge the possibility that female warriors might exist and flourish in a conducive environment.[49]

Many writers building on Jungian theory exclude women entirely from the study of the Hero archetypes, presuming that the Hero is always a male construct.[50] For example:

> Jungian psychoanalysis tends to assume that archetypal patterns derived from male experience are applicable to women's as well. As a consequence, female archetypes are interpreted according to male patterns and the male patterns may be allowed to eclipse women's experience altogether. The feminine may be reduced to an attribute of the masculine personality rather than seen as an archetype deriving from women's experience that is a source of power for the self.[51]

In literature, the feminist archetype critics by and large challenge the paternalistic constraints of the classic archetypes and expand gender roles by re-visioning female characters within the traditionally male archetypes such as Warrior. Madeleine L'Engle's *Kairos* series[52] and Ursula K. Le Guin's *Earthsea* series[53] are two 20th-century young adult book series that portray female characters in the Warrior role. In popular culture, characters such as Wonder Woman do this also. But certain distinctions are made between the female and male Warrior/Hero in the literary and cultural narratives. The typical heroic Warrior is one who "takes a long, usually solitary journey, saves the days, and rescues the damsel-in-distress by slaying a dragon or in some other way defeating the enemy"[54] after which he typically "marries the daughter of his predecessor and becomes king."[55] In contrast, the female Warrior/Hero, after defeating the enemy and saving the day, typically does not "marry the prince and become Queen."

Can this explain some of the gender gaps we see in healthcare leadership? I think so. I believe that unconscious bias built on what traits we perceive as being important for leaders to embody limits the ability of many women to achieve the highest leadership roles in healthcare organizations. As is also the case in many other industries, the representative heuristics we use to determine who and how someone is perceived to have the qualities necessary to be a good leader continue to be a constraint for women in the healthcare industry. Let's look at the Jungian archetypes in more detail to see how this might be playing out.

Archetype 1: The Huntress

The Greeks called her Artemis. She is the goddess of the hunt, the wilderness, wild animals, the Moon, and chastity. She has sworn to never marry. The Romans called her Diana. She carries a quiver of arrows and holds a bow. She is the daughter of Zeus and Leto and the sister of Apollo, the god of War.

The Huntress embodies freedom and sovereignty over her own body and life. She protects other women and does not need a partner to feel complete. The goddess of the hunt in Hinduism is Banka-Mundi, who protects wild animals, provides fertility, and removes fear. In Lithuanian mythology, she is Medeina, a single, beautiful huntress who protects the forest. The Inuit call her Pinga. In Africa she is Oya.

In all of these cultures, the Huntress archetype idealizes competency and independence (from men), and protects others. Of all the female archetypes, the Huntress is the least associated with a prototypical family role. She has freedom. She is a wild child. She is a tomboy. Although the Huntress is typically described as beautiful, the architype is asexual. It is that asexuality that provides her freedom. By not being a mother, daughter, sister, or lover, the Huntress is independent of a paternal relationship. She is not defined in relationship to a man.

For the Huntress, tools and weapons are allowed. As part of her competency, she can use a bow and arrow, change a tire, program a computer, perform an appendectomy, deliver a baby. Her innate competency allows her to focus on goals. She is not bogged down with responsibilities forcing her to be a perpetual caregiver to others, but she will use her power to protect victims.

The Huntress role can be incredibly powerful for women in the workplace. Competency, autonomy, goal-focus, and protectiveness in many respects represent ideal non-gendered leadership characteristics. However, the potential to be perceived as "aloof, emotionally unavailable, and potentially cruel" are also a risk for this archetype.[56] That is, the Huntress can quickly turn into the bitch, that most feared identity associated with women and power. Consequently, women will often back away from the full strength of this archetype.

Archetype 2: The Lover

The Greek goddess of sexual love and beauty is Aphrodite. The Romans called her Venus. The Aztecs called her Xochiquetzal. She has been known as Mami Wata (Nigeria), Hathor (Egypt), and Erzuli (Vodou). Each of these cultures associates these female deities with sexuality, passion, and creativity. In contrast, Carl Jung considered the Lover archetype as a male or gender-neutral archetype, focused on bliss, intimacy, and ecstasy. Associated with libido, the Lover archetype encourages you to indulge and delight in the things you love in life. The Lover is enthusiastic, sensual, and when performing their best, the Lover creates long-lasting, meaningful relationships.

Within the context of the work environment, the Lover archetype can be quite dangerous. In many world cultures, female sexuality outside the confines of marriage is considered strictly taboo. In patriarchal cultures, wives are the property of their husbands, and unmarried girls and women are the property of their fathers. Outside the family, including in the workplace, a woman perceived as actively sexual can be labeled as a seductress, or worse, a "whore." Female sex workers (prostitutes) have generally been shunned and punished throughout history. Within the context of the workplace, the risk for women participating in consensual sex remains high.

The risk for women participating in non-consensual sex is much greater. Sexual violence has been estimated by the World Health Organization to affect one-third of all women worldwide.[57] A 2017 *The Washington Post* poll found that 54% of American women report receiving "unwanted and inappropriate" sexual advances; 95% said that such behavior usually goes unpunished.[58]

When such behavior is reported, there often are reprisals for doing so. A 2016 Equal Employment Opportunity Commission report stated that although 25%–85% of women say they experience sexual harassment at work, few ever report the incidents, most commonly due to fear of reprisal.[59] Data from France indicated a person who makes a sexual harassment complaint at work is reprimanded or fired 40% of the time, while the accused person is typically not investigated or punished.[60] In Japan, as few as 4% of rape victims report the crime, and the charges are dropped 50% of the time.[61]

In the medical field, among U.S. academic medical faculty members, about 30% of women and 4% of men reported experiencing sexual harassment. Complaints by medical staff often have negative consequences on their careers.[62] One systematic review indicates up to 60% of medical students experience harassment or discrimination of some kind during their training, with women being targeted more than men. The harassment includes inappropriate sexual advances, requests for sexual favors, sexist jokes and slurs, exchange or rewards for sexual favor, and other verbal or physical conduct of a sexual nature.[63]

As in other fields, women who report episodes of sexual harassment in the healthcare industry often experience marginalization, retaliation, and stigmatization. Research indicates that women are more vulnerable to harassment when they are perceived as weak and when they are perceived as so strong that they challenge traditional hierarchies.[64] Among women physicians reporting harassment described as severe, 59% perceived a negative effect on their confidence in themselves as professionals, and 47% reported that these experiences negatively affected their career advancement.[65]

Archetype 3: The Maiden

Kobe (meaning Little Girl in Greek) is the original archetypal maiden in Greek mythology. She is innocent and virginal. When she is snatched to the Underworld, she becomes a married woman and is given the name Persephone. The archetypal Maiden is youthful, effervescent, uncorrupted, and playful. She has a sense of curiosity and is pure of heart and mind. She is not, however, independent of others. She is the daughter, protected by her parents, and her adventures are not her own. She is the damsel-in-distress. She is Sleeping Beauty, Rapunzel, Cinderella.

She is helpless in some way, whether through incapacity (asleep, tied to the railroad tracks), imprisonment (towers and dungeons), or mentally (bound by a curse or lack of knowledge about something important). She is young and powerless, and requires protecting and rescuing, usually by a male Hero. The Maiden archetype is built on innocence and pure intention, but the added element of female sexual possibility creates the tension and moves plot lines along in fairy tales and movies.

Within a work environment, young women may not be taken seriously if they are perceived as being naïve or inexperienced. This makes them vulnerable to being taken advantage of. Compliance and obedience are expected. Relationships may be based on codependency, creating risk of exploitation and forced silence. The silencing of the Maiden is as old as the most ancient of myths. In Ovid's *Metamorphosis*, Tereus rapes Philomela, then cuts out her tongue so she cannot speak about it.[66] Johannah King-Slutzky calls this Philomela, "the ur-text for women without tongues" and catalogues stories of tongueless or mute maidens unable to communicate their trauma, from young female martyrs, such as St. Christina, to Hans Christen Andersen's Little Mermaid.[67]

The #MeToo movement that has developed during the past decade focuses on exposing the silencing of women who have been sexually harassed or assaulted in the workplace, and who did not feel they had a voice to share their experience.

This silencing of women in the healthcare field due to discrimination is beginning to be offset by the large number of studies showing the prevalence of the problem. Survey data collected in 2021 from 7,000 emergency medicine residents showed that 45% of respondents reported experiencing workplace mistreatment in the most recent academic year, with the most common source of mistreatment being from patients and patient family members. Female emergency medicine residents reported higher levels of nearly all forms of mistreatment, with most of the reported gender-based mistreatment originating from patients and their families; the second source of gender-based mistreatment was from nurses and staff.[68]

Two years earlier, a Northwestern Medical study that surveyed trainees in all accredited 260 U.S. general surgical residency programs reported women surgical residents suffer more mistreatment leading to burnout and suicidal thoughts. In this study, the sexual harassment and verbal/physical abuse came from surgeons and fellow residents; 65% of all the women surgeons reported gender discrimination and 20% reported sexual harassment.[69] A large cross-sectional analysis from 2020 unmasked the high prevalence of sexual harassment among gastroenterology, internal medicine, and pediatric residents; 83% of female residents in the study reported they were subject to sexual harassment. Unfortunately, most residents were unlikely to report the offender (87% female, 93% male).[70]

Microaggressions are subtle, insulting, discriminatory comments or actions that communicate a demeaning or hostile message to nondominant groups. A 2021 study of the prevalence and nature of sexist and racial/ethnic microaggressions against surgeons and anesthesiologists who are female and/or racial/ethnic minority members in a large health maintenance organization found that 94% of the female respondents experienced sexist microaggressions, most commonly overhearing or seeing degrading female terms or images (86%), being pressured to intentionally appear less feminine at work and/or hide emotions (73%), and experiencing sexual objectification (44%). In addition, there was an 81% prevalence of racial/ethnic microaggressions., with 61% of female physicians from underrepresented minority groups reporting sexual objectification in the surgical workplace.

The prevalence of physician burnout was 54% for women (versus 43% for men) and highly correlated with surgical workplace mistreatment in the form of sexual or racial/ethnic microaggressions, especially for the female physicians from minority backgrounds who had experienced both sexual and racial mistreatment. Despite the tendency for individuals to minimize the impact low-level microaggressions have on them, the high correlation with implicit bias and physician burnout reveals significant unhealthy stigmatization in medical institutions.[71]

Archetype 4: Mother

The archetypal mother is universally recognized in all cultures. She is a nurturing, selfless caregiver who protects and provides for her children at any cost to herself. She is fertile and wise. She is the Christian Madonna, the Hindi Kali, the Greek Demeter, Egypt's Isis, and Nigeria's Yemanja. She is driven to provide for her loved ones and is persistent and compassionate. Her natural domain is the home, and she may not be welcomed outside of that domain unless the domain is identified as being a "nurturing profession":

> Mother finds her identity and fulfillment in cherishing, nurturing, and protecting. Her instinct is to assist all that is unfolding and in the process of becoming. She sees where other people need assistance or protection, and she goes to their aid. She encourages others to develop themselves, and she supports whatever is in need of nurturing or help. She attends to the comfort and security of whomever she nourishes. Mother will usually arrange her outer way of life to include marriage or a nurturing profession, such as teaching or nursing or social work.[72]

This concept of "nurturing professions" as being particularly appealing to women may box women into careers that are lower paid, including medicine. Although more than 50% of current medical students are women, female medical students are frequently discouraged from pursuing surgical careers and are told that surgical training is incompatible with having a family.[73]

For women who do choose to train as surgeons, those who became pregnant during residency perceived negative stigma related to childbearing, dissatisfaction with maternity leave policies, and inadequate lactation and childcare support. In a survey of 347 surgeons who were pregnant during residency, 39% seriously considered leaving residency due to these factors.[74] Attrition rates are high for both men and women during surgical training, but it is significantly higher for women than men (25% vs 15%) with uncontrollable lifestyle cited as the most common reason.[75]

In October 2021, Paula M. Smith, MD, PhD, Mina F. Nordness MD, MPH, and Monica E. Polcz MD, MS, published an editorial in *JAMA Surgery* calling for substantial changes to the American Board of Surgery's parental leave policy.[76] These women pointed out that the current American Board of

Surgery policy is non-compliant with the American Board of Medical Specialties requirements that residency training programs of member boards must allow six weeks of parental leave without exhausting other leave or extending training.

Becoming a parent during surgical residency is so difficult for women that female physicians and surgeons often delay childbearing. A recent survey of 850 surgeons in the United States found that compared to their non-surgical colleagues, 65% of female surgeons delay having children because of surgical training. On average they are two years older than their non-surgical peers at first pregnancy, have fewer children, have a greater use of assisted reproductive technology, and have nearly twice the number of major pregnancy complications (48% vs 27%). In fact, 42% of female surgeons had experienced a pregnancy loss (greater than twice the rate of the general population). Their nonelective cesarean delivery rate is substantially higher (26% vs 15%), and their postpartum depression rate is higher (11% vs 6%).[77]

Archetype 5: Sorceress

The Sorceress or Mystic is an archetype associated with both men and women. The Mystic focuses inward and is spiritual and derives power by tapping into natural sources of healing and renewal.

For women, the archetype can take on a much darker side than for men. She is the Enchantress, the Sorceress, the Witch. The role is not one associated with family or home. This woman has power outside the home. In the classic scenario of the male Hero doing battle in the world, the Mystic is an alternative source and type of strength.

Due to the apparent magical source of her power, the Mystic can evoke fear in patriarchal cultures. She is often set up as the antagonist to the male Hero in myths and legends. Typically, she is on the fringe of a society. She may be called upon to use her power for good but is rarely accepted by society in the long run in a leadership role. She is a nonconformist.

For women, being a nonconformist can be dangerous. In fact, a nonconforming woman who does not fit easily into one of the female roles typically perceived as positive (such as mother, maiden, or grandmother) frequently will be accused of being a witch and subsequently shunned, tortured, or murdered. Consider Joan of Arc. Mysteriously, this peasant from northeastern France received visions she said were from the archangel Michael and Saint Margaret and led the French army to victory at Orleans. But she was soon burned at the stake by her enemies. Consider the many wicked women unmasked as witches and subsequently killed in myths and legends: in Hansel and Gretel (burned to death in a hot oven), in Sleeping Beauty (burned to death with glowing hot iron shoes), and in the Wizard of Oz (melted with water).

In some cultures today, violence against women is associated with the accusation of witchcraft, where unexplained misfortunes are attributed to supernatural forces under the power of a human being (Witch).[78,79,80] In the last decade, the United Nations has reported a rise in women killed for witchcraft across the world. In India, women are targeted as witches as a pretext for seizing their land. In Saudi Arabia, women have been convicted of witchcraft in court, and in Ghana they have been exiled to "witch camps."[81] Around the world, conceptions of witchcraft share some common traits. Middle-aged women are the most common victims, and the accusations are typically patriarchal in etiology.[82]

Much anthropological work has demonstrated that the accusation of being a witch is associated with being poor, old, female, and powerless. However, there is also substantial precedence for accusing women who attain political power of being witches, including Cleopatra and Anne Boleyn. Hillary Clinton has been called a witch since she was First Lady in the 1990s, and during the 2016 presidential campaign the American social media was flooded with images of Clinton wearing a black hat and riding a broom. Speaker of the House Nancy Pelosi has had similar treatment, as has Julia Gillard, the first female prime minister of Australia.[83] In March 2021, the leader of Michigan's Republican Party referred to Governor Gretchen Whitmer and two other top Democratic elected women as "witches" that the GOP wanted to "soften up" for a "burning at the stake" in the 2022 election.[84]

Historically, an increase in the prevalence of accusations of witchcraft and the violence against women it perpetuates tends to occur in times of increased social instability and community anxiety.[85] Workplace violence perpetuated against female healthcare workers is common worldwide and has substantially worsened during the pandemic, perhaps with similar underlying sociological factors at play.[86] In a survey of 1,066 academic physicians in the United States, 30% of women reported experiencing sexual violence in the workplace compared with only 4% of men.[87] In one study of emergency medicine trainees, women experienced on average three nonphysical episodes of violence a day from patients and their families, compared to 0.9 per day for their male colleagues.[88]

Violence against women healers is not just a contemporary problem. Women often served as the healers in communities for centuries, presiding over childbirth, having specialized knowledge in plant-based medicines, including analgesics, sedative and digestive medicines, as well as preparations to relieve the pains of childbirth, in spite of the opposing positions of the church (who believed women should give birth with pain due to Original Sin). As medicine became professionalized in the Middle Ages, it became a male activity and these traditional women healers were pushed out, labeled as witches, and often killed:

> To understand the meaning of the witch-hunt, the explanation of the competence of the healers, the professionalization of medicine or the institutionalization and control of science by the established power is not sufficient. The witch-hunt was a conscious act of genocide by the elites of power that fed on a renewed misogyny that took hold from the fourteenth century. This misogyny was fed by the Church under the influence of the texts of Thomas Aquinas....This renewed misogyny would be accompanied by, at the beginning of the Modern Age, a backwards step for women in all aspects of their lives, coinciding with the Renaissance. The chronology of the witch-hunt coincides with these changes...Theologians and inquisitors stated 'where there are many women, there are many witches.'[89]

The 344 people who were residents of New England and accused of witchcraft between the years 1620 and 1725 were significantly different from their contemporaries: 78% were female (and roughly half of the 22% who were accused men were the husbands, sons, or friends of female witches). The majority of the women were over the age of 40 (past child-bearing years), single, widowed or divorced, and less likely to have brothers or sons. In other words, women who failed to fulfill the primary function of women in Puritan society — to bear children and serves as helpmates to men — were the most likely victims of witchcraft accusations.[90]

One strategic approach to understanding the power and danger of the Sorceress archetype is to approach it from the perspective of it being the source of creative disruptive ideas. In a world in which implicit and explicit bias impacts how women are perceived, creative disruption is both necessary and dangerous. The fear of those who disrupt the status quo frequently leads to violence. Understanding the implications of violence as a response to creative disruption can help us develop effective risk mitigation strategies.

Archetype 6: Queen

The Queen archetype is about legitimized feminine power. She is capable and has sovereignty. She is typically seen as married and is loyal to her husband, the King (unless, of course, there is no king, in which case she holds all the legitimate power herself). She is Hera, wife of Zeus, the Romans' Juno, the Hindu Parvati, the Norse goddess Frigg, Egypt's Hatshepsut, and the Queens Elisabeth I and II. She is a full-grown woman, resplendent in her power. When there are darker Queen Bees, Ice Queens, Evil Queens, Red Queens, and Wicked Queens, these women characteristically still display control and power that comes from the freedom to choose.

Queens typically are thought of as resplendent in their jewelry and finery. They stand above the other women around them, who may constitute their loyal court. The Queen has regal demeanor and asserts the natural confidence of leadership.

As with any feminine archetype associated with power, there is a shadow side. She may be seen as emotionally distant, vindictive, jealous, judgmental, controlling, or angry. But because they are leaders, Queens are responsible for the safety and well-being of their subjects. She has responsibilities. She is complex and mature.

When considering contemporary women who have achieved the highest success as leaders, Margaret Thatcher, Indira Gandhi, Golda Meir, Winnie Mandela, Jacinda Arden, Eleanor Roosevelt, Ruth Bader Ginsberg, Condoleezza Rice, Sandra Day O'Connor, Nancy Pelosi, Madeleine Albright, and Kamala Harris immediately come to mind. They are from different nations, cultures, and political perspectives, but they all have possessed the capacity to communicate confidently and effectively, inspire loyalty, negotiate the world of masculine hegemony, and carry themselves, not bejeweled in finery, but as strong, elegant women.

Much has been written about the double bind women leaders face in being judged by their appearance and dress. "Too feminine," "too masculine," "too formal," "too informal" are a constant barrage of judgment women leaders are subjected to. Kamala Harris was criticized for her Chuck Taylors. Hillary Clinton has been harassed for her pantsuits. Michele Obama received negative press for wearing a black sleeveless dress in her first official portrait as First Lady. Alexandria Ocasio-Cortez has been criticized for wearing tailored business suits and for wearing a sequined designer dress.

Not surprisingly, the most senior political leaders have chosen to blend in with respect to clothing choices rather than be subjected to the disproportionate criticism they face for their clothing choices. A few have figured out how to make a statement without the backlash. Madeline Albright did so with her lapel broaches. Ruth Bader Ginsburg's dissent collars may be the most ingenious fashion choice of any modern Queen.

The Reykjavik Index assess attitudes toward female leadership in the G7 countries as well as India, Kenya, and Nigeria.[91] The results of its recent survey of 20,000 people in these nations are disheartening. Angela Merkel, former chancellor of Germany, was perhaps the most effective leader on the world stage in the past five years, yet only 41% of the Germany people in the survey said they felt very comfortable with a woman being the head of government. The responses from the other countries were abysmal: 56% in Nigeria and Kenya, 38% in Japan were uncomfortable with a woman as the nation's leader.

An interesting insight from the Reykjavik study is that when researchers asked respondents, "For each of the following sectors or industries do you think men or women are better suited to leadership positions?" the majority in each country stated men were more suited, but when asked direct, explicit questions about prejudice against women leaders, many survey respondents deny their prejudice.[92]

There are positive trends reflected in the Reykjavik report with regard to pharmaceutical and medical research, in that the G7 average index score was higher (80) in terms of being perceived as having leadership roles equally suitable for women and women. Unfortunately, the healthcare sector scored lower (71), ranking 18th out of the 23 sectors surveyed. Results indicated that among general practitioners in the United Kingdom, the discrepancy in average earnings was the worst of any gender pay gap of any profession.[93]

More encouragingly, research focusing on unconscious gender bias is beginning to shed light on methods to address its adverse impact on advancing women leaders. Unconscious gender bias occurs when a person consciously rejects gender stereotypes but still unconsciously makes evaluations based on them.[94] Even people who view themselves as progressive on gender bias issues, including women themselves, have hidden gender-based biases.[95]

Those women who have managed to successfully attain leadership roles likely do so within the parameters of the Queen archetype. Recent leadership development work focused on unconscious gender bias acknowledges the rediscovery of the importance of the unconscious developed by Sigmund Freud, C.J. Jung, and other early psychologists, that until recently has been overshadowed by behavioral psychology. Strategies to develop an empirically based framework for diagnosing women's workplace experiences that impact their ability to attain leadership roles is beginning to focus on making them aware of specific manifestations of gender bias in organizations, such as few role models, suboptimal networks, and excessive performance pressure.

Developing women leaders will require organizations, including healthcare organizations, to identify their Queens and develop strategies for maximizing their numbers and effectiveness. Healthcare organizations need to undertake this strategic work because unconscious gender bias affects healthcare workers and patients. A study in Denmark showed women waited longer on average for a diagnosis than men 72% of the time,[96] with disbelief in women's symptoms and under-recognition of pain contributing to inadequate symptom management.[97] In the United States, implicit gender bias has been identified at the medical student level, with residents, with academic physicians, and for older women physicians throughout their careers.[98,99]

So how do we develop Queens (female leaders) in healthcare? A recent article in *Harvard Business Review* provides specific recommendations:[100]

- Institute family-friendly policies to eliminate the maternal bias that presumes mothers do not have time to be leaders by including 12 weeks of paid childbearing leave, 4-12 weeks of childrearing leave for all new parents, lactation rooms and protected time, onsite childcare services with emergency back-up care, paid catastrophic leave, and career schedule flexibility.
- Mitigate bias, discrimination, and sexual harassment through implicit bias training, annual salary review, more effective reporting systems for harassment, and legal assistance for family responsibilities discrimination.
- Improve mentorships, sponsorships, and targeted funding for women through formal mentoring programs, peer mentoring, facilitated sponsorships, development workshops specifically for women of color, and research support when women are caring for children or ill family members.

Of these recommendations, the first two are about leveling the playing field through structure change; the third is about developing our Queens.

Archetype 7: The Wise Old Woman

Sometimes she is a grandmother, loving and kind and wise. Sometimes she is a crone, to be shunned and feared. The Wise Old Woman is a storyteller. If you listen to her, you may learn from her wisdom. But sometimes she is ignored, deemed irrelevant to contemporary happenings, and sometimes feared. Carl Jung referred to the Wise Old Woman as a *mana personality*, representing a primordial spiritual energy, or life power, that could assist one in growth and transformation or, alternatively, in destruction and disintegration.[101]

The Great Mother exists in myths, fairy tales, and legends from around the world. She has reached a certain age and has learned from her experiences. She is self-contained, independent, and sometimes peculiar or eccentric. She is Hecate to the Greeks, Earth Mother to many, the Sage, the Wise Crone. She is not always physically decrepit but is always a woman with maturity. Some modern mythic Wise Old Women include Mary Poppins and the Good Witch Glenda. Some real modern women identified with the Wise Old Woman archetype include Maya Angelou, Oprah Winfrey, and Jane Goodall.

The Wise Old Woman archetype can be associated specifically with professions. Although in traditional Western culture the professions of teaching, medicine, law, and the priesthood were seen as male avocations, in contemporary culture, the embodiment of special knowledge within the guise of professionalism can work well for women as well as men.

Jung considered Logos, or knowledge, to be a feminine principle, embodied in the multitude of professions such as medicine, law, and teaching. In considering the definition of medical professionalism, "the values, behaviors and relationships that demonstrate a doctor's central determination to devote to his or her knowledge, skills and judgment to the protection and restoration of human well-being,"[102] the Wise Old Woman may be the archetype that best embodies the professional role for female physicians.

GENDERED ARCHETYPES AND SENSEMAKING IN PATRIARCHAL SOCIETIES

Feminist scholarship has focused on the development of a system that validates the experience of women, whether congruent with that of men or radically different. In this work, many scholars have wrestled with how to make sense of these repetitive motifs that pop up in multiple cultures as represented in the female archetypes. Jung disciple Toni Wolff described the four feminine archetypes — the Mother, the Hetaira, the Amazon, and the Medium[103] — which roughly correlate with some of the feminine archetypes we have flushed out in this analysis, but she then connects them to historical roles designated for women in ancient Greek society.

A *hetaira* is a form of courtesan, mistress, or prostitute in ancient Greek culture. These women were unmarried companions of men, with whom they engaged in sex, had educated conversations, even participation in the Greek Symposia along with male partygoers. Apollodorus considered them a part of his tri-partite division of the types of women: "We have hetaireia for pleasure, concubines for the daily tending of the body, and wives in order to beget legitimate children and have a trustworthy guardian of what is at home," described in the 59th speech of Demosthenes.[104] Ann Ulanov explains the four feminine archetypes in *The Feminine in Jungian Psychology and Christian Theology*:

> These fundamental archetypal forms of the feminine are described in the myths and legends of all cultures throughout history, as for example in the recurrent tales of the princess, the maiden, the wise woman, the witch, etc. In our everyday speech, when we describe women we know or know about, we often resort to typing them unconsciously using archetypal images. Common examples are the references to a woman as a "witch," "a man-eater," and so forth. The archetypal forms of the feminine describe certain basic ways of channeling one's feminine instincts and one's orientation to cultural factors. They also indicate the type of woman one is or the type of anima personality a man is likely to develop.[105]

Mary Daly and other feminists have challenged patriarchy's prefabricated set of meanings built into these archetypes. Archetypes give order to our experience and shield us from meaninglessness. Yet, Daly writes, the experience of nothingness is crucial for women to become authentic. "This becoming who we really are requires existential courage to confront the experience of nothings, a space that is not 'set apart' from reality, but from the contrived nonreality of alienation."[106]

Societies punish those who dare to live outside of prescribed roles. Within the context of the healthcare industry, we have already documented some of the impact these punishments play on the ongoing lives of healthcare professionals in contemporary 21st-century society. The inherent human need for order must be balanced by breaking down these archetypal hierarchies into their component parts, exposing them as "inner compulsions, psychic pulls, to be part of a collective view of women and men"[107] that has the ability to both enrich us and trap us in their rigidity.

USES OF ARCHETYPAL STRUCTURES IN ORGANIZATIONAL THEORY

Lest my work in flushing out the archetypes strike some of you as esoteric to understanding model healthcare organizations, it may be useful to look at some of the organizational theory work that draws on these Jungian principles to analyze the underlying operating dynamics of modern businesses. Gareth Morgan's *Images of Organization* identifies gender and the management of gender relations as one of 14 crucial sources of power to be managed in organizations.[108] His description of predefined gender stereotypes should look familiar:

Male Stereotypes	Female Stereotypes
Logical	Intuitive
Rational	Emotional
Aggressive	Submissive
Exploitative	Empathic
Strategic	Spontaneous
Independent	Nurturing
Competitive	Cooperative
"A Leader and Decision Maker"	"A Loyal Supporter and Follower"

What should also look familiar is his characterization of some strategies for management of gender relations by women and men. I have added a third column to his strategies categorization to make the link to archetypal theory more explicit:

Female Strategies		
Queen Elizabeth I	Rule with a firm hand, surrounding oneself as far as possible by submissive men.	Queen Archetype
The First Lady	Be content to exercise power behind the throne; a tactic adopted by many "corporate wives" such as executive secretaries and special assistants.	Wife Archetype
The Invisible Woman	Adopt a low profile and try to blend in with one's surroundings, exercising influence in whatever ways one can.	Spinster Archetype
The Great Mother	Consolidate power through caring and nurturing.	Mother Archetype
The Liberationist	Play rough and give as good as you get; be outspoken and always make a stand in favor of the role of women.	Tomboy Archetype
The Amazon	Be a leader of women. This style is especially successful when one can build a powerful coalition by placing like-minded women in influential positions.	Huntress Archetype
Delilah	Use the powers of seduction to win over key figures in male-dominated organizations.	Seductress Archetype
Joan of Arc	Use the power of a shared cause and mission to transcend the fact that you are a woman and gain widespread male support.	Heroine Archetype
The Daughter	Find a "father figure" prepared to act as sponsor and mentor.	Daughter Archetype

Male Strategies		
The Warrior	Bind women into roles as committed supporters. Frequently adopted by busy executives caught up in fighting corporate battles.	Hero Archetype
The Father	Win the support of younger women searching for a mentor.	Father Archetype
King Henry VIII	Use absolute power to get what one wants, attracting and discarding female supporters according to their usefulness.	King Archetype
The Playboy	Use sex appeal (both real and imagined) to win support and favor from female colleagues; often adopted by executives lacking a more stable power base.	Lover Archetype
The Jock	Use "display behavior" to attract and convince women of one's corporate prowess. Often used to garner admiration and support from women in subordinate or lateral positions.	Trickster Archetype
The Little Boy	Try to "get one's way" in difficult situations, especially in relation to female co-workers and subordinates. The role may take many forms, including the "angry little boy" who throws a temper tantrum to create a stir and force action; the "frustrated or whining little boy" who tries to cultivate sympathy; and the "cute little boy" who tries to curry favor, especially when he's in a jam.	Child Archetype
The Good Friend	Develop partnerships with female colleagues, either as confidants or as key sources of information and advice.	Brother Archetype
The Chauvinist Pig	Use various "degradation" rituals that seek to undermine the status of women and their contributions. Often used by men who feel threatened by the presence of women.	Villain/Bully Archetype

The feminist critique that Jung's archetypes are reductionist and stereotypical does not negate the fact that in our patriarchal society, men tend to dominate roles favoring aggression and women have been socialized to accept roles placing them in subordinate positions. Morgan asserts that organizations can serve as psychic prisons, where the dominant influence of the male is rooted in the hierarchical relations found in the patriarchal family, which can serve as a factory for authoritarian ideologies:

In many formal organizations one person defers to the authority of another exactly as the child defers to parental rule. The prolonged dependency of the child upon the parents facilitates the kind of dependency institutionalized in the relationship between leaders and followers and in the practice where people look to others to initiate action in response to problematic issues. In organizations, as in the patriarchal family, fortitude, courage, and heroism, flavored by narcissistic self-administration, as are often valued qualities, as in the determination and sense of duty that a father expects from his son. Key organizational members also often cultivate fatherly roles by actin as mentor to those in need of help and protection.

Critics of patriarchy suggest that in contrast with matriarchal values, which emphasize unconditional love, optimism, trust, compassion, and a capacity for intuition, creativity, and happiness, the psychic structure of the male-dominated family tends to create a feeling of importance accompanied by a fear of and dependence on authority. These critics argue that under the influence of matriarch values, organizational life would be far less hierarchical, be more compassionate and holistic, value means over ends, and be far more tolerant of diversity and open to creativity.[109]

We need to understand the significance of unconscious factors influencing our choices and behaviors in our organizations in order to break the bonds of these psychic prisons. The structures, rules, behaviors, beliefs, and patterns of culture that are hidden dimensions of our everyday realities can be recognized and our institutions can be fundamentally redesigned to reflect more balanced and equitable values.

CHAPTER THREE

Sorting Hats and Mindbugs

The modern social world in which we live would be unrecognizable to our ancestors The social contents of our minds, how we think about what's right and wrong as it involves other people, even those quite unlike us would be incomprehensible to them. Human values and aspirations have changed radically and rapidly, even within just the last few generations. Principles of equal rights and fair treatment, values essential to any modern democratic political system, have existed for barely a few centuries. The demands placed on us to survive in the past are not the same demands that allow us to thrive now.[110]

— Mahzarib R. Banaji and Anthony G. Greenwald

The female is, as it were, a mutilated male, and the catamenia are semen, only not pure; for there is only one thing they have not in them, the principle of soul.[111]

— Aristotle

And ain't I a woman? Look at me! Look at my arm! I have ploughed and planted, and gathered into barns, and no man could head me! And ain't I a woman? I could work as much and eat as much as a man — when I could get it — and bear the last as well! And ain't I a woman? I have borne thirteen children, and seen most all sold off to slavery, and when I cried out with my mother's grief, none but Jesus heard me! And ain't I a woman?[112]

— Sojourner Truth

Diagnostic excellence requires a comprehensive knowledge of diseases, skills in data gathering, competency in communication, and judgment in fact integration and problem solving. As such, diagnosis involves both the art and the science of medicine. At times, diagnosis involves fast thinking via pattern recognition (for people who have findings that are highly specific for a certain disease), whereas at other times, it involves slower thinking with iterative analyses. Putting it all together to achieve diagnostic excellence requires caring, curiosity, practice, experience, and feedback, all components of lifelong learning that contribute to the joy and satisfaction derived from the practice of medicine.[113]

— Allan S. Detsky, MD, PhD

J.K. Rowling's Sorting Hat is a sentient magical hat that determines which of the four school houses at Hogwarts a new student most belonged in. The first-year students are lined up one by one, and the battered old hat placed on their head. Then it speaks to the wearer in a small, quiet voice, interpreting their thoughts and feelings, and then pronouncing for all to hear which house the child had been assigned to, with no alternative future possible once the assignment had been made.

In *The Philosopher's Stone,* Harry Potter repeats "Not Slytherin, not Slytherin, not Slytherin..." with anxiety and dread, until he hears the happy pronouncement that he is to be in Gryffindor. The Sorting Hat is sometimes able to make an instantaneous judgment, determining Draco Malfoy belongs in Slytherin House immediately, while deliberating about Harry Potter's placement for several minutes in a so-called Hatstall (delayed decision) in which it carefully reasoned about his qualities such as cunning and determination; his history, based upon his parents' legacy as Gryffindors; and Harry's own dread at the prospect of being placed in Slytherin.

J.K. Rowling's seven-novel fantasy series is the best-selling book series in history, and in its fantastical adventures of dragons, witches, and flying cars, the basic underlying tension that drives the plot of good vs evil forward is the sorting of individuals into categories of beings, such as Muggles, Pure-Bloods, Gryffindors, Ravenclaws, speakers of Parseltongue, Dementors, and House Elves. All this sorting of people into categories and groups is something we have done as a human race since the beginning of recorded history. And, like the Sorting Hat, sometimes the sorting we do is instantaneous, and sometimes we sort after thinking and considering more slowly.

The archetypes that are inculcated into our cultural heritage are the constituent elements we use to sort. Heuristics are the rules of thumb we use to do the sorting. The power and weaknesses of the brain processes we use to do this sorting have been studied over the past half century by the collaborative team of Daniel Kahneman and Amos Tversky, who flushed out the two types of thinking we employ when we are sorting instantaneously or when we are in a Hatstall.

Kahneman and Tversky developed their work on the psychology of judgment and decision-making over a 30-year collaborative partnership. They performed thousands of experiments to research *cognitive bias* and *heuristics*. The story of their collaboration is told by Michael Lewis in *The Undoing Project* and the insights their research has taught us about how we are trapped by cognitive bias is summarized in Kahneman's 2011 bestseller *Thinking, Fast and Slow*.

Kahneman and Tversky identified two modes of thought that human beings use to make decisions. System 1 is fast, instinctive, and emotional. System 2 is slower, more deliberative, and more logical. Rational and non-rational triggers are associated with both types of thinking processes.

The process by which people use mental short cuts to arrive at decisions is called *heuristics*. Human beings use heuristics to decide within a short period of time when information is incomplete and uncertain. Types of heuristics that people frequently use in making quick decisions include the *availability heuristic*, whereby our judgments of probability and frequency of events rely on the ease by which we recall examples of those events; the *anchoring heuristic*, whereby people tend to accept and rely on the first piece of information they receive when making a decision; the *affect heuristic*, whereby people decide based on their emotional impressions rather than making laborious calculations and assessments; and the *representativeness heuristic*, whereby people tend to judge new things they encounter by comparing them to things or concepts that they are familiar with.[114]

Because they are mental shortcuts, heuristics can lead to cognitive biases. A *cognitive bias* is a systematic pattern of deviation from rationality in judgment. Individuals create their own subjective reality from their perception of an input. This construction of reality, not the objective input itself, dictates their behavior and enables faster decision-making, but can lead to errors due to inaccuracies and irrationalities.

In social identity theory, an *implicit stereotype* is an individual's pre-reflective attribution of particular qualities to a member of some group. Substantial research has demonstrated beyond reasonable doubt that implicit bias does predict socially and organizationally significant behaviors, including employment, medical, and voting decision made by working adults.[115]

The human brain is designed for quick pattern recognition, which is not necessarily a negative trait. There is a survival advantage to jumping quickly away when one sees a limbless, tubular shaped animal with a forked tongue and rattles on its tail underneath a rock, without having to deliberate whether all those traits probably signify a rattlesnake. But quick pattern recognition at its worse can lead to the fast, sloppy decision-making that creates cognitive errors, discrimination, and sometimes tragedy, such as the police shooting of 12-year-old African American Tamir Rice in Cleveland, Ohio, in 2014 when his water pistol was interpreted as a weapon.

Banaji and Greenwald have coined the term *mindbugs* to refer to a broad category of cognitive and social errors that people make that are assumed to have a basis in our evolutionary past as well as our cultural and individual histories.[116] These ingrained habits of thought lead to error in how we perceive, remember, reason, and make decisions.[117]

Archetypes are the psychological constructs upon which implicit cognitive biases are built. Archetypes are used to create recognizable, explanatory stories, and they can create mindbugs. They are universal, indestructible, intuitive ways to grasp the essence of attributes that connect directly with the unconscious mind.[118] As such, archetypes can be useful. The archetypes can empower you if you are able to spot them. By identifying situations and events where your actions are being interpreted through the unconscious archetypal presuppositions, you can alter the constraining storylines in which these archetypes typically move.

The archetypes can also be a trap. If they are not identified and managed, they limit your freedom. For example, a younger woman who is unconsciously linked to the Maiden archetype may not receive proper education, mentoring, or encouragement that would put her on a path for leadership positions. CEOs typically do not begin their storyline as damsels in distress. Some younger women with older male bosses get trapped into playing an archetypal "daughter" role. As a "protected daughter" they may avoid sexual harassment, but then they remain in a subordinate position that does not naturally progress to a leadership role.

In their popular book about cognitive bias, *Blindspot*, Banaji and Greenwald are quick to point out that we all carry the mindbugs of hidden biases as the result of a lifetime of exposure to cultural attitudes about age, gender, race, ethnicity, religion, social class, sexuality, disability statues, and nationality. Our perceptions of social groups shape our judgments about people's character, abilities, and potential. Our human brains sort by stereotypes, built on archetypes, and become self-fulfilling prophesies.

Stereotypes are rarely favorable, and are typically used to sort and discriminate. In western cultures, the white male adult is the "default" human being. All others, including women, ethnic minorities, and non-binary people, are sorted accordingly. Banaji and Greenwald draw seven conclusions with respect to how mindbugs create racial discrimination as part of a mental sorting process of black men and women:

1. **Black disadvantage exists.** Compared to white Americans, black Americans experience many consequential disadvantages, including on average less formal education, less satisfactory healthcare, less property ownership, lower employment, less pay for the work they do, and high rates of imprisonment.

2. **This disadvantage experienced by black Americans is at least partly due to race discrimination.** There is a broad range of evidence that establishes, beyond any doubt, that black Americans experience race discrimination — disadvantage that is caused just by their being black.

3. **Social differentiation exists.** The human mental virtuality allows people to instantly sort others into highly distinctive categories, such as black female Nigerian rap dancers or elderly white male Swedish furniture makers, and to immediately infer distinct characteristics that they associate with these categories. Stereotyping is inseparable from this remarkably refined human ability to recognize and categorize human diversity.

4. **Attitudes have both reflective and automatic forms.** Reflective or explicit attitudes are those we are aware of having; automatic or implicit attitudes are comprised of associative knowledge for which we may lack awareness.

5. **People are often unaware of disagreement between the reflective and automatic forms of their own attitudes and stereotypes.**

6. **Explicit bias is infrequent; implicit bias is pervasive.**

7. **Implicit race attitudes (automatic race preferences) contribute to discrimination against black Americans.** Implicit bias operates outside of awareness, hidden from those who have it, but the discrimination that it produces is clearly visible in research.[119]

Just as racial sorting creates the mindbugs that lead to racial discrimination, gender sorting creates sexual discrimination. The dominant social order of Western civilization is built on patriarchal concepts that remain largely invisible but, as demonstrated in the research of Gerda Lerner and others, "constantly reinforced metaphors around gender in which the male is perceived as the norm and the female as deviant; the female as unfinished, physically mutilated and emotionally dependent." Lerner's work illuminated five major assumptions about gender in patriarchal society:

1. **Men and women are essentially different creatures**, not only in their biological equipment, but in their needs, capacities, and functions. Men and women also differ in the way they were created and in the social function assigned to them by God.

2. **Men are "naturally" superior, stronger, and more rational, therefore designed to be dominant.** From this it follows that men are political citizens and responsible for and representing the polity. Women are "naturally" weaker, inferior in intellect and rational capacities, unstable emotionally, and therefore incapable of political participation. They stand outside of the polity.

3. **Men, by their rational minds, explain and order the world.** Women, by their nurturant function, sustain daily life and the continuity of the species. While both functions are essential, that of men is superior to that of women. Another way of saying this is that men are engaged in "transcendent" activities, women — like lower class people of both sexes — are engaged in "immanent" activities.

4. **Men have an inherent right to control the sexuality and the reproductive functions of women, while women have no such right over men.**

5. **Men mediate between humans and God.** Women reach God through the mediation of men.[120]

Lerner's work was a deep analysis of the development of patriarchy as the organizing cultural power structure upon which Western civilization was built, with a creation of feminist consciousness arising out of women's experiences with the limitations of this construct from the Middle Ages through the 19th century. Lest any dismiss Lerner's conclusions as being part of our history but not relevant to our contemporary world or our broader topic of the paucity of women in healthcare leadership, let's review some data from the past three years.

Both in primary care and specialty care, female physicians continue to experience pay discrimination. Female primary care physicians generate less revenue per visit because they spend more time with each patient on average, yet studies controlling for confounding factors such as specialty, age, academic degree, and number of sessions worked per week find that compared to male colleagues in the same practice, they spent more time in direct patient care per visit, per day, and per year.[121]

Female physicians have been found to be more likely to factor in past medications and psychosocial health when diagnosing disease, and diagnosis and prevention of certain conditions, including diabetes mellitus, tend to be more comprehensive when performed by female physicians, with patients of female physicians more likely to maintain control of blood pressure, glycemic index, and blood lipoproteins.[122]

A large population-based matched cohort analysis found small difference in surgical outcomes between patients treated by female and male surgeons, with the former having a small but statistically significant decreased risk of short-term postoperative death.[123] At the population level, evidence indicates that Medicare patients treated by male physicians have increased healthcare costs, adverse outcomes, and chance of hospital-related death compared to those treated by female physicians.[124]

Despite these statistically significant differences in outcomes, implicit biases negatively affect women in their medical careers by contributing to slower advancement, less favorable evaluations, underrepresentation in leadership positions, fewer invited lectures, lower salaries, impostor syndrome, and burnout.[125] In a cross-sectional study of nearly 40 million referrals to surgeons, female surgeons received nonoperative referrals more often than did male surgeons. Male physicians have a strong preference for referring patients to male surgeons; this disparity is not narrowing over time or as more women enter surgery. These preferences lead to lower volume of and fewer operative referrals to female surgeons and perpetuate sex-based inequities in medicine.[126]

I believe a deeper understanding of the female archetypes that undergird many of the discriminatory practices that are perpetuated through the mindbugs of implicit bias is crucial in eliminating the harm they cause. Recognizing when, where, and how these sorting archetypes serve as shortcuts in decision-making can empower women with a powerful diagnostic tool that can combat this ongoing implicit gender bias.

Just as pattern recognition of the various presentations of disease is a crucial skill clinicians must develop over the course of their training, pattern recognition of which archetypes are influencing behaviors in a professional setting can be a crucial skill to navigate the impact of implicit gender bias.

The diagnostic acumen that is a foundational clinical attribute of excellent physicians is built upon sorting ever-increasing amounts of available information. Clinicians are trained to gather and integrate data by relevance to form diagnostic hypotheses upon which an iterative Bayesian thinking process can be applied to assess various learned disease profiles against the patient's clinical story.

The art and science of medicine involves fast pattern recognition and slow analytic processes that good clinicians have learned to weave together to develop their diagnostic acumen. Clinical pattern recognition is based on listening to a story, making observations, and comparing and contrasting to stories one has heard before. Likewise, archetypal pattern recognition is built upon listening for stories one has heard previously and comparing and contrasting to them.

JUNG'S SORTING HATS AND
KAHNEMAN'S MINDBUGS

We need to describe in more detail the concept of archetypes as developed by Jung and subsequently refined by others in order to understand better how implicit bias occurs. Jung's concept of the collective unconscious is that every person in the world is connected by an understanding of patterns, symbols, tendencies, and situations, which are the archetypes. These archetypes are patterns that are universally recognized by people of different eras.

Jung describes four major archetypes that together shape the human personality.

1. **The self.** Jung considers the *self* to be the sum of the conscious and unconscious aspects of the total personality of an individual.
2. **The persona.** Jung describes the *persona* as a mask. It is the outward appearance a person displays: gender, social role, etc., who you appear to be, not who you are.
3. **The shadow.** The *shadow* is the unconscious aspect of an individual, repressed by social circumstances, such as rules, laws, ethics, cultural norms, and expectations. Jung took Sigmund Freud's concept of the shadow, the unconscious aspect of one's personality that the conscious ego does not identify with, and developed a broader concept of shadow to be the unknown dark side of the personality. Within that construct, he saw both positive and negative characteristics in every archetype. He believed that a person's life work is to achieve self-actualization through acknowledging, confronting, and assimilating all parts of oneself, including the shadow.
4. **The anima and animus.** Jung believed *anima* is the feminine side of a man and *animus* is the masculine side of a woman and argued that society repressed the natural femininity and masculinity of people, causing them to fail in the process of individuation. He proposed that the anima was a way for men to become more in touch with their emotionality and spirituality. His concept of animus is less cohesive than his analysis of the anima. He describes the animus as containing four developmental layers centered around collective strength romance, authority, and spirituality.

Jung further develops from the four major archetypes of self, persona, shadow, and anima/animus, a category of 12 separate *character archetypes* that represent behavior patterns that make up different ways of being. They are also cultural symbols and images that exist in the collective unconscious: *the leader, the caregiver, the creator, the explorer, the hero, the innocent, the jester, the lover, the magician, the member, the outlaw, and the sage.* Jung proposes that it is within these cultural symbols that an individual lives out their story. These archetypes are the original patterns of which all things of the same type are representations or copies.

Drawing in the insights of Kahneman and Tversky, we see that the archetypes underlie the biases built into the heuristics by which we make decisions. System 1 thinking involves associating new information with existing patterns, rather than creating new patterns for each new experience. Kahneman described several components that lead to errors in judgment built into System 1 thinking. *Anchoring* is a tendency to be influenced by irrelevant numbers and information. The *availability heuristic* is a mental shortcut that people use to make judgments about the probability of events on the basis of how easy it is to think of examples. The *substitution heuristic* is the propensity to substitute a simpler question for a difficult one. *Framing* is the context in which choices are presented.

Kahneman distinguishes between two selves: the *experiencing self* and the *remembering self.* He believes that the remembering self dominates the ultimate conclusion one makes in decision-making. Jung would agree and would contribute that the remembering self is composed of both the conscious and collective unconscious aspects of oneself and tells stories based on archetypes.

The short cuts we use in System 1 decision-making are built on recognizing these patterns and comparing and contrasting our present experience to them. Here is how that might work:

GENDER The person I am with is female.
AGE The person I am with is young.
POWER The person I am with is vulnerable.
KINSHIP The person I am with is a member of my family.
THEREFORE, THE PERSON I AM WITH IS MY DAUGHTER AND MUST BE PROTECTED.

GENDER The person I am with is female.
AGE The person I am with is mature.
POWER The person I am with is powerful.
KINSHIP The person I am with is not a family member.
THEREFORE, THE PERSON I AM WITH IS A QUEEN OR A WITCH AND I MUST BE CAREFUL.

Understanding how patterns of kinship, power, age, and risk intersect with these archetypes can be useful in identifying what archetype is unconsciously impacting a particular professional situation. Pattern recognition is built into fast-thinking System 1 by evaluating a particular person or circumstance against previously learned archetypes and stories. The heuristic relies on sorting. Therefore, understanding how the archetypes are sorted can provide useful insights.

SORTING THE ARCHETYPES BY GENDER

When sorted by gender, the archetypes are not symmetrical. Jung described archetypal events that human beings undergo during the course of their lives: birth, death, separation from parents, initiation, marriage, the union of opposites. And, he described archetypal figures: Mother, Father, Child, Wise Old Man, Wise Old Woman, the Trickster, the Hero.[127] He thought of the number of archetypes as being infinite and fluid, but he believed the 12 ones that specified character were primary.

Most of the 12 archetypes are typically identified as male: *the Creator, the Explorer, the Hero, the Jester, the Magician, the Member, and the Outlaw.* A few are androgenous: *Sage, Lover.* A single one is identified as female: *Caregiver.*

Other thinkers have elaborated on Jung's concept. Neo-Jungians Moore and Gillette modeled out archetypes of masculine psychology as consisting of four healthy masculine archetypes (King, Warrior, Magician, and Lover) and unhealthy shadow archetypes (Tyrant, Sadist, Detached Manipulator, Weaking, Masochist)[128] but they did not elaborate out comparable feminine archetypes.

Neo-Jungian Carol S. Pearson, PhD, conceptualized 12 archetypes as *the Idealist, the Realist, the Warrior, the Caregiver, the Seeker, the Lover, the Revolutionary, the Creator, the Sage, the Jester, the Magician, and the Ruler.* On Pearson's website, the photographic images associated with these archetypes are all male except the Caregiver, the Revolutionary, and the Magician, despite her "gender-balanced human development theory."[129]

Caroline Criado Perez's recent book *Invisible Women* put this into perspective not through Jungian theory, but in identifying the gender data gap in all facets of life as being the result of the presumption that the default human is male:

> One of the most important things to say about the gender data gap is that it is not generally malicious, or even deliberate. Quite the opposite. It is simply the product of a way of thinking that has been around for millennia and is therefore a kind of *not* thinking. A double not thinking, even: men go without saying, and women don't get said at all. Because when we say human, on the whole, we mean man.[130]

SORTING THE ARCHETYPES BY AGE

The three archetypes of the Divine Feminine are Maiden, Mother, and Crone. They are explicitly tied to a woman's reproductive stage. The Maiden is virginal, but a potential mother, who often must be protected, defended, rescued, or saved. Her rescue is often the object of the Hero's journey, but she herself traditionally is not depicted as being capable of undertaking a heroic journey herself.

The Mother archetype is the caregiver. As such, she is defined by her relationship to those she provides care for: her children, her spouse, and her own parents. In cultural traditions the world over, both historical and contemporary, women are expected to provide most of the caregiving tasks within both their family structures and often in their external work. Globally, 75% of unpaid work is performed by women.[131] In the UK, 70% of unpaid dementia caregivers are women, and female caregivers are more likely to help with bathing, dressing, using the toilet, and managing incontinence.[132]

Once a woman is past her reproductive years, she becomes a Crone. The older woman archetype is in its positive form, the grandmother, who "supports other women by setting up the Maiden with fine suitors, and helping the Mothers raise their little ones."[133] The post-menopausal Crone can be seen as the Wise Old Woman, representing intuition, wisdom, and inner knowing. But in literature, the Crone image is not entirely positive:

> The Crone: the ancient holy one. She holds the power of age and time, of retribution, and of transformation... Ancient, though not always aged, she may be beautiful, but she's not pretty.[134]

She is often associated with the image of the Hag and, as such, can be feared as representing aging and ugliness.[135] Our cultural obsession with preserving youthfulness coincides with the decidedly feminine nature of age bias. Gender disparity becomes more remarkable with advancing age. Among the population 85 years and older, 67% are women. In this age range, only 18% of women are married, but 58% of men are. The poverty rate of the oldest old is increasing, related to the gender bias among the most aged.[136]

SORTING THE ARCHETYPES BY KINSHIP

Mother, daughter, sister, grandmother, and aunt are family members. Their archetypal roles are filtered through the lens of kinship. When women are perceived within the framework of their familial role, the archetype is generally positive. Mothers are caregivers, grandmothers are wise, daughters are innocent. However, female archetypes that are non-familial are more often associated with the shadow aspects of the self.

In fairy tales and myths, there are countless Evil Queens and Wicked Step-mothers (not really part of the family). Crones are not wise grandmothers, but Hags and Witches. The Lover archetype, almost always positive in its male form, can deteriorate to the Whore or Slut in its female form, as sexuality outside the framework of the family and marriage is taboo.

In patriarchal societies, powerful women are to be feared, and the language used to describe them is pejorative and violent. Podcaster Taryn De Vere (who happens to be a mother of five children) wrote in 2018 that she has been called over the past several years "witch, bitch, slut, whore, murderer, cunt, up-yourself, dangerous, show-off, cult leader," which she attributes to her being perceived as a Powerful Woman:

> How this world hates and fears Powerful Women. I can't think of one con-temporary or historical woman who had power who wasn't vilified and, in some cases, murdered for it. Powerful Women upset the patriarchal order of things. Women aren't supposed to like themselves; they're not supposed to be happy; they're not supposed to live without a man, or have lots of chil-dren outside of marriage; they're not supposed to like sex and if they do then they're not supposed to talk about it.[137]

The term "bitch" has been used as a term of contempt toward women for over six centuries. As Yvonne A. Tamayo has documented:

> Originally, "bitch" referenced a sensual or promiscuous women, and later evolved to include a woman considered angry, spiteful or malicious. Today, the term includes a woman deemed aggressive, competitive, or domineering. Despite its definitional nuances, "bitch" remains an unequivocal expression of hostility used to denounce, harass, and insult women who, by acting out-side of their prescribed gender roles, threaten the established paradigm of power as an inherently "male" characteristic.[138]

Using "bitch" has been interpreted as a method of containment and disci-pline to disempower women:

> "Bitch" is not only **a defining archetype** of female identity but also func-tions as a contemporary rhetoric of containment disciplining women with power....Using the term "bitch" in casual conversation, political punditry, and public debate is the most recent incarnation of sexual containment in American pollical culture. Its use is widespread and the potential conse-quences for women are significant. "Bitch" is more than an epithet — it is a rhetorical frame, a metaphor that shapes political narratives and governs popular understanding of women leaders.[139]

Linguist Deborah Tannen states that "bitch is the most contemptible thing you can say about a woman. Save perhaps the four-letter C word."[140] In its original meaning, a bitch is, of course, a female dog that has given birth — in other words, a mother. But a bitch is not a mother in one's family and as such it is used to prohibit women from assuming power in the non-family space.

SORTING THE ARCHETYPES BY DANGER/SAFETY

Several years ago, I bought a book entitled *Women, Fire, and Dangerous Things* because I loved the title and presumed it would teach me stuff. Indeed, it did, but I was astonished when I opened it for the first time to discover it was not a book about feminist theory, as I had inferred from the title, but a deeply thoughtful book in the field of linguistics in which the author, George Lakoff, is exploring what categories reveal about the mind.[141]

Indeed, Lakoff predicted the inference that many others and I made, that the title of the book suggests women are fiery and dangerous or have some commonality. He states that the idea that things are categorized by what they have in common is a classical idea that has been with us since antiquity. More recently, a new theory of categorization has emerged called *prototype theory* that shows that human categorization is based on principles that extend far beyond the classical theory.[142]

Lakoff explains that the title of his book is taken from the Australian aboriginal language of Dyirbal, in which one category, *Bayi*, includes human males and nonhuman animates; one category, *Balan*, includes human females, fire, and dangerous things; a third category, *Balam*, includes edible plants; and a fourth category, *Bala*, includes everything else.[143]

The central argument of his book is that the purported relationships between categories in the world and their "mental representations" do not hold. He cites the Dyirbal categorization example as evidence that conceptual categories do not get their meaning only by virtue of corresponding to objectively existing categories in the world. Rather, "human conceptual categories have properties that are determined by the bodily natures and imaginative processes (metaphor, metonymy, mental imagery) that do not mirror nature."[144]

Nonetheless, he agrees with the classicists that "most categorization is automatic and unconscious, and if we become aware of it at all, it is only in problematic cases."[145] It is these problematic cases that Lakoff's predecessor, Hilary Putnam, called *stereotypes*. A stereotype for Putnam is an idealized mental representation of a normal case, which is not necessarily accurate. For Putnam, tigers have stripes, although there are examples in the real world of stripeless tigers.

For women, the underlying automatic and unconscious categorizations (archetypes) make us the "problematic cases." Consider the tongue-in-cheek tweet that went viral on Twitter in November 2021. "Men tend to choose high paying professions — like doctor, engineer, CEO, etc., while women naturally go toward lower paying careers — like female doctor, female engineer, and female CEO,"[146] or the tweeted photo of a man holding up a sign that said, "She's Someone's sister/mother/daughter/wife" with all of those categories marked out for the sign to then read "She's Someone."[147] Both tweets make the point that women are an exception to the general category.

Caroline Criado Perez's extensive study on the adverse impact of seeing men as the human default includes everything from anthropologists identifying most pre-historic human skeletons as male (proven incorrectly in later DNA studies) that skew our scientific understanding to drugs that do not work for one sex or the other.[148]

In 2021, researchers confirmed at the University of Southampton in the UK that personal protective equipment has not been developed for female healthcare workers and those from Black and minority ethnic backgrounds, leading to lower levels of protective performance for these populations. Facial dimensions differ between men and women and between people of different ethnicities, but face masks and respirators were developed predominantly for a white male population based on their anthropomorphic measurements.[149]

By being viewed as "problem cases" or "exceptions to the norm," women frequently are identified as dangerous when they hold roles outside the safe archetypes. And what are those safe archetypes? Most of them are family roles: grandmother, mother, sister, daughter. The Maiden must be rescued because she is outside the protection of her father. The woman Lover quickly becomes the Seductress or the Whore. Consider the term for an older woman pursuing a younger man in a sexual relationship: "cougar." Christian culture has historically associated cats with "the subversive power of the devil and particularly with women who are non-compliant with notions of feminine (and feline) compliance."[150]

The Wise Old Woman archetype is safe in the persona of the grandmother, wise and caring, and to be feared in the persona of the Witch, wicked and frightening. During the exceedingly misogynous era of 1450 and 1700 CE, approximately 100,000 people were tried and killed for being witches; more than 80% were women. Witches were persecuted during the height of male priestly power in Christian Europe, when the Church idealized the spotless Virgin. In contrast, the Witch is sexual. She is Satan's Whore who has agreed to become his mistress for the powers of necromancy.[151]

In contrast, the Huntress is one of the only female archetypes to be defined outside the confines of the family that is safe for women. She is powerful with natural physical strength, protective of the weak, action oriented. Even here, the role is one of category exception. Like "female CEO," she is a Huntress, not a Hunter. She is a tomboy, not a boy.

SORTING THE ARCHETYPES BY POWER/VULNERABILITY

Painting with a broad brushstrokes, the female archetypes who have power are the Mother, Queen, Huntress, and Witch. Maidens are vulnerable and must be protected or rescued. The Seductress has power that is to be feared. The Wise Old Woman has wisdom, but her power is ambiguous. In her personification as Grandmother, she is respected and loved and sometimes seen to be a protector. However, as Hag or Witch, she is outcast and shunned, although her powers are feared enough to have her killed as a Witch.

Among the male-gendered archetypes, nearly all possess some form of power, whether in the persona of Father, Grandfather, Hero, Trickster, Lover, King, or Villain. Among the 12 original Jungian archetypes (Innocent, Everyman, Here, Outlaw, Explorer, Creator, Ruler, Magician, Lover, Caregiver, Jester, and Sage), the gender-neutral Innocent is vulnerable. The female Lover archetype in its positive form is actually the "beloved" to be pursued and won over by her male counterpart. If she is depicted in a more powerful persona, she becomes the cougar, a dominating and manipulative woman. In contrast, the Maiden is obedient, innocent, passive, and easily manipulated.

SORTING THE ARCHETYPES BY SHADOW/LIGHT

Crucial to Jung's original concept of the unconscious archetypes which we use in our sensemaking is the idea of the shadow. Jung posited that the shadow is the unconscious aspect of the personality that the conscious ego does not identify with. In contrast to Freud's concept of the unconscious Id, Jung's shadow can be either positive or negative, but tends to be most associated with negative personality traits because it includes the least-desirable aspects on one's personality. "Everyone carries a shadow, and the less it is embodied in the individual's conscious life, the blacker and denser it is," he wrote.[152]

Among the general categories of the female archetypes, the Wise Old Woman's shadow is the Witch. The Mother's shadow is the Wicked Stepmother. The Queen becomes the Wicked Queen. The Lover becomes the Whore or Seductress. In more modern terms, the women who becomes the CEO, president, doctor, or other singular leader title traditionally identified as male has the feared shadow identity of the Bitch.

Some social research based on fieldwork and interviews during the 2016 election cycle identified explicit constructed narratives that portrayed presidential candidate Hillary Clinton as a "bitch-like personality," with implicit characterization that framed but did not directly call her a "bitch."[153]

This "bitch-whistling" with respect to Hillary Clinton goes back as far as the 1990s when she was First Lady, and Speaker of the House Newt Gingrich's mother, Kathleen Gingrich, said in an interview with Connie Chung: "She's a bitch."[154] In 1984, when former President George H. W. Bush was running for vice president, his wife, Barbara Bush, described her husband's political opponent, Geraldine Ferraro, very explicitly: "It rhymes with rich."[155] Female Republican politicians have had equal treatment, including more recently Marjorie Taylor Greene, Nikki Haley, and Sarah Palin.

THINKING FASTER AND SLOWER

Jung's postulated archetypes have long been criticized for an assumption that Jung presumed their innateness in the psyche as *a priori* structures. Certainly, reality is far more complex than these dualistic categorization schemes. But human beings still use archetypes, which are "nothing more than the deep structures in the psyche and social systems,"[156] to make sense of their life experiences.

Much progress has been made in the past decade by the LGBTQ+ community calling out the limitations of the binary nature of archetypal thinking.[157] However, many of our social systems are still built with the either/or, male/female, light/shadow, power/vulnerability, young/old, family/stranger, binary categories with all the inequalities and divisions they sustain. We unconsciously draw on them when we think fast; we do not adequately draw on them in our analyses when we think slow.

Recognizing them can help us learn how to use them to provide us power and can help us learn when they are trapping us. Then, we need to think slower and develop alternative storylines and strategies to prevent rigid archetypes from limiting the possibilities of our lives and leadership potential.

As Erik Goldwyn of the Billings Clinic points out, "There seems to be abundant evidence that the mind is crammed with innate predispositions, perceptual biases, recognition mechanisms, emotional and expressive subroutines, behavioral urges, and more....Jung's *a priori* archetype-as-such was perhaps not so misguided after all."[158]

JUNG'S SORTING HAT

Archetype	Gender	Age	Power	Kinship
Leader	♂	Adult	✚	Tribe
Creator	♂	Adult	✚	Tribe
Explorer	♂	Adult	✚	Tribe
Hero	♂	Adult	✚	Tribe
Jester	♂	Adult	✚	Tribe
Magician	♂	Adult	✚	Tribe
Everyman	♂	Adult	✚	Tribe
Outlaw	♂	Adult	✚	Tribe

(table continues)

Archetype	Gender	Age	Power	Kinship
Lover	♂	Young Adult	+	Tribe
Sage	♂	Old	+	Tribe
Wise Old Woman	♀	Old	+	Tribe
Grandmother	♀	Old	+	Family
Mother	♀	Adult	+	Family
Daughter	♀	Young	✕	Family
Maiden	♀	Young	✕	Family
Innocent	♀	Child	✕	Family
Queen	♀	Adult	+	Tribe

(table continues)

Archetype	Gender	Age	Power	Kinship
Wild Woman ✊	♀	Adult	✛	Tribe
Great Mother 🤰	♀	Adult	✛	Family
King 👑	♂	Adult	✛	Tribe
Mystic 🦉	♀	Adult	✛	Tribe
Witch 🍯 🐦	♀	Old	✛	Other
Whore 👠	♀	Adult	✕	Other
Bitch ⚡	♀	Adult	✛	Other
Tomboy 🌱	♀	Young	✛	Family

PART II

Who Is She?

In a world where the "default" human is male, the patriarchal imperative has always been to constrain the definition of what it is to be a woman. But from the pre-Homeric three-faced goddess Hecate to our contemporary Tomboys and Bitches, this strategy continues to fail.

CHAPTER FOUR

Tomboys, Maidens, and Daughters

You are old enough to leave off boyish tricks and behave better, Josephine. It didn't matter so much when you were a little girl; but now you are so tall, and turn up your hair, you should remember that you are a young lady.

— Louisa May Alcott, *Little Women*

One purpose of this book is to analyze differences in identity that women in the healthcare industry experience that impact their capacity to take on leadership roles and fully contribute their talents. In the previous chapters, we exposed an exhaustive litany of barriers to advancement, many the result of unconscious biases designed into the cultural fabric of our patriarchal history. As pattern seekers, people make quick judgments based on archetypal elements they have been socialized to recognize. Frequently, these judgments are dualist and binary: girl or boy, hero or maiden, caregiver or leader. But the dualism we have inherited as part of our intellectual tradition does not account for the rich variation in forms that make up our world.

At its best, human culture is built on "ands" not "ors": hero AND maiden, leader AND caregiver. Constructing the world of ands is a creative process, and one that permits people to embrace differences as providing richness of experience and talents, rather than limiting freedom and opportunities.

TOMBOYS

While I was growing up, people called me a tomboy. I liked to run and play outside with my brother and boy cousins. I preferred wearing blue jeans to dresses, playing with Lincoln Logs to dolls, mowing the yard to washing the dishes, riding my horse to twirling a baton. I loved climbing to the top of the enormous magnolia tree in my backyard and hanging upside down on the monkey bars.

In my high school band, every other girl chose to play the flute or clarinet except me. I chose the drum and the trumpet. My brother, cousins, and I played games that basically consisted of running around with sticks and pine cones in our hands saying "pow! pow!" and making machine gun noises we had heard on TV in various iterations of hide-and-go seek and tag.

We chose up sides and gave the games what we thought were impressive sounding names (and now very politically incorrect ones) such as "cowboys and Indians," "cops and robbers," and "army." We built forts, stacked up rocks, dug out little trenches. I was as comfortable in all these typically male roles as my cousins and brother were.

When my best friend Nell and I "played doctor," I refused the nurse role. In my imagination, the nurse was limited to assisting only by handing the doctor the toy medical instruments to operate on the patient. Nell typically agreed to play the nurse and we inevitably assigned the role of patient to my younger sister Pam, who was just glad to be included in our games at all. It was not uncommon for Nell and me to kill off poor Pam with a deadly illness we invented on the spot. Curing her was not really part of the plan. It was mostly about getting to use the little plastic toy medical instruments.

When people asked me what I wanted to be when I grew up, it was usually "a mad scientist" or "a horse jockey." In those pre-Title IX days, there were not very many sports options available for girls. I rode my horse Daisy everywhere, including one year riding from door to door with my Girl Scout uniform on to sell Girl Scout cookies, but did not have much opportunity to play competitive sports.

I grew up watching my brother Jack, two years younger than me, playing little league baseball and midget league (this name also now recognized as insensitive) football. In my community, there were no comparable athletic opportunities for girls. When I got to middle school, I was so excited with the possibility of being on the girls' basketball team, but I had never played organized sports before, was short and clumsy, and was cut from the team two years in a row.

I practiced basketball every afternoon in my yard with my brother and cousins and was able to make the junior varsity team my freshman and sophomore years of high school, where I sat on the bench both seasons, and was cut from the varsity tryouts my junior year. I also tried out for the girls track team in high school, but it folded when there was not enough interest to have a team, so I switched to the boy's track team, running the 440- and 880-yard events. I wanted to try pole vaulting, but was told by the coach that girls did not have the capability of pole vaulting because of our weak upper body strength.

As a point of fact, I do not have weak upper body strength. Even at age 60, I am able to bench press my weight. Nonetheless, back then, there were significant constraints on what I was permitted to do. And when I was successful, it had repercussions. On the track team, I started the year about middle of the pack in the 880. By the end of the year, all the boys I had beat had quit the team, so I was dead last.

The term *tomboy* isn't used much anymore. Its popularity has waxed and waned over the course of history. The *"tom"* part of tomboy comes from the 12th-century Middle English term *"thom,"* which meant "boy type," like the term "tomcat." Tomboy was coined in 1556 by Nicholas Udall in a play called *Ralph Roister Doister* to describe a rambunctious boy. By the 17th century the term had evolved to mean a "forward, immodest, or unchaste woman." Finally, by the 19th century, it derived its current meaning of "a girl or young woman who acts or dresses in what is considered to be a boyish way, especially one who likes rough or energetic activities conventionally more associated with boys."[159]

That certainly is a good description of me as a child. Back in the 1960s and '70s, the term did not have as strong an association with gender ambiguity as it does in the contemporary dialogues about gender identity, although the cultural approval of tomboys continues to swing positive or negative from one historical period to another.

Being a tomboy was quite a freeing identity for me as a child. I was not subjected to much pressure as a child to act only in traditional stereotypical female roles. I enjoyed play activities associated with adventure rather than care giving. I wore little black patent leather shoes with white anklet socks and frilly dresses to church on Sunday, but on the other days it was mostly jeans. In jeans, I didn't get embarrassed by exposing my underwear when I hung upside down on the monkey bars, which would happen in the jumper my mother occasionally convinced me to wear to school.

Although I started elementary school at a time when girls typically wore dresses and skirts to school, by high school, jeans were unisex and requisite for everyone. For the most part, my parents, teachers, and friends accepted my behavior. In contrast, I heard my brother and male cousins being told to not "be a sissy" or "throw like a girl." The underlying message they learned, and I learned to a certain degree by proxy, is that it was a bad thing for them to be perceived as feminine. The biggest compliment my parents would give my brother was "he's all boy." I would have not considered it a compliment to be described as "all girl."

I will not speak for my brother and cousins, but others who have thought deeply about the impact of patriarchy on men point out that just as patriarchal culture has narrowed what is acceptable for women, it also constrains men to reach the full spectrum of the humanity by conditioning them to repress such important qualities as emotional expressivity, empathy, and nurturing.

Tony Porter calls "the man box" an invisible inner prison that patriarchy has built for men, that sets them up for a false hero's journey, pushing men to seek external sources of fulfillment rather than learning how to express their authentic selves.[160] A recent study of men and women from over 70 countries shows that men universally put more value on independence, self-enhancement, and status, while women emphasize the well-being of their inner circle and people in general.[161]

Apparently, my childhood experience is not unique. In 19th-century American culture, the word *tomboy* referred to permitted conduct by young girls to exercise, wear "sensible clothing" and to eat a "wholesome diet."[162] The 19th-century feminist writer Charlotte Perkins Gilman asserted that "the most normal girl is a 'tom-boy' — whose numbers increase among us in these wiser days — a healthy young creature, who is human through and through; not feminine till it is time to be."[163] Playground advocate Joseph Lee advocated for tomboyism in 1915 as crucial to a girl's development:

> In short, a girl should be a tomboy during the tomboy age, and the more of a tomboy she is, the better. From eight to thirteen is indeed, according to the best authorities, the critical age with girls, and not, as is generally supposed, the period of the early teens; because it is during the earlier period that the issues of the later one are practically decided. If a girl does not become a good sport before she is fourteen, she never will, but will be condemned to premature young-ladyhood.[164]

In film and literature, tomboys remained popular through the mid-20th century. The 19th-century heroines like Jo March in *Little Women* and Laura Ingles Wilder in the *Little House on the Prairie* series foreshadowed Scout Finch in *To Kill a Mockingbird* (1960), Addie Loggins in *Paper Moon* (1973), and Amanda Wurlitzer in *The Bad News Bears* (1976).

But in post-WWII culture, a new push to "hypergender" boys and girls began to emerge. The baby boomers became the first American generation in which almost every child was raised wearing gender-specific dress.[165] The previous traditions of dressing young children in unisex clothing ended with highly differentiated clothing choices for the two genders, including the designation of pink as a color appropriate only for girls and blue as a designated color for boys' clothing.

The need for women to provide the labor workforce during World War II created a Rosie the Riveter character — a woman with independence. When men returned to the workforce after the war, women's and girls' clothing became frillier, curvier, and more constraining, returning them to a power-diminished state. 1950s *Parents* magazine articles explicitly told mothers how to raise girls to be wives and mothers so they would not be "seriously handicapped adults."[166] Tomboy behavior was considered an acceptable stage for girls ages 7–10, which they needed to grow out of by puberty in order to prepare for their roles as wives and mothers. *The New York Times* assured parents in a 1950s article headlined "'TOMBOY' PHASE CALLED NATURAL" up until puberty.[167]

By the 1980, the hypergendering of childhood had led to pink bikes, pink diapers, pink Legos, pink Barbie cars, pink everything for girls. For the Mighty Morphin Power Rangers American superhero series premiering in 1993, of the five teenage superheroes, two were girls: yellow ranger and, you guessed it, pink ranger.

The 1981 animated children's television series *The Smurfs* featured only blue characters. Of the original 20 characters, only one, Smurfette, is female. All the rest — Papa, Clumsy, Brainy, Grouchy, Hefty, Greedy, Jokey, Chef, Vanity, Handy, Scaredy, Tracker, Sloppy, Harmony, Painter, Poet, Famer, Natural, Snappy, Slouchy, Grandpa, Baby, Architect, and, of course, Doctor — are male. Subsequently, a second female, Sassette Smurfling, is created as the baby sister of Smurfette, and Nanny is created as an old flame of Grandpa Smurf. These three female characters, representing the three ages of womanhood without irony, are not "natural" Smurfs; they are created with sorcery.

Much of what is considered normal for girls and boys is created by culture and changes over time. The highly binary girl/boy gender divisions of the past several decades have been created around specific marketing strategies that have gendered nearly all toys, clothing, bedding, school supplies, and cultural role models.

The Powerpuff Girls characters created as an American superhero animated television series based on female characters centers around three kindergarten-age girls who have superpowers. Blossom, the leader is "sugar and spice and everything nice." Her color is...wait for it...pink. Bubbles is the "softest and sweetest" of the three with a blue designated color and blonde hair. Buttercup is the "tough hotheaded tomboy." Her personality is "spice," and her signature color is green. She is characterized as loving to "get dirty, fight hard and play rough; she does not plan and is all action."[168] Tomboy Buttercup was originally to be named Bud, but this was changed to Buttercup, perhaps to alleviate any hint of gender ambiguity.[169]

More recently, the media is starting to develop more diverse female protagonists, including non-white Disney princesses such as Mulan and Pocahontas, *Star Wars'* Rey and *Game of Throne's* Arya Stark. Yet in 2018, just 38% of main characters on kids' TV shows were female, and those female characters are twice as likely to use magic to solve problems as boys, who use physical power and STEM skills. Female characters are twice as likely as male characters to be portrayed sexually, based upon appearances such as breasts, long eyelashes, etc.[170]

Backlash against feminism and LGBTQ+ social movements that has developed since the 1970s has resulted in societal fears that tomboyism leads to lesbianism or transgender identity later in life, despite the lack of evidence that childhood and adolescent behavioral typical of boys but displayed by girls is an indicator of one's sexual orientation later in life.[171] For some transgender people, the freedom of non-gendered childhood play roles can certainly be a healthy and liberating experience, as Stephen Hutting recently shared:

> Growing up, I learned an additional function of play: identity formation. I viscerally cringed when I heard my female name, so I reinvented myself as a dog or dinosaur to whom names meant nothing. It should be noted that sexual differences in those species are far more subtle than in humans. For the hours in which I was fantasizing, I could except the body that abraded me, as well as any roles of "daughter" and "girl."[172]

However, an equal number of *cis*-gendered women proudly claim to have been tomboys as a child, including Janet Jackson, Cher, Ava Gardner, Jean Jennings, Hillary Rodham Clinton, Dolly Parton, and Julia Child.[173]

The term "psychologically androgynous" is a term coined by psychologist Sandra Bem in the 1970s to characterize individuals who combine personality traits that American culture has broken down into masculine and feminine. Her work has been criticized for defining some traits as masculine, such as dominance, forcefulness, competitiveness, and independence, and some as feminine, such as affection, sympathy, warmth, soft-spokeness, and tenderness, as being too binary. Why should there have to be a special name, *tomboy*, for independent, forceful, dominant girls? Nonetheless, data using the Bem Sex-Role Inventory (BSRI) does indicate that individuals identified as androgynous, as opposed to more polarly masculine or feminine, correlate with confidence, higher self-esteem, creativity, and career success.[174]

I believe my healthy dose of "psychological androgyny," i.e., tomboyism, provided me with certain skills that have served me well as an adult and possibly provided me with advantages that have led to my leadership roles in the healthcare industry.

The structural problems our society creates in hypergendering childhood via clothes, toys, and expected behaviors leads to girls curtailing certain activities and focusing on their appearance, and boys focusing on their skill sets.[175] For me, and those girls like me who never felt comfortable in polarizing feminine roles, we may have had greater comfort in "playing with the boys" in our adult roles and therefore were more accepted in leadership positions.

I also believe that it is decidedly wrong for the many highly talented women who are not comfortably tomboys to be constrained by unfair gender stereotypes that contribute to gender disparities throughout the healthcare industry. From that point of view, spaces in which women feel uncomfortable or excluded in which informal leadership opportunities may be arise need to be identified and mitigated.

DAUGHTERS

The subconscious ways in which one is perceived in the professional settings of the healthcare industry need to be recognized as part of the human tendency to structure experience. As delineated so effectively by Sylvia Brinton Perera,

> Often identity is based on personal adaptations to what the animus tells us should be, so we adapt to or rebel against the projections hooked onto us; thus, we have almost no sense of our own personal core identity, our feminine value and standpoint. In the West, women have too often been defined only in relation to the masculine as the good, nurturant mother and wife, the sweet, docile, agreeable daughter, the gently supportive or bright, achieving partner.[176]

That "sweet, docile, agreeable daughter" may be how some younger women are perceived in the work environment, limiting their ability to advance in leadership opportunities. My experience, even as a tomboy, like many girls growing up, had all sorts of pressures toward gender-conforming behavior. I knew very early that, although I could run wild and climb trees and whoop and holler as much as my brother, I always had to wear a shirt and he did not years before puberty ever set in. I had more chores, like drying the dishes, shelling peas, snapping beans from our garden, and dusting the house, that he was never required to do, in addition to outside work I enjoyed like mowing the lawn and feeding the horses and cows. I detested being told to "be more ladylike," which meant, among other things, I couldn't participate with the boys and men in castrating bulls, which seemed to me was the most mysterious and exciting aspect of our cattle farm.

Some of the data evaluating the tomboy phenomenon indicate that the older a child gets, the more pressure there is to "gender conform." I smile to myself sometimes at the very "unladylike" things I do as part of my internal medicine practice and wonder what my grandmother would think about them. My grandmother, who we called Big Mama (all 4 foot 11 inches and 98 pounds of her) constantly admonished me about the sports I played. She told me if I wasn't careful all that physical activity would make my "female organs" fall out.

Big Mama, born in 1908, was educated at home to prevent her exposure to the influenza pandemic of 1918. Her ideas of how a proper girl should behave did not include basketball, castrating bulls, or sweating. My dad teased me when Big Mama admonished me about the constant imperiled state of my female organs, saying that if I didn't behave, he would send me to "an all-girls' finishing school to get me finished!" My sister Pam and I would just giggle at the absurdity of it all, but we knew there were subtle gendering messages being conveyed, even in the teasing.

Big Mama would have declared the digital rectal exams, hemorrhoid excisions, and other minor procedures I perform as part of my primary care practice as "unladylike" as castrating bulls, I suppose. The 57 autopsies I performed as a pathology intern at Duke Medical Center in 1990 were not very ladylike either.

The type of activities I was restricted to participate in on the farm due to my gender were based on rigid cultural perceptions of what female versus male children could acceptably participate in. Much of modern-day medical culture still has some of these same biases built in. For example, I remember my fifth-grade math teacher, Mr. Poston, presented this riddle to the class:

> A man and his son are driving in a car one day, when they get into a fatal accident. The man is killed instantly. The boy is knocked unconscious, but he is still alive. He is rushed to the hospital, and will need immediate surgery. The doctor enters the emergency room, looks at the boy and says, "I can't operate on this boy, he is my son." How is this possible?

The answer is that the surgeon is the boy's mother, but just as was the case in 1971 when I first heard this riddle, most people today are stumped because they do not jump to seeing that the boy's mother could be a surgeon. In fifth grade, I remember shouting out the right answer in the classroom and being mocked by the boys in the room that a woman being a doctor was silly. The experience Dr. Joan L Thomas describes when she applied to an orthopedic residency program in 1978 was not much different from my experience in elementary school a few years earlier. The interviewer at a Midwest orthopedic residency program told her they had hired a female resident once and, although she was doing well in her private practice in Colorado, they were "not ready for another one."[177]

Ultimately, Thomas determined becoming an orthopedic surgeon was a glass ceiling she was unlikely to shatter in 1978, so she pivoted to cardiology and became one of the first female chiefs of cardiology in the United States before retiring in 2021. In 2022, orthopedic surgery remains the whitest, most male-gender-skewed specialty in the U.S. healthcare system.

Nineteenth-century childrearing manuals asserted that girls who were raised as tomboys "would surely develop the resourcefulness, self-confidence, and, most importantly, the constitutional vibrancy required for motherhood."[178] In this era, strong, energetic young girls were valued, but they were expected to abandon these tomboyish traits at the onset of adolescence. "Tomboy taming" is a literary theme seen in the transformation of Jo March in *Little Women* and Laura Ingalls in the *Little House* books. Louisa May Alcott was apparently forced by her editor to marry off Jo in *Little Women* in order for the novel to get published.

By the end of the 19th century, tomboyism had evolved from being perceived as behavior to be encouraged to promote strength and health to dangerous behavior that, if persistent into adulthood, could encourage women to delay marriage, get an education, and have a professional career.

The 19th-century male medical establishment argued that the "weaker sex" did not have the physical strength or intellectual capacity to handle the rigors of higher education or a professional career, and that, if young women were permitted to participate in these activities, they would ruin their health and reproductive abilities. (Just like Big Mama warned me!)

Dr. Edward H. Clarke of Harvard Medical School asserted in *Sex in Education* (1878) that women were "destroying their wombs and their childbearing potential by pursuing a course of higher education intended by nature only for the male sex."[179] But interestingly, *fin-de-siecle* feminists promoted the New Woman in literary fiction with stories of tomboys who grew up to become physicians.

The growing number of female physicians in the United States by 1900 was supported by such characters in novels as Caroline Simmons in Harriet Beecher Stow's *My Wife and I*, Dr. Cornelia D'Arcy in Lillie Devereux Blake's *Fettered for Life*, Lurida Vincent in Oliver Wendell Holmes' *A Mortal Antipathy*, Dr. Mary Prance in Henry James' *The Bostonians*, Nan in Louisa May Alcott's *Jo's Boys*, William Dean Howells' *Dr. Breen's Practice*, Sarah Orne Jewett's *A Country Doctor*, and Elizabeth Stuart Phelps' *Doctor Zay*.[180]

Tomboys, maidens, and daughters are three manifestations of the first phase of the female archetype, each emphasizing a slightly difference aspect of the form. The tomboy emphasizes gender fluidity and freedom. The daughter and maiden differ mostly in the primary male relationship in which they are defined: daughter with the father and maiden with the hero. These gender-linked archetypes can be seen as inner representatives of socially sanctioned roles and behavior patterns, which sometimes do not resonate with the real lives of real women and girls. The maiden is supposed to transform into the mother and then to the crone, identified as a triple deity.

The triple deity has been found in cultures and religions all over the world. Christianity's Father, Son, and Holy Ghost; Greek mythology's Zeus, Poseidon, and Hades; Hinduism's Brahma (creator), Vishnu (preserver), and Shiva (destroyer) are all Indo-European versions of tripod male-gendered triple deities. Carl Jung identified the arrangement of deities into triplets as an archetype in the history of religion: "Triads of gods appear very early, at the primitive level. The archaic triads in the religions of antiquity and of the East are too numerous to be mentioned here. Arrangement in triads is an archetype in the history of religion, which in all probability formed the basis of the Christian Trinity."[181]

The female-gendered triple deities take the form of the triple-faced goddess, representing the three stages of a women's lifecycle: maidenhood, motherhood, and crone in Neopaganism, although earlier forms of triple female deities do not correlate directly with these forms. The Greek Hecate was represented in triple form as a single body with three faces permitting her to see in all directions as the goddess guarding entrances and boundaries. By the Hellenistic period, she had become the Roman goddess Diana; the three distinct aspects were Diana the huntress, Diana of the moon, and Diana of the underworld.

Among indigenous peoples, medicine women guided young women into women's mysteries at menarche, introducing them to the three stages of a woman's life journey: the *way of the householder* (when a young woman develops independence and self-reliance), the *way of the mother* (when at the birth of her child she learns to master her world), and the *way of the teacher* (when she becomes the transmitter of spiritual and social wisdom). A separate path, *the way of the gatherer and the way of the ritualist*, is a path for those who choose the shaman role of extensive knowledge of seasons, weather, astronomy, healing, and spirituality. The Native American pantheon centers on the Great Goddess, called Thinking Woman or Spider Woman among the Navajo, who has two daughters or sisters, depending upon the particular tribal tradition: Changing Woman and White Shell Woman. Grandmother Spider thought the creation of the stars, sky, and earth or wove it like a web.[182]

In 1949, Jung and Kerenyi proposed the theory that groups of three goddesses in Greek mythology become a quaternity by association with a male god as either daughter, wife, or mother.[183] Many of the ancient goddesses were associated with the moon and its three cycles of waxing moon as maiden, full moon as mother, and waning moon as crone, including Hera, Athena, Hecate, and Demeter. Forms of the Neopagan religions such as Wicca have made this maiden, mother, crone structure a central component of their worship. But some feminists have criticized this trilogy as being too restrictive and founded on an androcentric view of femininity based only on a woman's relationship to a man.[184]

Other scholars have argued that patriarchy was built on religion creation stories designed to supplant female-centric goddesses as creators. Paula Gunn Allen noted that among Native American tribes, gynocentric cultures based on agriculture tend toward Great Goddess creators, such as Spider Woman, while hunting and gathering cultures project male creator deities.[185]

The archetypes reflect cultural assumptions of how human beings are related to one another and how they ought to behave. As Carol Pearson points out, the Warrior archetype is associated with masculinity and the Caregiver archetype is associated with femininity, so boys get reinforcement for warrior behavior and girls for altruistic behavior.[186] Carol Gilligan recognized that women are likely to see the world as webs of connectedness, while men perceive ladders and hierarchies to compete for power.[187]

The human wholeness we need our leaders to develop requires an integration of the elements of both caregiving and heroism. However, the politics of 2023 that manifest many efforts at unconstrained patriarchal power require us to develop a far stronger sense of an inner androgenous self that is distinct from prescriptive sex-defined roles. Again, Carol Pearson is describing the work to be done with prescience:

For many men and women today, finding out who they are requires moving beyond prescribed sex roles to find what it means to be a man or a woman at a deeper, more genuine level. In particular, the connection of Caregiving with women and Warrioring with men seems less connected for many men and women with a genuine sense of gender identity than with long-standing cultural roles (descending perhaps as far back as hunting/gathering societies.[188]

Patriarchal cultures create social models built on competition, war, sexism, racism, and class structure. Androgynous cultures, which bring feminine values of connectiveness and caregiving into the cultural model, can create stronger, more inclusive and sustainable societies. The resulting culture will be nonbinary in nature; that is, restrictive archetypes will be replaced with more holistic ones that permit development of the positive aspects of caregiving and heroism.

The static nature of the specific archetypes gives rise to assumptions that individuals have a "fixed, essential identity, one with which the person is born, rather than one which is achieved dialogically, through complex processes of self-construction in conditions not of one's own choosing."[189] The story arch of the three-fold goddess is that a female child comes of age as a young maiden who is innocent and vulnerable. She must be protected by her father and rescued by a hero, who then marries her. She becomes a mother, who is the caregiver for her family, until she becomes the older crone, either welcomed for her wisdom or cast out as a witch.

This story arch does not account for tomboys, except as a prepubescent transitional stage. Michelle Ann Abate's in-depth cultural analysis of the tomboy exposed that the American version as developed in the 19th century was based on a racialized construct. Femininity had come to be equated with fragility and invalidism for upper- and middle-class white women. The classic tomboy's code of conduct built around sensible clothes, exercise, and a wholesome diet was intended to strengthen white women.

The literature often described tomboys as having a "brown" complexion and dark hair. Female gender rebellion, as developed in the tomboy, pushed boundaries transgressing contemporary conceptions of black/white, male/female, heterosexual/homosexual, savage/civilized, adult/child, different/same.[190] For those of us who were or are tomboys, pushing these boundaries may provide us with certain leadership development skills that can be effective in C-suites and boardrooms that are still constructed within patriarchal design constraints.

However, to ensure there is much greater gender equality in leadership positions, we need to call upon more women than just self-described tomboys.

To do so, the stereotypical storylines built around a women's development into the childbearing and caregiving roles need to be addressed head-on, particularly as they relate to both conscious and unconscious barriers embedded in patriarchal cultures.

Merlin Stone's landmark exploration of the ancient worship of the Great Goddess and eventual suppression of women's rights evaluates prehistoric and early historic periods of human development when religions existed in which people worshipped female Creator deities. According to Stone, female Creator deities were worshipped from the early Neolithic period of 7000 BCE to as late as the closing of the last Goddess temple in 500 CE. Stone believes female Creator deities have been inaccurately interpreted by the male-dominated early archeological texts as "fertility cults."

As Stone asserts, "In most archaeological texts the female religion is referred to as a 'fertility cult,' perhaps revealing the attitudes toward sexuality held by the various contemporary religions that may have influenced the writers. But archaeological and mythological evidence of the veneration of the female deity as creator and lawmaker of the universe, prophetess, provider of human destinies, inventor, healer, hunter and valiant leader in battle suggests that the title 'fertility cult' may be gross oversimplification of a complex theological structure." [191]

Stone argues that men initially gained control "that now allows them to regulate the world in matters as vastly diverse as deciding which wars will be fought when, to what time dinner should be served" as resulting from societies that for centuries have taught young children, both female and male, that a male deity created the universe and all that is in it, producing man in his own divine image, and then as an afterthought created women to be his obediently helpmate.

The image of Eve, created for her husband, from her husband, brought about the downfall of humankind. Her work emphasizes the use of the Adam and Eve myth as justification for patriarchal social hierarchy being called on to justify the brutal massacres called "witch hunts." In a 16th-century church report, the story of Eden was put to use in the following passage: "Woman is more carnal that man: there was a defect in the formation of the first woman, since she was formed with a bent rib. She is imperfect and thus always deceives. Witchcraft comes from carnal lust. Women are to be chaste and subservient to men."[192] Thus, the maiden is to be controlled by men, to be protected by men, and to serve men.

Not all scholars agree with Stone's assertion that a prehistoric female deity was replaced with a male deity as patriarchy became the dominate culture structure in Western European civilization. Sarah B. Pomeroy, who focused her scholarship on women in classical antiquity, notes that very little evidence exists that prehistoric Greek women ever enjoyed equal status to men, with basic demographic evidence establishing that women's lifespan was at least 5–10 years less than men's.[193]

Pomeroy notes that, although there are four times as many neolithic female figurines as male ones, and females predominate in Minoan frescoes, that does not mean that real human women had high status or that prehistoric worship of a Mother Goddess implied female dominance in religion or other aspects of culture.[194] Certainly medieval Christianity's emphasis on the Virgin Mary has demonstrated that a Mother Goddess may be worshiped even in patriarchal misogynist societies. When women are identified in ancient or medieval societies with power, they typically are interpreted along patriarchal lines as evidence of exceptionalism rather than evidence that social change needed to occur.

MAIDENS

For the past 35 years, the avant-garde feminist activist artistic group Guerilla Girls has exposed gender and ethnic bias in art and corruption in politics, art, film, and pop culture using humor and outrageous visuals. They remain anonymous by wearing gorilla masks in public. Their mission has been to mitigate the stereotypes that limit women's choices, challenging labels that "makes you less or more than you really are."[195]

They point out the enormous number of stereotypical categories our culture produces for women relative to men: Daddy's Girl, Girl Next Door, Tomboy, Bimbo/Dumb Blonde, Femme Fatale/Vamp, Bitch/Ballbreaker, the Mother, the Wicked Stepmother, the Old Maid, The Hag/Crone, Supermom, Soccer Mom, Bull Dyke, Feminazi, Bombshell, Foxy Lady, Whore/Prude, Cocktease, Ice Queen, Fag Hag, Bra Burner, Biker Chick, Gold Digger, Trophy Wife, Diva, Lady Boss, Supermodels, among others.

Most of these stereotypes are negative labels signaling a woman is behaving in ways that do not adhere to the standard story line moving from maiden to mother to crone. I believe that in the workplace, these stereotypes are used to lock women into the Maiden role and out of a leadership role.

"She's not ready." I have heard that phrase used more than once to deny a competent younger woman a pathway to leadership. By the early 2000s I was the president and CEO of a large and growing multispecialty medical group in North Carolina called Cornerstone Healthcare. I had been the only women on the 12-person board of directors since its inception and then served as its chief executive officer for 16 years. It was a physician-owned company; the shareholders voted for new shareholders and the board of directors.

Like much of the medical profession at the time, the majority of our physicians were men, although the number of women physicians was growing. We had finally recruited an excellent young female internist to the group who had been with us for two years and was up for the vote. I had presumed unanimous consent but was surprised when that turned out not to be the case. She received a couple of "no" votes, one which had written on the ballot "she's not ready."

Although I was shocked at the time, I shouldn't have been. This young internist was highly competent. She was also beautiful — something that seemed to make some of her male colleagues uncomfortable, although they constantly alluded to it. Flash forward 15 years and a large international company I had an association with announced their new North American leader would be a woman. One of the men in the company I knew commented at the time, "She's not ready." A few years later I listened to a physician leader comment that a new female chief medical officer "was not ready."

All three of these highly competent early- to mid-career women absolutely were ready to move up in leadership positions, yet in each case someone felt perfectly comfortable deeming them "unready" with no explanation as to why that might be so. I believe in all three cases it was pure gender bias, when each of them trapped in subconscious personas of the Maiden, ever young, beautiful, and "unready." Becoming an effective leader requires credibility, and young women often are not bestowed credibility.

Dr. Joan L. Thomas has had the insight that leadership roles are often denied women because "women do not generally remind men of their younger selves."[196] She notes in her wonderful memoir, *The Heart of the Story*, that she had witnessed male leaders giving promotions to favorites, typically younger males who remind them of themselves. Rebecca Solnit, in her insightful essay "Men Explain Things to Me" cogently describes the experience of having an older man lecture her about her own book, unaware she was its author, and become "so confused the neat categories into which his world was sorted that he was stunned speechless." She shares:

> Men explain things to me and other women, whether or not they know what they're talking about. Some men. Every woman knows what I'm talking about. It's the presumption that makes it hard at times, for any woman in any field; that keeps women from speaking up and from being heard when they dare; that crushes young women into silence by indicating, the

way harassment on the street does, that this is not their world. It trains us in self-doubt and self-limitation just as it exercises men's unsupported overconfidence.[197]

The silencing of young women has been part of the Maiden's story line for a long time. The Disney version of "The Little Mermaid" deleted the song "Silence is Golden" from the animated feature. The sea witch Ursula was originally supposed to sing to Ariel:

You won't sing. You won't speak
Not a word, not a squeak
Not a peep, not a squeal
That's the price. Love. That's the deal.

But silence, silence is golden, my dear
Up there, they hate chatter
So, what does it matter
If you become mute
Nobody likes a loudmouth!

I mean it
Silence, silence is golden, my dear
Don't you think you should try it
They'll say she's so quiet, so shy and cute!
Well take it or leave it. That's all, that's the bargain
Go on, take a stand, make a choice

Remember you'll get the legs and the lungs and the prince
All I get is the voice
And you'll be
Silent, but silence is golden. Sign here
There's no choice for you since
You're in love with a prince
but relax. I've been told Silence is gold![198]

Silencing goes hand in hand with powerlessness and young women are often silenced to prevent them from telling stories of predation and violence. The power of the *#MeToo* movement has been the power of women to speak up and tell the stories of how they were silenced and exploited.

Unfortunately, women sometimes have learned to silence themselves. Carol Gilligan identified a gendered division of morality between the masculine and the feminine, with the masculine voice identified as individualistic and rational, free from the nuance of emotion; in contrast the feminine voice is relational-dependent and considerate of others, characterized by moral obligation to maintain harmony within a network or relationships. Gilligan identified an alarming lack of women's voices in the political, societal, and individual spheres she studied. Women were not only omitted from patriarchal public discourse, but were found to have internalized the inequality by silencing themselves.[199] This process of internal restriction has been linked to depression, anxiety, low self-esteem, perfectionism, disordered eating, and loss of self.[200]

The historical, cultural, and political forces that have kept women's voices out of the public sphere are alive and well. The long tradition of silencing women can be attributed to the societal belief that women are inherently responsible to care for those around them. Starting in childhood, both men and women are conditioned to think of women as relationship beings, as daughters, sisters, wives, and mothers. Research finds this conditioning begins early with both young boys and girls endorsing traditional gender roles for women. However, boys report stronger adherence to the belief that women should be subordinate and self-silence in order to maintain harmony.[201]

Self-silencing in women is strongly predicted by the level of women's adherence to traditional gender norms. Women who displayed passive acceptance of the oppression of women were less inclined to respond to a sexist remark as opposed to a nonsexist remark, were far more likely to engage in higher levels of self-silencing.[202] Current research on gendered online harassment has revealed that targeted women are more likely than targeted men to become more cautious in expressing their opinions publicly. Furthermore, the gender differences increase as the harassment becomes more aggressive and directed toward group characteristics.[203]

Women who share their stories are stepping outside of the boundaries that have been created for them. Suzanna Quintana, in sharing her story of her own experience as an abuse survivor, found herself being attacked online for speaking about it:

> *"She's crazy." "Bitter." "Resentful." Vengeful." "Just another bitch with an ax to grind."* These words are designed for one purpose only: to silence women... What is it about a woman speaking up that makes some people want to cover their ears, to the point where they can't stand it and so use the ammo in their arsenal to make it stop: *using words designed specifically for women with the sole intent to make them shut the hell up*...women are oftentimes fairly easy to shut up because our society has reinforced the belief that it's not a woman's place to raise a ruckus, speak out of turn, or god forbid not "be nice." And *why don't you smile more often while you're at it? Put up with whatever I'm serving you and then I want you also to like it.*[204]

Stereotypically, women are perceived as talking a lot. But statistically, men talk more, in both professional settings and in school. Studies indicate that women speak less than men, regardless of their position of power; women who voice their opinion more frequently than other coworkers risk backlash. In addition, women's suggestions are more likely to be discounted.

In a Harvard study, Catherin G. Krupnick researched gender's influence on participation within various classroom settings at Harvard College and across the board male students spoke more often that female students.[205] Facebooks' Sheryl Sandberg and Wharton professor Adam Grant highlighted that the reasons women tend to stay quiet at work include the fact that they walk a "tightrope" when they do speak at work because they are either barely heard or judged as too aggressive.[206]

Women who have become intolerant of the silencing of women have begun to call it out in ways that allow us to identify the behavior more readily. Rebecca Solnit's *Men Explain Things to Me*, gave rise to "mansplaining" to describe the act of a man explaining something to a woman in a condescending way that assumes she has no knowledge of the topic. The tendency for men to take credit for an idea put forth by a woman has been termed "bropropriating" and the unnecessary interruption of a woman by a man has been termed "manterruptions."

MeToo is about the even deeper injustices of sexual coercion, rape, and violence against women that has been silenced in the workplace. Sexual assault survivor and activist Tarana Burke first used the phrase "Me Too" on social media in 2006. The purpose of this social justice and empowerment movement is to empower sexually assaulted individuals to break their silence through empathy, solidarity, and strength in numbers, especially young and vulnerable women, especially in the workplace.[207]

The World Health Organization estimates that sexual violence affects one-third of all women worldwide. A 2017 *ABC News* and *Washington Post*[208] poll found that 54% of American women report receiving "unwanted and inappropriate" sexual advances, with 95% saying that such behavior usually goes unpunished.

MeToo has increased the public dialogue about sexual harassment in medicine. Among 1,000 U.S. academic medical faculty surveyed, about 30% of women but only 4% of men reported experiencing sexual harassment; medical staff who complain often suffer negative consequences to their careers.[209] Reshma Jagsi, the author of the study, wrote in a commentary that none of the medical women who contacted her had previously revealed the abuse they suffered; some questioned their self-worth and wondered if they brought it on themselves. The women who do report sexual harassment experience marginalization, retaliation, stigmatization, and worse.[210]

Unfortunately, about 75% of men who sexually harass women persistently deny any wrongdoing. Men identified with a high score on an anonymous questionnaire regarding their likelihood to use their power over women to extract personal favors were more likely to find a woman attractive if primed with words like "authority," "boss," and "power" than if primed with neutral words. Sexual harassment is thus a tool in the general misuse of power.[211,212]

Kate Manne, author of *Down Girl* and *Entitled,* argues that "misogyny should not be understood as a monolithic, deep-seated psychological hatred of girls and women. Instead, it's best conceptualized as the 'law enforcement' branch of patriarchy — a system that functions to police and enforce gendered norms and expectations and involves girls and women facing disproportionately or distinctively hostile treatment because of their gender."[213] Misogyny discourages girls and women from straying out of bounds of expected gendered behavior. When they do, they know what they will be in for: hostility and often violence.

Manne distinguishes misogyny from sexism, which is the "ideological branch of patriarchy: the beliefs, ideas, and assumptions that serve to rationalize and naturalized patriarchal norms and expectations — including a gendered division of labor, and men's dominance over women in areas of traditionally male power and authority."[214] Whereas sexism is what an individual may believe or feel, misogyny is what a woman experiences or faces. In our patriarchal culture, women are *expected* to be *givers:* of care, nurturing, sex, reproductive labor. Men are *entitled* to be *takers*: of power, authority, claims to knowledge, sex.

The consequences for girls and women who stray outside the borders of gendered boundaries can be far-reaching, including sexual harassment, rape, other forms of violence, and death. A 2015 survey by the Centers for Disease Control and Prevention found that 43.6% of women have experienced some form of sexual violence in their lifetime. A 2010 study on victimization by sexual orientation found that 44% of lesbian women, 61% of bisexual women, and 35% of heterosexual women experienced rape or physical violence.[215]

From a global perspective, one in three women worldwide have experienced physical and/or sexual violence in their lifetime, with 38% of murders of women committed by a male partner. About 100 million girls are "missing" from the world's population — the victims of infanticide, femicide, malnutrition, and neglect. Women between the ages of 15 and 44 are at a higher risk of rape and domestic violence than of cancer, car accidents, malaria, or being injured in war. In addition, 30% of females globally have reported that their first sexual experience was forced.[216] During the COVID-19 pandemic, violence against women has intensified, a "shadow pandemic" according to the United Nations.[217]

Yet, the remonstrations of those accused of sexual harassment in the workforce has continued to damper any legitimizing of outrage: "You are making a big deal out of nothing," "Things were different back then." As Jacqueline Rose notes, "Sexual harassment consists of unwelcome sexual advances which, pace the mostly — though not exclusively — male protests, are never innocent, a mere trifle, playful or a joke. And that is because however minimal the gesture, it nearly always contains the barely concealed message: 'This is something which I, as a man, have the right to do to you.'"[218] Women and girls are rendered powerless by cultural constrictions of gendered roles and male privileges. Those that push the boundaries are subject to misogyny in both of its forms: psychological and physical violence.

I learned about rape before I learned about sex. I was that nine-year-old tomboy I described at the first of this chapter, playing alone at recess at my elementary school. The other children were up on the basketball court playing games: kickball for the boys and some sort of girl game (like pretending to be the Brady Bunch girls) for the girls.

But I hated playing the girl games and the boys didn't like me playing kickball with them. I therefore went around the corner of the schoolyard to my beloved monkey bars and was hanging upside down when a car pulled slowly up about twenty feet from where I was playing. A man called me over to his car. I walked over to the car and then something made me stop about five feet from it. He called me closer. Suddenly I felt frightened and ran back up to where the other kids were playing.

I told the teacher there was a man in a car on the other side of the playground asking me to get in his car for some reason. I remember that she fussed at me for not being with the other children but did not express any alarm about this man. That night at dinner, I mentioned the weird man in conversation. My parents immediately called my grandfather, a retired sheriff, and soon they were asking me to describe every detail of the man's face, the car, asking about whether I knew the license plate number. I was very confused about all of this, not quite sure why there was such a fuss. So, the next day, my mother asked me if I knew what rape was. I did not. I was told.

I had a hard time describing the car to them. It was a pale aqua blue sedan with fins on the back and I didn't know they were called fins. I remember my parents taking my younger brother, sister, and me on a Sunday afternoon drive, and driving into a neighborhood and asking me if a car they pointed to was like the one I had seen at the school yard. It was not, but I saw one across the street that was like that and that's when I learned what fins were — after I had learned about rape.

Over the course of the next few days, I told the other girls in my class about the man in the car and we began pretending we were Nancy Drew (and Bess and George) or Alfred Hitchcock's Three Investigators. (Pete, Bob, and Jupiter), or the Boxcar Children (Henry, Jessie, Violet, and Benny) and were "sleuths" on a mystery to catch a bad guy. When, a few days later, the man showed back up at the school yard we were ready. We got his license plate number.

To this day, I know the man's name, the make of the car, and that license plate number. I know it because several days after we saw him back at our elementary school, he was arrested with a sixth-grade girl in his car. Apparently, with the information I shared over the dinner table and the license plate number we remembered, law enforcement nabbed him when he returned.

And just like that, the tomboy had to understand the dangers of being a maiden, which in my case, was the risk of real abduction/rape, apparently. All the archetypal elements are there: innocent maiden, evil abductor, rescued by a father figure (my grandfather, Big Daddy). But the way I defined myself in this story was not as a victim, which I easily could have been, but as a girl adventurer, sleuthing and participating in the capture of the bad guy, and rallying other children to help me.

I have no idea how much of this I am remembering incorrectly after 50 years, but the basic elements are true: playing alone on the monkey bars, being ignored by the teacher, later getting the license plate number, and being told about the other girl he as picked up in his car. Perhaps, because of this event and the way it figured into how I was told about female vulnerability and sexual violence, I always have had trepidation in playing the innocent maiden role.

I remember Big Daddy absolutely shaming me when I was about 11 years old because I was riding on the back of a horse with one of my male classmates and holding on with my arms around his abdomen. I felt ashamed because he told me I was not behaving "like a lady." It had never crossed my mind that I was supposed to act "like a lady" until he shamed me. I was just riding as a second rider on a horse with one set of stirrups.

Carol Pearson reprised her *Persephone Rising* in 2018 to counter her concern about "headlines documenting instances and abuses of unrestrained patriarchal power, as well as new efforts to redefine and assert feminine ways of gaining influence and power."[219] She specifically focuses on the power of the Demeter–Persephone story.

Demeter's beloved Kore (*girl* in Greek) is stolen away by Hades, God of the Underworld, who rapes her. Demeter, Goddess of the Harvest, will not let anything grow until Hades relents and releases her daughter. Zeus intercedes because the people are starving, and Kore, now transformed to Persephone, powerful Queen of the Underworld, returns to her mother with springtime each year, descending to the Underground every winter.

Pearson interprets the Persephone archetype as providing energy that helps us when we are feeling trapped or stuck to find a path to personal success and fulfillment. Persephone creates new possibilities out of her trap, a young heroine with energy that can be tapped by "women as a group who are just now beginning to recover from the limitations of male-dominated attitudes and social institutions."[220]

The importance of exploring these distinctions between tomboy, maiden, and daughter roles is crucial in getting at some of the important questions about the differences between men and women, male and female, sex and gender. At a basic biological level, those born with two X chromosomes are phenotypically different from those born with an X and a Y. The former has the reproductive organs that allow them to give birth and breastfeed children. The later on average are taller, with more muscle and physical strength and larger larynxes, which leads to deeper tendered voices. Women are the sturdier sex and live longer than men, which is a difference found across mammal species.[221]

While these sexual differences are dimorphic in our species, most aspects of ourselves as human beings are not distinguished by our sexual dimorphism, including our moral reasoning and intelligence. Gender, as opposed to sex, is not dimorphic. It refers to the learned overlays that turn a biological female into a woman and a biological male into a man, and, in contrast to sex, which is bimodal; the differences in gender move across a spectrum based on cultural norms.[222]

In the United States, the color pink used to be considered a masculine color and blue a feminine one, until Madison Avenue switched the gendered messaging. In some societies, boys and girls take care of infants, cook, and perform other domestic chores, while in others, these tasks are assigned solely to girls.[223]

In a study of six cultures across the world, Whiting and Edwards concluded that "there are universal sex differences in the behavior of children 3–11 years of age, but the differences are not consistent nor as great as the studies of American and Western European children would suggest." They caution that learning environments may well be responsible for the behavior frequently attributed to the innate characteristics of male and female primates as inherited by their human descendants."[224]

Primatologist Frans de Waal argues that the doctrine of mind-body dualism "upheld by a two millennia-long slew of male thinkers to elevate their souls above the rest of creation, including women, is unlikely to be helpful in dismantling gender prejudices." He argues that "few human behaviors are rigidly preprogrammed," with obvious gender relations variance from culture to culture, subject to education, social pressure, custom, and example. He asserts:

> Even the few aspects of gender that resist change and seem inalterable offer no excuse to deprive one gender of the same rights and opportunities as the other. I have no patience with notions of mental superiority or natural dominance between the genders, and I hope we'll leave those behind. It all comes down to mutual love and respect and appreciation of the fact that humans don't need to be the same to be equal.[225]

We will have a much better performing human society if de Waal's insights can become culturally embedded, because the vast potential of the half of the human race who has been excluded from positions of leadership and power because of patriarchal assertions that male dominance and female subordination are "nature" will be able to develop richer, more resilient communities. In healthcare, we may begin to reverse our shameful resurgence of infant and mother mortality, domestic violence, male deaths from violence, sexual assault, and female impoverishment.

Common Vocabulary In Relation to Sex and Gender

Terminology	Definition
Sex	The biological sex of a person based on genital anatomy and sex chromosomes
Gender	The culturally circumscribed role and position of each sex in society.
Gender Role	The typical behavior, attitudes, and social functions of each sex resulting from an interplay between nature and nurture.
Gender Identity	A person's inner sense of being either male or female.
Transgender	Referring to a person whose gender identity does not match their biological sex.
Transexual	Referring to a person who has undergone hormonal and/or surgical gender reassignment.
Intersex[226]	Referring to a person whose sex is ambiguous or intermediate since their anatomy, chromosomes, and/or hormonal profile don't fit the male/female binary.

CHAPTER FIVE

Bitches and Witches

It is a fundamental truth that we still live in a world where the division of labor is uneven. At work we also still have to work to lean in, in daily professional life to make sure our voices are heard, to understand that a strong woman leader is often viewed as a bitch, while a strong male leader would never be viewed in that way. The key is to be an effective leader, and we make incremental progress through our effectiveness every day.[227]

— Elisabeth Stambaugh, MD, MM
Chief Medical Officer
Atrium Wake Forest Health Network

*The problem then and today is that the mere act of speaking up in a confident voice often brands women as troublemakers rather than team players. After the episode with that doctor, I sometimes wondered if I had a red "B" emblazoned on my white coat — a "B" that was both invisible and visible, that stood for **Bossy** or maybe something even worse. No matter, I would not back down. I considered it my duty to ensure that patients receive the best treatment available.*[228]

— Joan L. Thomas, MD, CPE, FACC
Chief of Cardiology, Unity Hospital

"Well, what did the bitch say about it?" I stopped dead in my tracks. It was the end of the workday, and I was rushing into the doctors' lounge at the hospital to grab my white coat and stethoscope on my way up to see a patient who had been admitted by the hospitalist service. The two doctors talking to one another were not aware I was behind them at the cloak closet, and they were talking about me.

The woman who was asking the question was a specialist in my medical group, someone whom I greatly admired for her clinical excellence, and someone whom I had gone out of the way to help with a tricky hospital administrative matter that had impacted her personally just a couple of years before. But here she was using the "B" word about me, as the two of them dissected a conversation I had had with the other physician, a man, about an income distribution formula issue impacting our medical group. Before he could answer her, he saw me. His face grew white as a sheet as I looked him in the eyes and nodded to him.

"Well, hello, Grace!" he said, a little too loudly. I just smiled a greeting and walked past the two of them, hearing her whisper as I was nearly out of earshot, "Do you think she heard us?" Yes, I heard you. And the incident must have impacted me enough that I am still remembering it 15 years later.

I also remember the time I called to speak to one of our orthopedic surgeons about a patient concern, and the receptionist who answered the phone asked me, "Now who did you say you were, Sweetie?" I was CEO of the medical group, which she should have known. My signature was on her paycheck. Because I personally find women's use of "Sweetie" and "Honey" when addressing other women offensive, I politely asked her to call me Dr. Terrell from now on, rather than "Sweetie." I figured if she was using that language with me, she was using it with patients, many of whom would be as put off by it as I was.

Yet, the orthopedic surgeon was already laughing about it by the time he got to the phone to talk to me. Apparently, he thought that it was a great joke that the receptionist had been called out by me. What was interesting to me is that she had told him about this when it had been private, polite feedback to her.

What is interesting to me now in reflecting on my internal dialogue at the time: My immediate response to the knowledge that the orthopedist and the receptionist communicated about this was an irrational fear that they were perceiving me as a bitch for providing this feedback to her. I had not been rude to her. In fact, most would argue she was being rude to me, although in the part of the country I am from, the pervasive use of "honey" and "sweetie" when addressing another woman is usually just ignored or accepted. My observation through the years is that these terms are almost never used when addressing a white man, unless he is elderly, but commonly used by waitresses, nurses, clerical staff, clinicians, in grocery stores, retail settings, and restaurants, when speaking to women and often also to older black men. And for those of us who are offended by it, to call it out carries risks. The risk for women when they call out discriminatory language patterns is to be labeled with the Big B.

It is dangerous for women to be perceived as aggressive. The year 2020 was deemed by *The Guardian* as "the year of the Karen" because Karen became the new pejorative term denoting white women using their privilege to demand their own way. A Karen's defining characteristics include "a sense of entitlement, a willingness and desire to complain, and a self-centered approach to interacting with others."

Videos surface on the internet showing white middle-aged women behaving horribly, weaponizing false victimhood to assert power over black men, such as the Central Park birdwatching incident. According to Heather Suzanne Woods, a researcher at Kansas State University, a Karen "demands the world exist according to her standards with little regard for others, and she is willing to risk and demean others to achieve her ends."[229]

But there is no agreed-upon parallel name for a white man who behaves in the same manner. Over the course of the past year, the term Karen has become less about describing behavior than controlling it and telling women to shut up. Hadley Freeman, columnist for *The Guardian*, argues that the term Karen is sexist, ageist, classist, and anti-woman.[230] Jennifer Weiner, writing in *The New York Times* during the pandemic, said the Karen meme had succeeded in silencing her, saying she had had to balance her desire to complain about a nearby man coughing into the open air, hawking and spitting on the sidewalk, with her fear of being called a Karen.[231] The fear of being called a Karen is the fear of being perceived as strident. It is the fear of being a Bitch.

What is so powerful and fearful about the B word? Analyzing this in 2007, Kate Figes noted that when it comes to negative stereotypes, women "win hands down."

> Girls are "bossy" and grow into women who "nag," while boys of all ages are "authoritative" and "natural-born leaders." When men go out for a drink together it is considered positive social interaction or "networking"; when women get together, they "gossip." But the stereotype that many women hate the most is "bitch".... As the actor Bette Davis once said: "When a man gives his opinion, he's a man; when a woman gives her opinion, she's a bitch."

> For centuries, the straight definition of the word bitch was simply a sexually promiscuous woman. Then as women became more powerful throughout the 20th century, the definition expanded to include being duplicitous. Now men tend to call women bitches when they do not get what they want from them. So, if a woman turns a man down for a date, she is a bitch. If she climbs the career ladder faster than him, she is a bitch. If she becomes his boss and turns down one of his ideas, she is — you guessed it— a bitch.[232]

Figes is one of a number of feminist writers who disagree with feminist writers asserting that Bitch should be "reclaimed" and worn proudly by women who find subordinate roles unacceptable. The pro-Bitch group was articulated in the 1960s with the Bitch Manifesto, that declared:

Bitches are "aggressive, assertive, domineering, overbearing, strong-minded, spiteful, hostile, direct, blunt, candid, obnoxious, thick-skinned, hard-headed, vicious, dogmatic, competent, competitive, pushy, loud-mouthed, independent, stubborn, demanding, manipulative, egoistic, driven, achieving, overwhelming, threatening, scary, ambitious, tough, brassy, masculine, boisterous, and turbulent" but nonetheless "Bitch is Beautiful" because "they are subjects, not objects" who "often do dominate other people when roles are not available to them which more creatively sublimate their energies and utilize their capabilities. More often they are accused of domineering when doing what would be considered natural by a man.

A Bitch is a threat to the social structures which enslave women and the social values which justify keeping them in their placed....Bitches are not only oppressed as women; they are oppressed for not being like women. Because she has insisted on being human before being feminine, on being true to herself before kowtowing to social pressures, a Bitch grows up an outsider....By definition Bitches are marginal beings in this society. They have no proper place and wouldn't stay in it if they did."[233]

Kate Taylor asserts that "bitch is a word many women fear because it is hurled at women who are non-compliant, assertive, not willing to smile when you harass them on the street...and it's all about a woman's behavior. If a woman is called bitch, it's because she isn't acting in the way someone else wants, in a way considered complaint with traditional femininity." Taylor acknowledges that "bitch is a lever used to push people down. It's a weapon to belittle and dehumanize....Bitch is a word that follows women from place to place. It arrives before you and stays long after. People you've never met will hear the tale of your bitchiness whether or not it's true." She acknowledges that she can't remember the first, nor the last time she has been called a bitch, "because the word has been used against me so often in my 38 years it would be impossible to count every instance." Nonetheless, she declares, "Bitch now means the other person realizes I'm not a doormat...Bitch tells me I'm standing firm, standing up for myself, and most importantly, that I'm being heard even though others don't like what they hear."[234]

Taylor's point is that the term "bitch" is based on a woman having power that someone is attempting to take away from her by characterizing her behavior as unfeminine, but accepting the term may allow women to identify when they are actually being perceived as powerful and therefore threatening. It is the threatening aspect of the term that likely creates the fear many women feel when they hear it.

The rise of the term "bitch" as an insult against women accelerated in the 1920s with the successes of the suffrage movement. In 1915, most of the books and articles published using the word "bitch" referred to a female dog. However, by 1925, there were a significant number of articles and books that used the word as a slur against women. By 1930, the number of references that called a woman or women "bitches" outnumbered those that used the word in reference to dogs.

As women have gained political power, the term "bitch" is frequently used as a metaphor that signals backlash, particularly when women are on the cusp of achieving power. We saw this in the 2016 election with phrases like "Trump that bitch" and "Life's a bitch, don't vote for one" hurled at Hillary Clinton, and Representative Ted Yoho calling Representative Alexandria Ocasio-Cortez a "fucking bitch" after the two members of Congress had a heated debate about police reform.[235]

Women fear being called a bitch because it is a form of hate speech that is designed to curb their behavior. Hate speech is "speech which intimidates, stigmatizes, abuses, denigrates, or inflicts intention emotional distress on individuals or groups on the basis of race, color, national or ethnic origin, alienage, sex, gender identity, religion affectional orientation/preference, disability, or other characteristic unrelated to individual merit."[236] The purpose of hate speech is to "inflame the emotions, denigrate the designated outclass, inflict permanent and irreparable harm to the opposition, and ultimately to conquer."[237] Hate speech tells its victim that "you are not as good as I am. You belong back in the black part of town, on your back sexually serving us, on the reservation where we put you, in the closet, in the ovens of 50 years ago, silent, enslaved, second class, or dead — as you were before."[238]

Hate speech attacks people at their core and data indicate those who have experienced such language have symptoms as far reaching as psychological symptoms and emotional distress with rapid pulse rate, difficulty breathing, nightmares, post-traumatic stress disorder, hypertension, psychosis, and suicide.[239] Hate speech aimed toward women has not been studied as much as has hate speech directed toward someone's race or religion, but when it has, the data indicate women experience hate speech with increased fear and often fall silent, unable to speak for themselves, especially if the speech is sexual in nature.

In contrast to ethnic-directed hate speech, hate speech toward women is viewed as the woman's own fault, something she has brought upon herself.[240] As a form of hate speech, labeling a woman a "bitch" is a strategy for keeping a woman in her "proper" role.[241] Women who are not in traditional roles are perceived more negatively than those in traditional roles. Asbury observes that "by labeling a woman as a 'bitch,' one is trying to make a woman feel like an outcast, as if she does not fit into society's mold of an ideal woman. A woman who is labeled a 'bitch' is someone who is in control, and this culture seems to find that offensive."[242] The end result for many women, is that they learn to temper their behavior in order to be perceived as less aggressive.

Research has shown that women suffer consequences for their lack of confidence, but when they do behave assertively, they suffer another set of consequences. Women pay a heavier social and professional penalty than men do for acting in a way that's seen as aggressive:

> If a woman walks into her boss's office with unsolicited opinions, speaks up first at meetings, or gives business advice above her pay grade, she risks being disliked or even — let's be blunt — being labeled a bitch. The more a woman succeeds, the worse the vitriol seems to get. It's not just her competence that's called into question; it's her very character.[243]

Women fear the bitch label because they know being perceived as a bitch can harm them. The business strategist Jennifer Fitta transparently talks about how she used to "try and hide from being called a bitch" because society had taught her that "it is a shameful character flaw." She speaks about a painful incident at work where she had been given a seat at the table for the first time and overly prepared to present a pitch for a budget increase, which was received positively. However, after the meeting a coworker, unaware she was right behind him, said that her presentation would have been better if she "wasn't such a bitch."

She did exactly what many women would do in that situation: spending her evening picking apart her presentation and questioning what was bitchy about her. Over time, Fitta learned to recognize that women are called bitches when they are asserting power. Rather than accepting the term as pejoratively standing for a woman who is being "loud, nagging, or shrill," she proposes a new definition:

> Bitch/biCH/noun: A powerful woman who stands firm in her position despite adversity and opposition. Bitch/biCH/verb: to express power or strength in one's position.

Fitta observes that the common denominator for all references to the term "bitch" apply to a woman in power. She proposes to "own our power and share that power with the young women in the future — teaching them and those around them that defining a woman's position as powerful is never derogatory and positioning the word bitch in that light simply won't work anymore."[244]

Some other women are coming around to a similar point-of-view. Florence Given posted this declaration on Instagram in 2020:

Fear controls us and keeps us small. For me, it took being confronted with what I feared most (coming across as a "bitch") to realize the effect that fear was having on my life. The first time I stood up to my ex was also the first time I was called a bitch. He could feel me slowly gaining self-respect and autonomy outside of the relationship and knew the EXACT word to shame me "back into my place"...but it didn't work. It burst the bubble of the distorted reality I was living in and gave me the courage to leave. I realized in that moment the word "bitch" had been held over my head my entire life to keep me from asserting myself and remain a submissive doormat for people to wipe their feet all over.

Fear of being a bitch kept me SMALL! I usually stayed quiet when I was disrespected by others to appear "nice." I'd internalized the belief that there was some form of pride to gain in having my entire existence geared up for the service and pleasure of others. Finally, being called a "bitch" by a man and matching it with the experience that led to being called a bitch, FREED me. It all finally made sense. I learned that "bitch" is a myth we use to shame women into submission. A bitch is just a woman without boundaries. [245]

Business executive coach Carol Lempert recalls leading a workshop of a group of high-potential women in digital media in which a vice president of one of the companies stated, "Look, I appreciate that many of my colleagues need to learn to 'Lean In' and all that, but that's not my issue. I'm not afraid to speak my mind. I never have been. My issue is that when I speak up, I'm called a bitch." Lempert's advice to this executive included "owning it" in order to take the sting out of the word, quoting comedian Tina Fey's famous line, "Know what? Bitches get stuff done." But many women continue to feel the weight of the b-word and have not learned or wanted to "own it."[246]

Tamara Payne, founder of Ensemble, tells her story in a way that illustrates the hesitancy of even confident, assertive women leaders:

I own two businesses, both of which require strong leadership skills and the ability to manage various types of clients; from heavy involvement and strong hand holding to completely hand off and doing what I know is the right thing for the client...I am also a leader in the small business community. I have led multiple networking groups, for chambers of commerce, international organizations, national companies and on my own. I have been an organizer for startup events, mentored over one hundred micro and small business owners, and developed and executed small to large scale events.

I feel that I am respected in the community for my marketing knowledge and experience (20+ years), small business ownership (18 years), and community building (16 years). However, as I have sat in committee meetings, big and small, where everyone is invited to share and give input, I am hesitant to share freely for fear of being perceived as bossy, and even a bitch sometimes...

All it takes is a few people (mostly men) to say that I am a bitch (when I'm really just being a leader) and then I've got that reputation. The word bossy is synonymous with bitch when it comes to women in business. It's negative and leaves a mark on women like me. It causes me to hesitate in sharing my thoughts and my expertise when I'm in certain situations because I don't want to be perceived as a bitch. [247]

Calling a woman a bitch is a form of hate speech intended to silence her, remove her power, and control her actions. It is a form of verbal abuse that can escalate to threats, sexual harassment, bulling, slander, character assassination, and sometimes rape or violence. It saddens but does not surprise me that a female physician who chose to write about being called a bitch at work did so anonymously.

She related the experience of dropping her young daughter off at school, then being at the bedside of a patient who made a racist comment the day prior. She was speaking to the patient fairly tentatively due to his racist comments from the previous day, when a male colleague came in the room, interrupted her in midsentence, and told the patient an offensive sexist joke. The colleague and patient laugh loudly and then the colleague pointed to her and said to the patient, "So how is she treating you?" The patient's response? "Oh, she's a real bitch!"

She walked out of the room enraged and confused, but professionally confronted her colleague the next day. She asked him if she had daughters, and then said "I want you to consider the kind of culture you are creating for women and men. You can't tell inappropriate jokes and be respected. You cannot diminish my authority as the patient's physician by telling sexually inappropriate jokes. You cannot laugh after a patient calls me or any woman a bitch." She concluded "it is unacceptable to objectify women or to condone prejudice against women. This type of behavior can have a cumulative effect on well-being and career trajectories."

Unfortunately, this impressive woman must have believed that sharing her story more openly could affect her career trajectory, otherwise she would have provided her name.[248] Fear makes women quieter, and the objective of hate speech is to send women back to their "place," which is the private sphere or, in the workplace, a subordinate sphere.

Widespread fear of being called a "bitch" is not delusional. Women have centuries of historical precedence of being punished for being assertive. There is evidence that one reason the gender gap exists is because women fear being assaulted. The fear of rape and sexual assault can act as a professional barrier to women. Among higher-paying blue-collar jobs in which the employee interacts with individuals at their homes, the number of women in the professions is miniscule. Women make up only 1.5% of plumbers, 1.6% of carpenters, 2.6% of maintenance and repair professionals, 3.7% of telecommunications installers, because these positions require house calls. The number one cause of death for women at work is homicide.[249]

Employment situations associated with high rates of harassment include working for tips, working in an isolated context, working in settings with significant power differentials, and working in a male-dominated job, including construction workers, the military, and women faculty and staff in academia in science, engineering, and medicine.[250]

The blending of Bitch with Witch is just under the surface in many stereotypes and underscores the danger women feel about the bitch label. Although there are those who embrace the bitch label as something women should reclaim because it delineates a woman with power, the patriarchal acceptance of female power is only within traditional caregiving roles, and women with political, professional, and economic power can be delegitimized in a blink by moving the perception into the Witch realm of power, which is disenfranchised and outside the patriarchal hierarchy.

During the 2008 U.S. presidential campaign, a John McCain supporter referred to Hillary Clinton by asking, "How do we beat the bitch?" When reporting on the incident, CNN's Rick Sanchez said, "Last night, we showed you a clip of one of his supporters calling Hillary Clinton the b-word that rhymes with witch."[251] Sanchez would not use the word "bitch" on television.

Every culture around the world has some sort of threatening malevolent being who uses magic to influence others for personal gain. Being labeled a "witch" created a "less than human" persona for women, typically widowed, usually on the fringe of society. Witches were perceived as threats to society, and thousands of women have been tortured and killed through history for being characterized as witches. The labels "bitch" and "witch" are weapons used to limit women's power through vilification and ostracization.

Powerful women throughout history have been vilified in ways that are quite distinct from how powerful men are attacked by their enemies. After the murder of Julius Caesar, Octavian battled Marc Anthony and Cleopatra for control of the Roman Empire. Octavian (later Augustus Caesar) attempted to create "an enduring grotesque" in characterizing Cleopatra. He called her "brutal and bloodthirsty," "this pestilence of a woman," and told his soldiers that it was their obligation "to conquer and rule all mankind" and "to allow no woman to make herself equal to a man."[252] Joan of Arc was burned to death after being tried and convicted of being a witch, in addition to leaving home without her parents' permission, wearing men's clothes, and cutting her hair short.[253]

Women in history who have led their states as Warrior Queens may become "honorary men" if they successfully survive the crucible of war because the "unnatural, even bizarre aspect of a woman in such as role" is "terrifying."[254] Boudica, the queen of the British Iceni tribe who led an uprising against the conquering Romans in 60 CE after her daughters were raped and she was flogged, was described by Cassius Dio this way: "In stature she was very tall, in appearance most terrifying, in the glance of her eye most fierce, and her voice was harsh."[255] Women with power are "terrifying," like evil, ugly witches. By making them less than human, they are not only marginalized, they can also be tortured and killed. The fear women have of the bitch label is justifiable. It can be dangerous to be labeled a Bitch or a Witch.

Workplace gender bias takes one of two forms. *Descriptive bias* ascribes certain characteristics to women. They are supposed to be caring, warm, deferential, emotional, sensitive. Women who demonstrate these traits are often said to have "lack of fit" for a leadership position. *Prescriptive bias* describes what happens to women who break through and claim a traditionally male position. Eric Jaffe says:

> Here the empirical evidence is also overwhelming. Studies have found that women who succeed in male domains (violating incompetence) are disliked, women who promote themselves (violating modesty) are less hirable, women who negotiate for higher pay (violating passivity) are penalized, and women who express anger (violating warmth) are given lower status.[256]

In three experiments, negativity was directed at successful female managers in ratings of liability, interpersonal hostility, and boss desirability, but it could be mitigated if they were perceived of having communality, such as being a mother.[257] The experiment involved a memorandum about a company's female vice president, attesting to her "outstanding effectiveness, competence, and aggressive achievement focus." Subjects in the study rated a male vice president described in identical terms consistently higher.

However, the descriptive paragraph was appended with the language stating "Although Andrea's co-workers agree that she demands a lot from her employees, they have also described her as an involved manager who is caring and sensitive to their needs. She emphasizes the importance of having a supportive work environment and has been commended for her efforts to promote a positive community." With that addendum, the ratings equalized.

Four experiments show that gender differences in the propensity to initiate negotiations may be explained by differential treatment of men and women during negotiations. Male evaluators penalized female candidates more often than male candidates for initiating negotiations, with perceptions of niceness and demandingness explaining the resistance to female negotiators.[258]

Men who expressed anger in a professional context have been found in research to confer higher status than female professionals. This was the case regardless of the actual occupational rank of the target, whether the person was a female trainee or a female CEO. Also, whereas women's emotional reactions were attributed to internal characteristics, men's emotional reactions were attributed to external circumstances.[259] Other data tell us that male and female leaders are liked equally when behaving participatively and including subordinates in decision making. But when they are acting authoritatively, women leaders are disliked much more than men leaders.[260]

Women are not necessarily always disliked when they are successful, but they are penalized when they behave in ways that violate gender stereotypes. If women are expected to be warm, nurturing, nice, and friendly, a women leader pushing her team to higher performance can be seen as assertive, aggressive, or abrasive. She may be perceived as "too masculine," an Ice Queen, Ballbuster, Bitch, Witch.

Consider the former executive director of *The New York Times*, Jill Abramson. Publisher Arthur Sulzberger Jr., replaced her in that role in 2014, several weeks after she challenged the publisher over what she perceived was unequal pay and benefits relative to the male editor, Bill Keller, whom she had replaced. Abramson previously had been publicly profiled as overly aggressive and strong-willed. Her staff described her as "impossible to work with" and "not approachable" in a *Politico* article published just a few days after the paper won four Pulitzer Prizes, the third highest number ever received by the newspaper.

Dean Baquet, who replaced Abramson at the *Times*, had been seen to burst out of Abramson's office, slam his hand against a wall, and storm out of the newsroom. Yet it was Abramson, not Baquet, who was accused of being overly emotional, with an anonymous staffer sharing, "Every editor has a story about how she's blown up in a meeting." Baquet, himself, dismissed the stereotype but interestingly used the "B word" to do so: "I think there's a really easy caricature that some people have bought into, of the bitchy women character and the guy who is sort of calmer. That, I think, is a little bit of an unfair caricature."[261]

Shortly after she was named as the first woman to appear at the top of *The New York Times* masthead in its 160-year history, Jill Abramson was profiled in the *The New Yorker*. The second paragraph was spent describing her "white dress and black cardigan with white flowers and red trim" as well as her "pale complexion" and "deep dark lines under her eyes." Her voice was described in paragraph nine as "the equivalent of a nasal care honk." Further down in the article she has "an abrupt manner" then "too rough with underlings." Yet, she had previously received criticism for publishing a book about her dog, *The Puppy Diaries: Raising a Dog Named Scout*. "Being executive editor is a full-time job, you shouldn't be writing a book, especially one called *The Puppy Diaries,*" said one editor.

The New Yorker article went on to describe her colleagues commenting about her "brusque manner" and about "concerns about her assertiveness and whether it would stifle discussion and dissent, and about her presentation skills, including her voice.[262] Three years later, Abrahamson was out as executive editor, with the *Atlantic* speculating that "If it's true that Sulzberger and others were perturbed by Abramson's 'aggressive' style, their dynamic is representative of a series of findings from management psychology, which show that female leaders are disproportionately disliked for behaving forcefully."[263]

Abramson may have felt trapped by the limited patterns of conduct deemed favorable for women in leadership positions. There is a narrower band of acceptable behaviors for female than male leaders in the workforce. Women have made strides in recent years as being considered more effective leaders than in the past, but only so long as they do so by manifesting perceived "feminine" leadership styles of behavior.

A study of 60,000 people in 2011 found that those who had female managers did not give them lower ratings than those who had male managers. Sadly, however, of 46% who expressed a preference for their boss's gender, 72% stated they wanted a male manager.[264] Another 2011 study demonstrated that "leadership now, more than in the past, appears to incorporate more feminine relational qualities, such as sensitivity, warmth, and understanding."[265] In other words, leadership is more recently accepting of "feminine" qualities, not necessarily of women with "masculine" qualities.

A woman might be accepted as a leader provided the organization's or group's performance is stellar. Nonetheless, she may still be seen as deviant. Olga Khazan states:

> You could be satisfied that a leader has fostered organizational productivity, while still believing that she's a *shrill bitch*. So, while authoritative female

leaders might still be far from being well-liked, it's a pretty big deal to know that female bosses in general are viewed as just as effective — and sometimes more so.[266]

The narrow band of acceptable female behavior is a survival strategy. Women's "pathological politeness as described as an everlasting ploy of the patriarchy" is a result of girls and women being socialized to be polite as a learned behavior. "Girls are taught to prioritize other individuals' comfort and emotions over their own," according to Dr. Leela Magavi, regional medical director for Community Psychiatry in California. Politeness in women becomes a problem. When they do speak their minds and demand to be heard, they're often labeled difficult or nasty.[267] The actress Joan Collins describes how she was relegated to roles in Hollywood as a teenage star because "I wouldn't be 'nice' to studio heads, and it gave me a reputation of being a bitch."[268]

A 2002 meta-analysis of physician gender effects in medical communication found that female physicians engage in significantly more active partnership behaviors, positive talk, psychosocial counseling, psychosocial question asking, and emotionally focused talk than their male counterparts, with no differences in the amount, quality, social conversation, or manner of biomedical information giving.

The analysis concluded that women physicians disclose more information about themselves in conversation, have a warmer and more engaged style of nonverbal communication, encourage, and facilitate others to talk to them more freely and in a warmer and more intimate way. They take greater pains to downplay their own status in an attempt to equalize status with a partner, in contrast with men's tendency to assert status differences.[269]

In other words, most female physicians use normative female patterns of communication in their communication with patients. This pattern of communication has been linked to a variety of positive outcomes, including higher levels of adherence to therapeutic recommendations, but it is not necessarily conducive to promotion into leadership positions in healthcare organizations.

Men getting promoted faster and being paid more than women has been described as due to a "confidence gap" that women have, with concerns this leads to perfectionism and action paralysis in women. Perhaps this female reticence is conditioned from the fear of being assigned to the role of the bitch. If we do not perform perfectly, we will likely be harmed.

Authors Katty Kay and Claire Shipman observed in *The Confidence Code: The Science and Art of Self-Assurance — What Women Should Know*, that "underqualified and underprepared men don't think twice about leaning in. Overqualified and overprepared, too many women still hold back. And the confidence gap is an additional lens through which to consider why it is women don't lean in." [270]

The underlying assumption is that lack of self-confidence hurts a woman's chances of success, and that if they can just be a bit more self-confident, they can break through the glass ceiling. However, other research disputes this perspective. Margarita Mayo, Natalia Karelaia, and Laura Guillen have shown there is no gender difference between men and women in self-reporting of self-confidence. Instead, irrespective of how self-confident a woman feels, it is the extent to which others perceive a woman as self-confident that determines its impact on her organizational influence as well as her need to be perceived as pro-social (warm, nice) — something that was not required of men.[271]

In the details of this study, the authors conclude that "while self-confidence is gender-neutral, the consequences of appearing self-confident are not. Where men are allowed to focus on their own objectives, women are expected to care for others as well." The authors conclude that "this prosocial (double) standard does not appear in any job description, but it is, indeed, the key performance indicator against which access, power, and influence will be granted to successful women. Men are held to a lower standard."[272]

In *On Liberty*, John Stuart Mill defends freedom because only free people can take full command of their own lives. He argues that it is good to be self-created, to be someone who "chooses his plan for himself."[273] As Kwame Anthony Appiah points out, "for a long time— since the Enlightenment, we might say — the great liberal struggle was to get the state to treat its members as individuals only, without favoring or disfavoring particular ethnic or religious or gender identities."[274] But each of us has to find the freedom of our *self-identifies* within the *social identities* into which we are culturally born.

There are numerous kinds of human beings and numerous categories we use to label people. The expectations we have of men and women are placed with the conventions of how we expect them to behave in their social identities. That's the rub. For women to be successful, their narrower range of acceptable behaviors still include the need to be "pro-social" that is, warm, nice, care-giving, mothers, grandmothers, sisters...AND have the necessary leadership skills.

Appiah points out that American anti-discrimination laws use the concept of "stereotypes" to cover three distinct ideas:

1. **Statistical Stereotypes**: The idea of ascribing a property to an individual on the basis of the belief that it is characteristic of some social group to which she belongs, where there is indeed a statistical correlation between that property and being member of that group, but where, in fact, she does not have that property.
2. **Simply False Stereotypes**: The idea of a false belief about a group.
3. **Normative Stereotypes**: The idea that how a person behaves is grounded in a social consensus about how they ought to behave in order to conform appropriately to the norms associated with membership in their group.[275]

It is this normative stereotype that creates the constraining boundaries of acceptable female behavior, and those who fall outside those boundaries are thus bitches— or, in past time, witches. And witches will be burned at the stake. However, in the words of Emily Dickinson:

Witchcraft was hung, in History,
But History and I
Find all the Witchcraft that we need
Around us, every Day.[276]

And within that context, we need to be able to identify the power of the Bitch label — as a signaler of women behaving in ways outside normative stereotypes — in order to own it, use it, manipulate it, reject it, whatever we wish, whenever we want, every day.

CHAPTER SIX

Queen CEO

I've had hundreds of conversations with women across various industries who are forthcoming and candid about the cost of patriarchy distress disorder perpetrated by their companies. Men are seen as assertive when they speak up; women are seen as aggressive. When a woman asserts her boundary, she's labeled a bitch.

In the medical field, women physicians are often mistaken for nurses. In venture capital presentations, women are assumed to be men's assistants. A gender stereotype that nails women on the cross of being "caring" and "nurturing" sustains an expectation that we will carry responsibilities outside of our scope of duties.

Women are under greater scrutiny in leadership roles. Many women have to deal with sexual harassment in their workplaces and are often rumored to have slept their way to the top. All of these keep the patriarchy stress disorder machine. That is extremely taxing on women and ends up costing organizations big — in lost and underutilized talent, high turnover, poor public image, lawsuits, and higher medical and legal costs.[277]

— Valerie Rein, PhD

On January 20, 2000, I became president and chief executive officer of Cornerstone Healthcare and held the title of CEO in that company and eventually three others for 21 years. There was no announcement in the press about my position at Cornerstone, which at the time was a smallish physician-owned multispecialty medical group in High Point, North Carolina. Cornerstone's first CEO, Dr. Doug Blazek, served in that role from the group's inception in 1995 until I stepped into the role in 2000. He found that five years of leading the medical group, including addressing behavioral issues with his medical partners, was not conducive to referrals to his surgical practice from his colleagues, nor did the stipend he was paid for the position make up for the income he lost from his surgical practice. In contrast, my internal medicine practice was not dependent on my relationship with my colleagues, and my primary care level compensation accommodated the stipend substitute much more readily.

While I was at Cornerstone, the group grew from an initial $16 million in revenues generated by 42 physicians in 16 medical practices to $300 million in revenues generated by more than 300 providers in 93 practice locations. We were one of the first medical groups to successfully transition to full electronic medical records, one of the first patient-centered medical homes in the country, one of the first medical groups to move to value-based models of care and payment, and a winner of the prestigious AMGA Acclaim award in 2015 for outstanding quality in a medical group.

Like much of the independent medical groups, Cornerstone was eventually incorporated into a larger hospital-owned integrated delivery system in 2016, but not before we had spun off a couple of other companies: CHC Realty LLC, responsible for constructing a couple of 100,000 square foot state-of-the-art medical office buildings, and CHESS (Cornerstone Health Enablement Strategic Solutions), a population health company successfully managing more than 150,000 lives in full-risk value-based contracts.

I initially served as CEO of those two companies, too, and later in my career I served as CEO of Envision Genomics, a biotechnology startup focused on whole genome sequencing with a machine-learning diagnostic technology permitting rapid diagnosis of rare diseases, and Eventus WholeHealth, a medical group that provides integrated primary care and mental health care to medically vulnerable adults who are homebound or residing in long-term care facilities.

I believe one reason I have been able to have a long career as a CEO for multiple companies is that the original role at Cornerstone Healthcare was not seen a particularly prestigious or competitive. The president and CEO of a smallish multispecialty medical group, particularly one that initially was more primary care and medical specialty focused rather than broadly surgical subspecialty focused, was initially a low-status leadership position in the medical community hierarchy when I assumed the role in 2000. Cornerstone was not on anyone's radar for all the innovations it has subsequently been known for, and the CEO of the medical group answered to a board of 12 physicians with limited authority in our governance structure who in turn answered to all the shareholders for many significant group decisions, such as any capital expenditure over $100,000, addition of new shareholders or member groups, and changes in the income distribution formula.

The initial stipend I received for the position was minimal, meaning I still had to practice medicine full time to maintain my primary care physician income as well as my credibility with my physician colleagues, most of whom dismissed management roles for physicians as a sellout if one did not continue to practice medicine. To get anything accomplished at Cornerstone Healthcare, I had to build consensus with multiple constituents and do so with soft power rather than assumed authority. For a southerner, my speaking style is direct and to the point, but the male-dominated medical group I led with its all-male board of directors meant I had to hone my listening skills, because my natural tendency to speak early in a debate did not always serve me well.

Some research data from Penn State in 2021 found that the more companies praise and tout the past accomplishments of their incoming women CEOs when announcing their hiring, the more likely it is for these women to have shorter tenures in the CEO role. That resonates with me, and the fortuitousness of the low status of my first CEO role allowed me the years of experience I needed to improve my leadership skills without the constant scrutiny that many women experience.

Many women encounter the double-binding effect, or catch-22, in their professional lives, where they are trapped by two interconnecting stereotypes. Women are stereotypically seen as being sensitive and nurturing and thus not fit for leadership roles; when women show that they are competent for leadership roles, they are criticized as not fulfilling the stereotypical expectations for what women should be. The author of the study observed: "When women act confident and leader-like, it can violate these societal expectations of what a women should be, which is highly problematic. Organizations may want to help women by touting their accomplishments, but as soon as they do, it can trigger a backlash."[278]

This research resonates with me, because I have found through the years that touting my own accomplishments can be risky. At graduation every year at my rural North Carolina high school, they gave awards for the top English student, the top math student, the top history student, and the top language student. In 1979, I graduated the top of my class, won all of those awards, as well as a prestigious merit-based Morehead scholarship to the University of North Carolina at Chapel Hill, but the principal chose to give me the awards the next day rather than draw attention on stage to the fact I had won them all. The boy who was class president, rather than the valedictorian, gave the senior speech.

That experience is one of many through the years, where I was encouraged not to draw attention to my accomplishments if they made me stand out too much from those around me. I did not think about it as a gender issue at the time I graduated, that it would be considered "immodest" for me to receive each of the awards on stage; but, in retrospect, I believe it was. Had the roles been reversed, would the principal have held off presenting the boy who was class president with all the academic awards out of a need for "modesty"?

Even after a woman has obtained the CEO role, challenges remain with respect to differences in behaviors they experience. Female CEOs face more aggressive questions on earnings conference calls than male CEOs, according to research from the University of Exeter Business School. Researchers analyzed recordings of 39,209 earnings calls with U.S. firms over a 13-year period ending in 2018. They defined "verbal aggressiveness" in four measures: the frequency of follow-up questions, the use of preface statements, the number of direct questions, and the questions that begin with assertions like "aren't you."

When the CEO is female, the male analysts use 5.3% more direct questions, 9.5% more follow-up questions, and 3.4% more preface statements. Verbal aggressiveness of analysists' questions is significantly associated with both the gender of the analyst asking the question and the gender of the CEO fielding the question. Male analysts are more verbally aggressive than female analysts, and male analysts' questions to female CEOs are more aggressive than their questions to male CEOs.[279] The cultural pressures for women to not stand out too much, especially if it overshadows a male, are ubiquitous.

Harvard psychiatrist Chester M. Pierce coined the term "microaggressions" in the 1970s to describe the type of insidious, toxic, but brief everyday insults African-American people experience. The term is now applied to denigrating messages regularly experienced by any socially marginalized group based on race, gender, sexual origination, social class, or ability status. The person, group, organization, or culture sending these messages is doing so unconsciously and is unaware of their effect, and those experiencing them are often unaware of them, also.

However, Stanford psychologist Claude Steel found that priming African Americans and women with racial and gender performance stereotype information (such as women not being as good at math as men) negatively affects their academic performance. Within the context of objective data, such as the more aggressive questions female CEOs face on analyst calls or that 66% of all interruptions by other justices at the Supreme Court were experienced by the three female justices over a 15-year period, the conservative criticism that microaggression is "pseudoscience" is demonstratively unfounded.

In the healthcare arena, evidence shows that physician gender influences patient satisfaction survey results. Female gynecologists were 47% less likely to receive top patient satisfaction scores than their male counterparts according to 909 patient satisfaction survey results.[280] A recent study of 1,505 physicians on the clinical faculty at Stanford University School of Medicine found that 1 in 4 physicians experienced workplace mistreatment, with patients and visitors the most common source of mistreatment. Among those reporting mistreatment, twice as many were women. Overall, 31% of women surveyed experienced one or more forms of mistreatment compared with 15% of men, especially sexual harassment and verbal abuse.[281]

When I was 10 years old, my favorite television show was *The Brady Bunch*. I liked the symmetry of three girls and three boys: Greg and Marcia, Peter and Jan, Bobby and Cindy. My classmates and I obsessed on the show, which was teaching us how children our age should look and behave in a contemporary "cool" (albeit white) family.

But there were subtle design elements in the show that in retrospect reinforced patriarchal stereotypes supporting male dominance, such as each of the male children in the blended family being slightly older than their female counterpart. Consider the episode where Greg and Marcia unintendedly find they are running for student body president against one another at their school. The family conflict over the competition is resolved when Marcia withdraws from the contest because Greg was older and "she would get her chance later." Never said, but certainly inferred by all of us 10-year-old Friday night TV watchers, is that Greg should be the student body president because he was a boy.

The father in the show, Mike Brady, has a clearly defined professional career as an architect. Carol Brady, his wife, does not have a professional career. She has ill-defined activities like freelance writer, sculptor, political organizer, and singer. Whatever she is doing, there is always Alice the housekeeper to help with meals, cleaning, and minding the children.

In more contemporary media depictions of men and women, even when women break role barriers, the stereotyping of acceptable behaviors persists. A recent analysis of superhero roles in movies shows these persisting gender differentiating messages:

> It is important to understand the content of media, as media can promote stereotypes that communicate what gender roles, appearances, and acts of

violence are acceptable in society. This content analysis of 147 superheroes in 80 movies found that male heroes appeared much more frequently than female heroes. Females were more likely to work in a group while males were more likely to work alone. Males were more powerful, muscular, violent, and evil while women were more attractive, thin, sexy/seductive, innocent, afraid, and helpless.

Compared to males', females' clothes (both costumes and non-costumes) were more revealing on both the upper and lower bodies. Although both genders frequently have special abilities and use weapons, male characters are more likely than female characters to have more than one special ability and use more than one weapon.

Males more often had super strength and resistance to injury, while female characters more often were able to manipulate elements (e.g., fire). Males were significantly more likely to use fighting skills, fire/flame weapons, and guns than females.[282]

Accepted sources of standardized information in contemporary online media continues to be confined by its predominately male-gendered writers. Wikipedia is the online encyclopedia that "anyone can edit," but only 8-15% of its editors are women, despite it being the seventh most-visited site on the web with over 18 billion page views.[283] Wiki's "diversity problem" has been attributed to the demographic composition of employees in STEM (science, technology, engineering, and mathematics) fields which remain overwhelmingly white and male.

Researchers identify STEM's "chilly climate" of subtle sexism women experience during education and employment, its competitive environments, grueling work schedules, and emphasis on after-work socializing as barriers that make it difficult for women to achieve work-life in a successful STEM career. This chilliness is deemed unconscious bias that permits "brogrammar" cultures of sexual harassment, assault, discrimination, and exclusion. The metaphor of "leaky pipelines" is invoked to suggest that due to personal "choices" (like child-rearing), women tend to "fall out of" STEM fields at faster and higher rates than their male colleagues.

Chilly climates leading to leaky pipelines metaphorically defines gender discrimination in terms of environmental factors that dissuade women from being available for leadership roles. In education, men are more often viewed as more valued students. Teachers generally call on men more often, asking them more questions, and not calling on females as much, even when they raise their hands. White males generally get the most questions, then minority males, then white females, with black females receiving the least attention. Teachers nod and gesture more when male students speak and often look elsewhere when females talk.

In the classroom, women and girls receive less eye contact. Teachers more often praise women for their attractiveness and males for their achievement rather than for the way they dress or look. Females are more likely to be asked factual questions, while men and boys are more likely to be asked harder and more open-ended questions. Comments focus on a woman's appearance or gender, such as "I'd like to hear from that charming young woman in the front row" or "what is the woman's point of view of this?"

Women are interrupted more often in class, and once they are interrupted, they tend to stay out of the discussion for the remainder of the class. Women are expected to be more modest about their achievements; men are expected to brag. In conversation, men are expected to analyze, explain, clarify, and control the topic; women are expected to reinforce and maintain the conversation to reduce tensions and restore unity.[284]

The rhetoric and strategy of perceiving gender gap as a "woman problem" arising from leaky pipelines places the burden of workplace transformation on the shoulders of women rather than on society to do the actual cultural work necessary to create equitable work environments. Cultural misogyny reinforces expectations to conform to sexist norms in the workplace where women are expected to adapt to the environment or get out, creating the leaky pipelines.[285]

These biases lead to significant imbalances such that women hold only 8% of CEO positions across Fortune 500 companies and 6% of CEO roles in S&P 500 companies. Although on a global average, girls outperform boys in science test scores, women make up only 8% of enrollment in manufacturing, construction, and engineering courses globally, and only 5% of all mathematics and statistics enrollment.

Boys score higher than girls on standardized math tests, but their gender gap in math performance has been demonstrated to be substantially affected by teachers' implicit stereotypes. Girls are more likely to consider themselves bad at math at the end of middle school if they are assigned to a teacher with stronger stereotypes, even controlling for their ability measured by standardized test scores.[286] Cross-cultural evidence suggests the gap in mathematical testing scores is likely due to cultural and social conditioning rather than biologically based differences in brain function.[287]

Given these barriers, it is not surprising to find that women comprise only 29% of the STEM workforce even though they make up 52% of the college-educated workforce. The percentage of women in board positions in STEM-related industries in 2020 was 19.2%. Women make up 3% of STEM industry CEOs.[288] This gap begins in education, fueled by gender stereotypes and expectations regarding "women's work" and "women's brains." The few women who begin careers in STEM face male-dominated workplaces with high rates of discrimination. Their contributions are often ignored; they experience isolation caused by lack of access to women peers, role models, and mentors; and they are paid less than their male-co-workers.

Among working parents, women in STEM leave their careers at dispropor-tionately higher rates than men.[289] More than 40% of women with full-time jobs in science leave the sector or go part time after having their first child, according to a study of how parenthood affects career trajectories in the United States. By contrast, only 23% of new fathers leave or cut their work-ing hours.[290] Even though 90% of people in the United States become parents during their working careers, STEM work is often culturally less tolerant and less supportive of caregiving responsibilities. Women balancing family and professional work often face workplace cultures where they are expected to make a choice between their personal and professional lives, hence creating another "leak" in the pipeline to leadership positions.

One might not expect leaky pipes to be a barrier in the healthcare industry where 85% of healthcare workers are female. However, when leadership positions are evaluated, the gender discrepancies are no better than the so-called STEM industries. Women hold only 15% of CEO roles in healthcare organizations, but when they do, they appear to positively influence gender diversity across their organizational leadership teams. Companies with female CEOs are more likely to have more women sitting on the board and more women in other senior positions.

A study published in *JAMA* in November 2021 reviewed more than 3,911 healthcare executives and 3,462 board members representing 161 health systems and 108 health insurance groups. Only 15.3% of CEOs of health systems were women and 15.8% of CEOs of health insurance companies were women. Among board chairs, 17.5% in health systems were women and 21.3% in health insurance companies were women despite the fact that 70% of the healthcare industry employees are women, thus making up a larger pool from which to draw leadership talent.[291]

The problem we need to solve is how to ensure we design our cultural and social environments so that all people, irrespective of gender or ethnic-ity, are able to maximally develop their capabilities. Achieving this would create larger talent pools, accelerate innovation, and augment the human resources we need to solve our most wicked 21st-century problems, such as climate change, health and economic inequities, and environmental collapse. Solving these problems requires broader access to power for underutilized groups of people than what our current patriarchal culture has permitted.

Breaking through the constraints of the traditional architypes, or perhaps enhancing the power of the archetypes by broadening their current limitations, will be crucial. One place to start may be understanding in more depth the power and constraints of the Queen archetype, which is the closest we have to the CEO role within the traditional historical contexts.

In *Women Who Run with the Wolves*, Clarissa Pinkola Estes emphasizes in discussing female naivete about male predators that "as long as a woman is forced into powerless and/or is trained to not consciously register what she knows to be true, the feminine impulses and gifts of her psyche continue to be killed off."[292] Patriarchy is predatory when it forces women into powerlessness. Identifying how to operate powerfully in the Queen role is an antidote to the patriarchal disease.

The Cambridge classical historian Mary Beard masterfully tells the story of the Roman Empire in her bestselling *SPQR* by demolishing the myths we've come to believe about ancient Rome and replacing them with a more richly woven story that incorporates women, slaves, and conquered people into the narrative. Women in ancient Rome were married as early as age 10 or 11 to men in their mid-20s or much older, augmenting their subordination through great equilibrium in age. In addition, by law, all freeborn women had to marry; most spent the rest of their lives in pregnancy and childbirth with high rates of death from childbirth for both infants and mothers.

Women who were raped often were killed by their fathers, husbands, and brothers to assuage their "dishonor." After giving birth to three live children, thus fulfilling their traditional roles, women were allowed to transact contracts and own property without having to have a male guardian.[293] Beard's scholarship provided her with the tools to write her astonishing manifesto *Women and Power* in 2017, in which she traces misogyny to its ancient roots and challenges the ongoing cultural assumptions about women's relationship to power.

> But this is still treating power as something elite, coupled to public prestige, to the individual charisma of so-called "leadership," and often, though not always, to a degree of celebrity. It is also treating power very narrowly, as an object of possession that only the few — mostly men — can own or wield... Of those terms, women as a gender — not as some individuals — are by definition excluded from it.

You cannot easily fit women into a structure that is already coded as male; you have to change the structure. That means thinking about power differently. It means decoupling it from the public prestige. It means thinking collaboratively about the power of followers not just of leaders. It means, above all, thinking about power as an attribute or even a verb ("to power"), not as a possession.

What I have in mind is the ability to be effective, to make a difference in the world, and the right to be taken seriously, together as much as individually. It is power in that sense that many women feel they don't have — and that they want. Why the popular resonance of "mansplaining" (despite the intense dislike of the term felt by many men)? It hits home for us because it points straight to what it feels like not to be taken seriously: a bit like when I get lectured on Roman history on Twitter.[294]

Beard points out in *Women & Power* that the silencing of women in public discourse is as far back as our historical records go. In Homer's *Odyssey*, Penelope bravely fends off suitors and waits for Odysseus for 20 years but is rebuked by her adolescent son for speaking in the Great Hall of their palace: "Mother, go back up to your quarters, and take up your own work, the loom and the distaff.... Speech will be the business of men, all men, and of me most of all; for mine is the power in this household."

In Ovid's *Metamorphoses*, the god Jupiter silences Io by turning her into a cow; the nymph Echo is punished so that her voice is never her own; the rapist of Philomena silences her by cutting out her tongue. Beard challenges the strategy of gradualism as a remedy for "the deep cultural structures" legitimating women's exclusion from power:

We have to be more reflective about what power is, what it is for, and how it is measured. To put it another way, if women are not perceived to be fully within the structures of power, surely it is power that we need to redefine rather than women? ...I have followed the usual path in discussions of this kind, by focusing on national and international politics and politicians — which we might add, for good measure, some of the standard line-up of CEOs, prominent journalists, television executives and so on. This offers a very narrow version of what power is, largely correlating it with public prestige...It is very "high end" in a very traditional sense and bound up with the "glass ceiling" image of power, which not only effectively positions women on the outside of power, but also imagines the female pioneer as the already successful superwoman with just a few last vestiges of male prejudice keeping her from the top.[295]

I would go a step further than Beard here, and state that women have been excluded from traditional positions of power because the archetypal tropes upon which we have designed our culture are themselves the instruments of power that have limited women from assuming roles of public power. I wholeheartedly agree with Beard that we need to "change the nature of power" rather than "change the nature of women." But learning from women who have succeeded in legitimized power roles can help us overcome the "strategy of gradualism" Beard aptly dismisses.

"The nature of women" is, in fact, the issue at hand. Are we different or are we the same? If we are different, is that justification for patriarchal power dynamics? Are Queens equivalent to Kings? The nuanced argument that we are the same — and therefore deserve equal opportunity and equal rights — more than we are different is used in some arguments to move equity policies forward. But the argument that we are different, and therefore bring something more to the table, is used just as often in moving equity policies forward.

Around 150,000 years ago, high numbers of healthy females began to die in childbirth for the first time in history, making it the leading cause of female death. No female of any other known species has as much difficulty giving birth as human beings, and no other species requires as much assistance from others during the delivery.

Studies in the 1960s by Washburn, Trevathan, and Rosenberg determined that human infants are born far more immature than other species because of the rate-limiting factors of fetus brain size to birth canal size.[296] If human newborns were as mature as other species at birth, the gestational period would need to be at least 18 months, which the brain is too large to accommodate.

Other unique aspects of female humans, compared to other animals, include orgasms, face-to-face copulation, being sexually available all the time, the ability to refuse a hard-wired receptivity for sexual intercourse, menstruation, and menopause.[297] In contrast to other animal species, human females have a relatively short fertility period with a potential to live long periods of time after menopause if they survive childbirth. Thus, Grandmothers, Queens, Priestesses, Healers, and other non-childbearing/rearing roles are more readily built into the human female life cycle than would be possible if our reproductive patterns were more consistent with other mammalian species.

It is the female of our species who bears the biological risk of death in childbirth and who has borne the responsibility of carrying for biologically immature infants for prolonged periods of time, keeping them alive through lactation. These roles did not exclude women historically from other crucial work. Harvesting wild plants and turning them into food, medicine, baskets, and clothing is a nearly universal female gendered activity.[298]

Although women have historically been written out of accounts of art and technologies, prehistoric evidence points to strong associations between women and plant-based knowledge as far back as is traceable.[299] The handprints found on the walls with European pre-historic cave paintings of game hunting have been demonstrated to be those of women. Dismissed by male archeologists of previous generations, there is now substantial evidence that Minoan civilization was matriarchal.[300] Compared to the Greeks and Romans, who disproportionately provided food calories to men rather than women, DNA data from neolithic towns demonstrate a relative gender parity of diet and health and ritual treatment of both female and male bodies in death.[301]

The Westernized version of human history starts with a version of a "primitive" hunter/gather tribe, where the physically stronger males hunted for game and women gathered plant foods and stayed close to the hearth with the children they bore. These societies supposedly were replaced by agriculture-based civilizations and then city-states, gradually organizing into kingships until the post-Renaissance modern states evolved, with patriarchies dominating the culture during all of this.

More recent data, such as that amassed by Graeber and Wengrow, indicate far more nuanced and diverse cultural legacies that have, unfortunately, been interpreted through limited Westernized lenses. Consider, for example, Jean Jacques Rousseau, the Enlightenment philosopher whose *A Discourse on Inequality* influenced much later thinking on human culture.

Rousseau imagined an innocent "state of nature" — levels of social and moral development corresponding to historical changes in modes of production, transitioning from foraging, to farming, to industry. Rousseau's 1762 novel *Emile* describes the ideal education of a young boy to prepare him to develop his natural faculties in the best possible way. For Emile's sister Sophie, however, Rousseau did not believe such an education was necessary. He emphasized that a woman's physical nature means that the business of her life is to bear and rear children. "The male is only a male now and again, the female is always a female, or last all her youth: everything reminds her of her sex. She should bear as many children as possible because half of the children will die young."

Sophie was to be educated to be docile and gentle, to submit uncomplainingly to injustices. Girls were to be educated in practical matters because he assumed men can move from the factual to the abstract, but women cannot. Like he believed the women of ancient Greece behaved, Rousseau thought women should first and foremost be mothers, spend their time at home, and be educated to prepare them for subordinate roles in a republic where all public activity is reserved for men.[302]

The prohibition of women from public spaces has been directly tied to their roles as mothers at least as early as the ancient Greeks. The earliest Bronze Age Mycenaean Linear B script lists the tasks of women as fetching water, spinning, weaving, grinding corn, and reaping. A few generations later, women could remain within public rooms without scandal but only in the presence of escorts. Politically, the Greek city-states focused mostly on military preparedness for defense, with men serving their families in the military and women expected to bear and rear future soldiers. All mature women were expected to marry.

The gender roles in which men ideally were warriors and women were child bearers persisted through the classical Greek era. The law of Lycurgus forbade the inscription of the name of any deceased person on a tomb except for a man who had died at war or a woman who had died of childbirth.

In the 6th century BC, Solon banned the right of male guardians to see women and children into slavery except for an unmarried woman found to have lost her virginity. All citizen women were perpetually under the guardianship of a male — either their father, husband, or male next of kin. Female infanticide was a widespread practice. There were disproportionately far fewer women than men in ancient Greece due to infanticide and childbirth mortality, with some scholars asserting evidence the ratio of males to females in ancient Greece was a high as five to one.

Women who were slaves, courtesans, and prostitutes were able to go about in public spaces, but all free "respectable" women were secluded from public with the exception of certain festivals and funerals. Women had separate quarters than men. Intruding upon a free woman in the house of another man was a criminal act.[303]

Although by the Roman era women were allowed more access to public spaces, Stoicism, the most popular Hellenistic and Roman philosophy, directed women's energies to marriage and motherhood. The Sophists argue that motherhood required women to be confined to the domestic sphere. Food rations for a woman in the Greek era were half that of men, unless she was pregnant, in which case her rations were increased as the "mother's portion."

Public records from Rome only apportioned food rations to men. Women were mostly confined inside their homes, with inferior nutrition, insufficient physician activity, and life expectancies 10 years shorter than men. And from this legacy, the Western intellectual tradition, from Aristotle to Rousseau excluded women from public spaces, equal education, and health equity.

In 2020, prior to the pandemic, the U.S. workforce was comprised of more women than men (50.4%),[304] but a year later, women comprised more than 80% of those who left the workforce, bringing their participation in the workforce to its lowest level since 1988. Many were forced to leave the workforce due to the closing of schools and day care centers during the pandemic.[305]

One unanticipated consequence of the pandemic has been the Great Resignation; economic recovery coming out of the pandemic has been slowed by the huge portion of the labor market who have left their jobs. A 2022 Global Workforce Hopes and Fears Survey surveyed 52,000 workers in 44 countries. The study found one in five workers are likely to switch jobs in the next 12 months, with "job fulfillment" being a motivating factor in their decision-making.

It should be no surprise that this is a gender-differentiated problem. In the survey, women are 7% less likely than men to say they are family compensated, yet 7% less likely to ask for a raise. They are 8% less likely to feel that their managers listen to them, and they have been far quicker to leave the workforce during the Great Resignation.[306]

In the healthcare labor market, this circumstance is particularly striking among nurses. A Relias/Brandware survey of 2,516 nurses in November and December 2021 found that the pandemic led to a precipitous increase in the number of nurses considering leaving the profession — 29% of the current survey's respondents compared to 11% in 2020. The survey found that staffing shortages were pushing nursing salaries higher, but RNs identifying as male, consistent with previous Glass Elevator-type analyses, had median salaries $14,000 higher ($90,000) than the median salary of RNs identifying as female ($76,000). In addition, 40% of the men stated they "always" or "most of the time" attempt to negotiate a higher salary, compared to 30% of women. Nurses who identify as Black, African American, American Indian, or Alaska Native reported the lowest levels of satisfaction with their current salary.[307]

The U.S. Social Security system still functions as if the workforce consists mostly of male breadwinners who work outside the home while their wives stay home and rear children. The "motherhood penalty" refers to the reduced earnings potential a woman experiences when she becomes a mother, which becomes even larger with each additional child and permanently reduces earning throughout mothers' work lives.[308]

Social Security's retired worker benefits are based on an individual's average career earnings. Because mothers tend to earn less than other women, their average Social Security benefit at retirement is less. A spousal benefit designed to compensate stay-at-home wives who missed out on accumulating a meaningful history in paid work has been muted by the lower marriage rates and higher divorce rates than was present when the law was enacted. The share of women receiving a spousal benefit decreased from 35% in 1960 to 18% in 2019. The medial earnings for childless women in 2019 was $3,850 per month, compared to $1,409 for women with children — 37% less than that of childless women. The difference in Social Security income for mothers is $785 per month compared to $1,301 for childless women.[309]

So cultural structure put into place at least 3,000 years ago that kept women in seclusion at home to rear children still impacts our policies and culture today, to the detriment of women who made up the majority of the pre-pandemic workforce. The no girls allowed/boys only spaces are often where deals get transacted in business, whether in private clubs, golf courses, locker rooms, fishing boats, or deer stands. There is nothing wrong *per se* with having separated gendered spaces, provided they are not utilized as the "old boys clubs" where informal business gets transacted in exclusive networks and provided that the women's space is not structured such that it is a powerless space.

In her book *The Moment of Lift: How Empowering Women Changes the World*, Melinda Gates tells the story of a 22-year-old woman named Champa living in central India whose 2-year-old daughter Rani was suffering from severe acute malnutrition. The child required special treatment in a Malnutrition Treatment Center two hours away by bus. Champa's father-in-law would not permit Champa to take Rani to the center, saying "She can't go. She has to stay and cook for the family." Gates describes how the mother was so "chained down by household duties and social norms that she didn't have the power to protect her child."[310]

The balance of the unpaid work the world over is done by women on average, putting in twice as many hours as men. In India, women spend six hours a day doing unpaid work, while men spend less than one. In the United States, women average more than four hours of unpaid work every day; men average just two and a half. During the pandemic, this imbalance of unpaid work responsibilities has meant that women have experienced greater financial penalties as they have left the workforce to perform necessary caregiving responsibilities. It also augments the difficulties of having balanced participation in leadership in business and governance and contributes to the absence from old boys' networks that often serve as the pathways to power.

What can we learn from those women who have broken glass ceilings, reached the highest levels of influence and power in roles from which women have traditionally been excluded? First, they often are skilled at standing out from male colleagues by highlighting their differences as well as the crucial similarities. My favorite example of this is Margaret Thatcher. In 1982, I had the fortune of working in the Liberal Whip's Office at the House of Commons in Great Britain. I was a rising college senior, and it was a remarkable time to be in the United Kingdom seeing world events up close. That was the year of the Falkland's War between Great Britain and Argentina, Ronald Reagan's visit to Parliament, Pope John Paul II's visit to London, the soccer World Cup, and Margaret Thatcher's term as prime minister.

I was able to spend some time in the upper gallery of the House of Commons watching Thatcher speak and debate with the Tories, Labor Party, and Lib-Dems. She was remarkable. She was the longest-serving prime minister of the 20th century and changed the course of British politics. She was the first prime minister with a science degree (chemistry) and moved the UK politically from a welfare state to a neoliberal (conservative) policy platform.

She experienced many of the same challenges of other women operating in a predominately male public space. In 1951 and 1952, she lost her first two elections as a Conservative candidate, the youngest and only female candidate in the country. In 1953, she qualified as a barrister and delivered twins, prematurely by C-section. She sat out the 1955 general election because, she stated, "I really just felt the twins were only two, I really felt that it was too soon. I couldn't do that."[311]

She was elected an MP (Member of Parliament) in 1959 and rose through the ranks of Conservative party politics to Parliamentary Undersecretary to the Ministry of Pensions and National Insurance in 1961, and the sole female member of the Conservative Shadow Cabinet in 1966. She became Secretary of State for Education and Science in 1970, although at the time she stated, "There will not be a woman prime minister in my lifetime — the male population is too prejudiced."[312] She was wrong about that, being elected prime minister nine years later, in 1979, and serving until 1990.

Shortly after Thatcher became leader of the British Conservative Party in 1975, she delivered a foreign policy speech in which she was highly critical of the Soviet Union, prompting the Soviet Army Journal *Red Star* to headline a rebuttal "Iron Lady Raises Fears." Thatcher immediately embraced the epithet: "I stand before you tonight in my Red Star chiffon evening gown, my face softly made up and my fair hair gently waved, the Iron Lady of the Western world. A cold warrior, an amazon philistine, even a Peking plotter. Well, am I any of these things? Well, yes… I am an iron lady, after all it wasn't a bad thing to be an iron duke. Yes, if that's how they wish to interpret my defense of values and freedoms fundamental to our way of life."[313]

Her iron lady metaphor became a generic term for other strong-willed female politicians, and further extended as any determined, strong, or unyielding woman.[314] As a 20-year-old watching Thatcher from the upper gallery of the House of Commons, I noticed she was always dressed in exquisite pastel-colored skirted suits that summer and, as was astonishing to my American eyes, often the same suit several days in a row. The men, no doubt wore the same suits as well, but their black and gray and blue suits made their clothing indistinguishable from one day to the next.

Thatcher's embracing of the Iron Lady moniker, while contrasting her "chiffon evening gown" and "fair hair gently waved" is reflected in her use of her handbag, almost as a stereotypical feminine trope. She was seldom seen without a British brand Launer handbag in her left hand. Her speeches were printed on paper cut to fit into her bag, and at cabinet meetings she would draw out notes of advice or instruction. "Whenever this happened, the cabinet secretary would pale, and the minister would raise his eyes to the ceiling. Many are the ministers who have cursed the contents of that wretched blue handbag," said secretary of education Kenneth Baker. Edwina Currie, who served in Thatcher's government, referred to the handbag as a "weapon." Forceful rebukes to cabinet members became "handbaggings," a term now in the Oxford English Dictionary as a verb, "to handbag" meaning to treat a person ruthlessly or insensitively.[315]

The handbag was an iconic symbol of her power, noted by a biographer as "the scepter of her rule." In 1997, now Baroness Thatcher stated, "Of course, I am obstinate in defending our liberties and our law. That is why I carry a big handbag."[316] In the political space where men dominated and no woman had ever held the highest office of state, Thatcher learned to utilize the handbag to signify her femininity and help her stand out, but this certainly caused anxiety amongst male politicians. She was ridiculed for her clothes and her voice, for her "middle class manner and appearance" and as "harsh and unfelling, even un-feminine"[317] But Thatcher used the handbag to augment her power as a woman in a man's world.

Soviet President Gorbachev and U.S. Secretary of State George Shultz both joked about the contents of the bag. In July 1990, Thatcher stated that anything she had wanted to keep quiet was in the bag, "the safest place — the only leak-proof place — at Number 10 Downing Street."[318] U.S. Secretary of State Colin Powell noted that Thatcher "exuded influence and power, the hair style, the dress, her manner, the way in which she carried that handbag — when she walked into a room, you knew that somebody had arrived and you'd better be careful."[319]

Thatcher's genius at "exuding power and influence" by finely honing her feminine brand of Iron Lady with Handbag is foreshadowed by an earlier female British leader, Queen Elizabeth I, who publicly highlighted both her feminine and masculine traits to increase her power and influence. To rouse support as England was about to be besieged by the Spanish armada, she traveled to Tilbury and addressed the troops directly,

> And therefore, I am come amongst you at this time, not as for my recreation or sport, but being resolved, in the midst and heat of the battle, to live or die amongst you all; to lay down, for my God, and for my kingdom, and for my people, my honor and my blood, even the dust. I know I have but the body of a weak and feeble woman; but I have the heart of a king, and of a king of England, too.[320]

Elizabeth ascended to the throne of England in a time of tremendous political upheaval. Her father, Henry VIII, had beheaded her mother, Anne Boleyn, when Elizabeth was two years old, and Elizabeth, declared illegitimate, spent much of her childhood secluded and at risk of assassination. Her younger half-brother, Edward, ascended the throne at her father's death, but died soon thereafter, and her half-sister, Mary Tudor, was crowned Queen.

Queen Mary attempted to restore Catholicism to England, burning 280 religious dissenters at the stake during her five-year reign. "Bloody Mary's" short, bloody reign had left the country in turmoil and augmented the already enormous doubt that a woman was fit to reign when Elizabeth ascended the throne in 1558. Elizabeth faced deep-seated, centuries-old prejudice that women were naturally inferior to men in every respect. She set out to prove them wrong with a series of actions including re-establishment of the Church of England and religious moderation, overseas territorial expansion, flowering of the cultural arts epitomized by William Shakespeare, and military victory over the Spanish, the greatest military power of the age.

Her refusal to marry was initially shocking to her subjects, who assumed as a woman she would not be able to make her way in the world without the guidance of a husband. But Elizabeth declared, "I will have but one mistress here, and no master," and utilized her position as the Virgin Queen to play more powerful nations off against one another.

In a deeply misogynist age, Elizabeth shared many of the opinions of her peers, but saw herself as an exception to this. She set out to confound her doubters, presenting herself as a "mere woman" when she did not want to act. On one occasion, a diplomat praised her fluency in foreign languages, to which she demurred, "no marvel to teach a woman to talk but far harder to teach her to hold her tongue." Among men preconditioned to believe she was a "mere woman" of less intelligence, Elizabeth was willing to encourage this underestimation, which made her stronger because her opponents did not consider her formidable intellect.[321] On other occasions, Elizabeth used the strategy of winning over her misogynistic subjects by referring to herself time and again in masculine terms. She was a "prince" who reigned in a "kingdom."[322] Her reign, one of the longest in British history, is considered the Golden Age of the kingdom.

Catherine the Great of Russia, who reigned as Empress Regent from 1762 to 1796 after overthrowing her husband Peter III in a coup, used a decidedly non-virgin strategy. Over the course of her reign, she had 12 lovers, dismissing them when they bored her. Her recent biographer Robert K. Massie assesses that "perhaps if she had been the daughter of a great king, as Elizabeth I of England had been; perhaps if she like Elizabeth, had been able to use virginity and abstinence as prizes to tempt and manipulate powerful men, the lives of these two preeminent woman rulers in the history of European monarchy would have been more similar."[323]

But Catherine II of Russia's experience was very different than Elizabeth's. She has been born in Prussia to a prince in the ruling family of Anhalt, educated by a French governess. In her memoirs she declared herself a tomboy and trained herself to master a sword. But at age 14 she was brought to Russia and chosen to be the wife of her second cousin Peter III, a psychologically damaged adolescent who did not consummate the marriage due to mental immaturity and who abused her emotionally. Just six months after his ascension to the throne, Peter was overthrown in a coup d'état organized by his wife, who had him arrested and forced him to sign a document of abdication eight days before he was assassinated.

During her subsequent 34-year reign, Russia's culture was revitalized, extending the territory of the Russian empire by 200,000 square miles, engendering the Russian Enlightenment under the influence of Voltaire, and centralizing medical administration, including the administration of 2 million smallpox inoculations. Like Elizabeth I's, Catherine the Great's reign has been deemed a "Golden Age" in imperial Russia. She was apparently accepted as a female ruler by the elite in Russia, although some in western Europe were skeptical, as suggested by the snarky observations of James Harris, First Earl of Malmesbury, a foreign ambassador to the Russian court:

Her Majesty has a masculine force of mind, obstinacy in adhering to a plan, and intrepidity in the execution of it; but she wants the more manly virtues of deliberation, forbearance in prosperity and accuracy of judgment, while she possesses, in a high degree, the weaknesses vulgarly attributed to her sex — love of flattery and its inseparable companion, vanity; an inattention to unpleasant but salutary advice; and a propensity to voluptuousness which leads to excesses that would debase a female character in any sphere of life.[324]

The "problem of the female ruler" as the 18th-century saw it, was how to resolve the political problem of widespread concern about female rule in general with the more specific problem of Catherine in particular. Catherine had several illegitimate children, but her son, Paul, was deemed Emperor Peter III's true son until Peter decided not to name Paul as his heir. After her husband's dethronement and death, she was criticized for not being able to withstand her passions and presumed to be a failure as both ruler and mother. She countered these misgivings with a strategy quite similar to the one Elizabeth had used: emphasizing her feminine traits when useful and masculine traits when useful.

The widely shared misogyny of the 18th century was countered by projecting androgynous identities and male traits onto female sovereigns. In her first memoir, Catherine assigned herself certain male traits (a tomboy's nature and a strong-willed character), while also describing her identity as a mother of the future heir, with a large part of the memoir dedicated to Paul's birth. Paintings were carefully designed to show her publicly represented in allusions to female warriors and classical goddesses with an androgynous nature. She frequently promoted an image of herself as a benevolent matriarch deeply concerned with her subjects, describing herself as a loving mother endowed with divine grace: "Her Imperial Highness's maternal heart, which is so fond of her people, was very pleased to see how heartily her command was taken by every kind of person, and one might say, all spirits untied to contribute with their ideas to that great undertaking for which they were told to dispatch you to this ancient capital."[325] The Russian Legislative Commission bestowed the title of "Great and Wise Mother of the Fatherland" upon her.

The need for women in leadership roles to carefully balance masculine and feminine traits in their public messaging derives in part from the misogynistic assumption that women do not have the traits necessary for the role, and those who succeed are exceptions. Indeed, both Margaret Thatcher and Queen Elizabeth saw themselves as "exceptions to the rule" when it came to female capabilities for leadership. Often, even when role models exist that counteract the widespread assumptions, they are dismissed as minor characters in a larger stage of more important male leaders. Two Frankish queens from 1,400 years ago suffered this historical fate.

Queen Brunhild and her sister-in-law Queen Fredegund are two Frankish queens who during their lifetimes grabbed and sustained power, convincing warriors, landowners, and farmers in feudal Europe to support them. Although history has dismissed their achievements as minor queens in a minor historical era, they in fact shared an empire that encompassed modern-day France, Belgium, the Netherlands, Luxembourg, western and southern Germany, and swaths of Switzerland. They both ruled longer than almost every king and Roman emperor who had preceded them.[326]

As far back as the Code of Hammurabi, from Babylonia 1776 BCE, western culture has established patriarchal laws and systems where women were considered inferior to men. The code divides people into two genders and three classes: the *amelu* (superior people), the *mushkenu* (commoners), and *ardu* (slaves). Members of each gender and class were assigned different levels of worth. The eye of a man was considered to be twice as valuable as the life of a woman. So, remarkable women who have reigned as Queens in patriarchal societies are viewed as exceptional, often described in ambiguous or male-gendered power language. But by being seen as exceptions, their success does not necessarily disrupt patriarchies or break glass ceilings.

For the Queens we have studied, the deliberate effort to appear regal was a crucial part of their strategy to maintain power. And there is always a risk that one's regal persona can be stripped away at moment's notice. I once saw this happen to Carly Fiorina when she was one of the keynote speakers for the annual meeting of the American Medical Group Association in 2014. This incredible woman, CEO of Hewlett-Packard from 1999 to 2005, was the first woman to lead a Fortune Top-20 company and she was about to announce her run for President of the United States in the 2016 Republican primary.

She came on the stage with an audience of 3,000 healthcare executives and physicians and gave a thoughtful speech without any notes and without using a podium. After her speech, microphones were placed in the aisles for people to queue to ask questions. The very first person was a white man who began his question by first commenting on her physical attractiveness. I saw her shoulders slightly slump, and then she answered his question effectively. I cannot imagine anyone ever beginning a question to a male presidential candidate by commenting on his physical attractiveness. Yet there we were.

Substantial research supports the differences between the biological sexes in preferences for conflict and cooperation across cultures and geographies. In the political realm, women are more directly conflict averse, and democracies in general become more willing to engage in non-confrontational forms of conflict resolution as women suffrage is instituted and women become more active in the political sphere.[327] Female political leaders, typically a gender minority among their peers, may often be *more* willing to participate in conflicts, with some speculation that the "tough" international actions of Indira Gandhi and Margaret Thatcher may have been a form of "male posturing" necessary to prevent their actions as appearing to be a form of "weakness."[328]

We never had the opportunity to evaluate how Carly Fiorina might have navigated any need for "male posturing" because she never got the opportunity to lead in the political sphere. Joyce Benenson, Christine Webb, and Richard W. Wrangham of Harvard's Department of Human Evolutionary Biology recently reported their research:

> We found that females exhibited stronger self-protective reactions than males to important biological and social threats; a personality style more related to threats; stronger emotional responses to threat; and more threat-related clinical conditions suggestive of heightened self-protectiveness. That females expressed more effective mechanisms for self-protection is consistent with females' lower mortality and greater investment in childcare compared with males. In addition, females more than males exhibit a lower threshold for detecting many sensory stimuli; remain closer to home; overestimate the speed of incoming stimuli; discuss threats and vulnerabilities more frequently; find punishment more aversive; demonstrate higher effortful control and experience deeper empathy; express greater concern over friends' and romantic partners' loyalty, and seek more frequent help.[329]

Steven Pinker of Harvard's Department of Psychology sees the gender differences as being:

> ...two sets of forces that can pull in opposite directions. One set comprises the common interest of men on the one hand and women on the other. Men tend to be more obsessed with status and dominance and are more willing to take risks to compete for them; women are more likely to prize health and safety and to reduce conflict. The ultimate (evolutionary) explanation is that for much of human prehistory and history, successful men and coalitions of men potentially could multiple their mates and offspring, who had some chance of surviving even if they were killed, whereas women's lifetime reproduction was always capped by the required investment in pregnancy and nursing, and motherless children did not survive.[330]

Elena L. Botelho and Kim R. Powell are leadership advisors at a firm called ghSMART and have done extensive research on what behaviors are associated with success as a CEO. Their research is based upon robust evaluations of over 17,000 C-suite leaders including five-hour interviews and analytic evaluations. One conclusion they derive is that, although only about 4–6% of the largest companies are led by female CEOs, female CEOs succeed by exhibiting the same four crucial behaviors as successful male CEOs: *decisiveness, engaging for impact, relentless reliability*, and *adapting boldly*. They found that women may deploy leadership styles and exhibit attributes different from men's, but statistically, gender has no impact on the probability of delivering strong results as a CEO. Female and male CEOs appear more similar than different.[331]

So, what is it then? Different or same? I believe the answer is both/and. Distribution of traits overlaps among the two genders, but archetypes are categorical distinctions. The crucial lesson I have learned through the years is to become hyper-attuned to the patterns of archetypal behaviors, languages, and customs in situations I find myself in, and use slow thinking to choose how to alter the paradigm.

Women remain underrepresented in every position in the corporate pipeline, as identified by a McKinsey and Company survey in 2015 that examined the employee pipeline of 118 U.S. corporations, and it is worse at the senior level.[332] Unconscious bias no doubt plays a role in sustaining this disparity. For example, data show the ratio of male to female characters in television and film has been the same — 3:1 — since 1946, with 81% of characters with jobs being male.[333] Among physicians' specialties, women are underrepresented in all of the highest-paid surgical and medical specialties (see Table 1).[334]

TABLE 1. Gender Representation in Medicine

Specialty	Percentage Female	Average Compensation
Pediatrics	58%	$244k
Ob-Gyn	57%	$336k
Diabetes & Endocrinology	52%	$257k
Dermatology	48%	$438k
Family Medicine	45%	$255k
Psychiatry	42%	$287k
Infectious Diseases	42%	$260k
Internal Medicine	39%	$264k
Pathology	38%	$334k
Public Health and Preventative Medicine	37%	$243k

(table continues)

TABLE 1. Gender Representation in Medicine *(continued)*

Specialty	Percentage Female	Average Compensation
Rheumatology	36%	$289k
Physical Medicine and Rehabilitation	34%	$322k
Oncology	33%	$411k
Neurology	33%	$301k
Ophthalmology	32%	$417k
Critical Care	31%	$369k
Allergy & Immunology	31%	$298k
Emergency Medicine	31%	$373k
Anesthesiology	29%	$405k
Otolaryngology	25%	$469k
Gastroenterology	24%	$453k
General Surgery	24%	$402k
Radiology	23%	$437k
Nephrology	23%	$329k
Pulmonary Medicine	21%	$353k
Cardiology	16%	$490k
Plastic Surgery	16%	$576k
Orthopedics	11%	$557k
Urology	8%	$461k

Margaret Thatcher's formidable and ubiquitous purse is an example of a woman leader using the design element of contrast in a cultural application of design thinking (see chapter eight strategies).

CHAPTER SEVEN

Doctor Mom

In each case, her children are not abandoned outright; they are left in the care of fathers and other relatives. When a man leaves in this way, he is unexceptional. When a woman does it, she becomes a monster, or perhaps an antiheroine riding out a dark maternal fantasy. Feminism has supplied women with options, but a choice also represents a foreclosure, and women because they are people, do not always know what they want. As these protagonists thrash against their own decisions, they also bump up against the limits of that freedom, revealing how women's choices are rarely socially supported but always thoroughly judged.[335]

— Amanda Hess

When I started medical school at Duke in 1985, I was 23 years old. Tim and I had married two years earlier, the week we graduated from UNC Chapel Hill. We had spent the first two years of our married life in Richmond, Indiana, where Tim was getting a master's degree in Quaker Religious History at Earlham School of Religion. When we moved back to Durham for me to start medical school, he first took a job at the Duke University faculty bar as a bartender (quite a humiliation for a UNC graduate!) and then got a job with the North Carolina Commission of Indian Affairs helping high school students from North Carolina's indigenous tribes take the necessary steps to get into college.

Then, during my third year of medical school, he went back to school at NC State University to get a second master's degree in the burgeoning new field of computer science. We were getting some tuition assistance from our parents during the time we were both in school, but also borrowed money from the federal student loan programs to cover our living expenses. Jobless and both in school full time, we decided we wanted to start a family. Our daughter Katy was born in 1988 at the end of my third year of medical school.

Having a baby in medical school is not something that was encouraged in 1988. My class of 108 students at Duke was less than 40% female. One other woman in the class had children. When Katy was born, I took eight weeks off, then did my fourth year "in reverse," rotating through the sub-internships at the end of the fourth year rather than at the beginning. The year Katy was born Tim took all his classes at NC State University on Tuesdays and Thursdays so he could be home with her on the other days. On Tuesdays and Thursdays, my sister Pam, an undergraduate journalism major at UNC, drove over to Durham to watch the baby and study. We also found an affordable babysitter who provided childcare in her home for the few hours each week that Pam or Tim could not be home with Katy.

I had learned in medical school that breast feeding was better for a baby's nutrition than formula and I was determined to do this. But in those days, there were no designated private areas for nursing mothers in the workplace. I did everything I could to hide from my colleagues the fact that I was a nursing mother, because I assumed I would receive reprisals. I used a portable breast pump in the bathroom stalls, and Tim at times would bring Katy to me to feed her in the car in the parking lot, stealthily, under a blanket. Although I had not had much interest in surgery as a specialty, I was told without my asking that having a child "excluded me" from the possibility of a surgical career.

After I graduated from medical school, I stayed at Duke Medical Center an extra year and did an internship in pathology, reasoning that without night call I could be at home with the baby in the evenings, giving Tim time to finish his degree. My year as a pathology intern still seems surreal. Katy walked early, talked early, and was like a little Tasmanian devil full of energy. I hated missing any part of her development during my working hours, although her irregular sleeping and eating patterns kept us all perpetually exhausted.

I spent my workdays doing surgical and autopsy pathology. It was an incredibly rich learning environment and a year of unique experience in my medical career that I would not trade for any other. But it was not easy for me to perform autopsies on fetuses and children without feeling some degree of emotional exhaustion. I still remember how I felt entering the autopsy suite to view one particular case. The little girl was almost the same age as my Katy, her lifeless body in a nightgown, still clutching a teddy bear.

Somehow, between my sister Pam, Tim, Tim's cousin Dan (an undergraduate student at UNC the year I was a pathologist), and Mrs. Lopossy, the parttime sitter, we managed to have Katy taken care of almost entirely at home for the first two years of her life without being in an institutional day care center. This was important to me at the time, because the societal message I was receiving implied institutional day care was not good for children.

That message has been refuted by well-designed studies, such as the National Institute of Child Health and Human Development that looked at the influence of both childcare and the home environment on over 1,000 typically developing children. They found that "children who were cared for exclusively by their mothers did not develop differently than those who were also cared for by others" and "parent and family characteristics were more strongly linked to child development than were child care features."[336]

The study found that two family features had a more significant influence on children's development: the quality of mother-child interactions and the family environment. Children's outcomes were better when mothers were responsive, sensitive, attentive, and provided good stimulation during interactions. In the NICHHD study, children had better social and cognitive outcomes when the family environment was one where families had organized routines, books, and play materials, and engaged in stimulating experiences both in and out of the home.

After I graduated medical school and completed the internship in pathology at Duke, I decided to do my internal medicine training at NC Baptist Hospital in Winston Salem, North Carolina. My reasons for choosing that program had less to do with its special primary care track, which I was excited about, and more to do with the fact that it was 20 minutes from the home of my in-laws, Drs. Eldora and Eugene Terrell. Tim, Katy, Rosie (our beagle), and I moved in with Eugene, Eldora, Sara (a.k.a. Mammy, Tim's grandmother) and their dogs Mopsie, Maggie, and Boomer for a year.

That crazy four generation, four dog, one toddler, three doctor household made perfect sense to me, as there were a lot of people to help Tim, Katy, and me while I was spending every third night at the hospital on call and Tim was starting his job in researching computing at the same medical center. Tim and I had both grown up in three-generation homes, so living in a four-generation home during my second internship in a row with a toddler made perfect sense.

Initially, I was the only woman among my group of fellow internal medicine resident colleagues at NC Baptist Hospital who was a parent. As in medical school, it was more common for the male residents to be starting a family, although not common for the men either. During my second year of internal medicine residency, one of the interns got pregnant. Unfortunately, she had a terrible case of hyperemesis gravidarum and was quite sick the whole year. Her husband was a third-year resident and took all of her call and all of his call most of that year as she was too sick much of the time to do so. I have often thought about that doctor/parent couple through the years and wonder how their careers and family life have progressed through specialty fellowship training and then medical practice. I was pregnant with my second daughter, Robyn, the last half of my third year of internal medicine residency, but fortunately did not have nearly the difficulties my colleague experienced.

On July 1, 1993, four days after completing my internal medicine residency and seven months pregnant with Robyn, I began my private practice with my in-laws at Quaker Internal Medicine. I took my medical boards that September before promptly going into labor a couple of days later. The next eight weeks of maternity leave were some of the sweetest of my life. I was able to walk Katy to the neighborhood elementary school for her first days of kindergarten. I also got to spend some very quiet and special time with my new little girl.

Robyn was born in 1993, the year of the Family Medical Leave Act, which allows up to 12 weeks of unpaid family leave for parents of newborns. I never assumed such an option would be possible for me. Although as grandparents, my in-laws were interested in the welfare of their new granddaughter, as medical practice partners, they were equally eager for my return to work. I marvel at the improvement in maternity leave benefits that my daughter Katy, now a mother herself, has just had, compared to my own experience. She was able to take a full 12 weeks of paid maternity leave from her law practice in Boston.

The International Labor Organization specifies guidelines for maternity leave standards. The guidelines call for a minimum 12-week maternity leave, with at least 14 weeks recommended, and specifies that women should be paid at least two-thirds of their earnings while on leave and receive full health insurance benefits. Currently these standards are observed by 199 countries with more than 120 countries offering paid maternity leave and health benefits by law. The United States is a disappointing exception to these international standards.[337]

I began my internal medicine practice when primary care started to lose status and get slogged by the economic forces of managed care. Quaker Internal Medicine had very thin financial margins and my in-laws were relying on my productivity to keep us financially stable and to cover my share of our grueling night call. I did not take night call for the two weeks prior to Robyn's birth or during the eight weeks after her birth. Our once-a-week call meant taking all the calls after hours for the seven internists in our call group, including from the three nursing homes in which my partners had medical directorships; calls from High Point Regional Hospital for the inpatients of all seven of us; and calls from the emergency room for patients who showed up needing care who did not have a primary care physician.

There were no nurse triage services in those days, no hospitalists taking on the inpatient work, and no advance practice providers taking first call. The paradigm was still for the internist to be the center of all activity in the middle of the medical universe, despite the degradation of both reimbursement and status with the evolving specialist-focused healthcare system. The work load was far more brutal in many respects than that I had experienced during my residency, but it was also more rewarding.

The intensity of the experiences with patients in the office, the hospital, and the nursing home in that era has been unsurpassed. It was comprehensive and I had been trained to be effective in a multitude of settings. In areas where I had not, the 40 years of experience of my in-laws filled in the gaps left in my training. They are two of the finest physicians I have ever practiced with, practicing "patient-centeredness" before there was a fancy name for it.

I remember feeling so angry when a gastroenterologist from our community kept calling me a "part-time" physician during this period of my career. My days started at 7:00 a.m. when I rounded on my patients at the hospital. Then I began seeing patients in the office at 8:00 a.m. I did not take a lunch break so I could complete my patient schedule and be home by 3:00 p.m. when Katy arrived home from school and Robyn's nannie went home. I also took the full call schedule like the rest of the seven physicians in my call group and frequently went back to the hospital in the evenings if I needed to round a second time, once Tim arrived home after 6:00 p.m. My so-called "part-time job" was 40–45 work hours every week, not counting the grueling night and weekend call schedule. In most situations, such a schedule would be considered full time. My gastroenterologist friend, however, did not see it that way.

Based on these experiences juggling my early medical career and motherhood, I have great empathy for the younger women in healthcare who are balancing work and caregiving roles during the pandemic. The COVID-19 pandemic has adversely affected female physicians more than their male colleagues. A November 2021 study published in *JAMA* evaluated a cohort of 276 physicians during the COVID-19 pandemic and found "mothers were more likely than fathers to be responsible for childcare or schooling and household tasks, to work primarily from home, to reduce their work hours, and to experience work-to-family conflict, family-to-work conflict, and depressive and anxiety symptoms. A gender difference in depressive symptoms was observed among physician parents during the COVID-19 pandemic that was not present before the pandemic." The authors concluded that pandemic conditions are associated with an increase in gender inequalities within medicine and signals the importance of further attention and resources to mitigate the potential adverse consequence for the careers and well-being of physician mothers.[338]

In contrast to many women physicians, I have not had a family culture built on the expectation that I would play a dominant caregiver role at home. Tim was usually the one who stayed home with the children if they were sick and couldn't go to school. And, thankfully for our nutrition, he is the cook in the family.

My experience, and that of contemporary young physician mothers parsing the challenges of advancing their careers and raising a family, has been shaped by professional and social expectations and norms that create substantial barriers to successful advancement into leadership roles, and also create disparities in financial compensation. Mothers with children under age 18 earn 69 cents for every dollar earned by working fathers, which is a much larger pay gap than the one that exists between working women and men not taking into account parenthood.[339] The gender pay gap for American physicians is one of the largest in the U.S. labor market. Compared with male physicians in their own ethnic groups, white women earn 77 cents on the dollar, Black women earn 79 cents, and Asian women 75 cents, even after adjustment for potential confounders.[340]

In analyzing the reasons for the compensation inequity, Amy Gottlieb and Reshma Jagsi observe that "much of this gender disparity can be attributed to prejudices embedded in the unconscious beliefs about what leaders look like, how men and women should behave, and how women's work is assigned and valued in our profession institutions and society." They note that in healthcare, women tend to advance in areas that are consultative and supportive rather than those with quantitative or significant managerial responsibility that incubate dean and chief executive officer positions. Female medical trainees are directed toward certain specialties seen as requiring traditionally "feminine" attributes (nurturing qualities, relationship orientation) and away from procedural and more technical specialties. Gottlieb and Jagsi point out that

> Long-standing cultural expectation regarding women's behavior remain at odds with well-accepted traits of leaders and high performers, even though organizations with female leaders often outperform those with male leaders. Women in the workplace are expected to be both directive and participative, decisive and caring, and executive and approachable, and they face backlash when their behavior violates these stereotypes. Women are consistently evaluated more negatively than similarly qualified men as they navigate the expectations of femininity while simultaneously fulfilling requisites of advancement and leadership.[341]

These unconscious social demands impact women in 2022 no less than they did in 1963, when Betty Friedan first published *The Feminine Mystique*, in which she explored the "schizophrenic split" between the "reality" of women's lives in which they were told their role was to seek fulfillment as wives and mothers who nonetheless felt unfulfilled by the limitation of these traditional roles.[342] Friedan noted that

> There is only one way for women to reach full human potential — by partici-pating in the mainstream of society, by exercising their own voice in all the decisions shaping that society. For women to have full identity and freedom, they must have economic independence. Breaking through the barriers that had kept them from the jobs and professions rewarded by society was the first step, but it wasn't sufficient. It would be necessary to change the rules of the game to restructure professions, marriage, the family, the home. The manner in which offices and hospitals are structured, along the rigid, separate, unequal, unbridgeable lines of secretary/executive, nurse/doctor, embodies and perpetuates the feminine mystique.[343]

As a physician who is a woman, who is also a mother and wife, and who has served as a CEO in several organizations, I might argue that there has been substantial progress in the 60 years since Friedan first described the "rigid, separate, unequal, unbridgeable lines of secretary/executive, nurse/doctor" perpetuating the feminine mystique. But here we are, six decades years later, with female academic physicians making 78 cents on the dollar compared to their male colleagues, all the while more likely to be responsible for child-care, schooling, and household tasks during the global pandemic.

Freidan called for a restructuring of society so that "women, who happen to be the people who give birth, could make a human, responsible choice whether or not — and when — to have children, and not be barred thereby from participating in society in their own right."[344]

Betty Friedan's point in 1963 was that the post-World War II "ideal woman" living a life defined entirely by her identity as a wife and mother who stayed at home in a suburban dream house was an incomplete and sometimes miserable experience for many women who had been told this was what they were to aspire to. She linked the attempt of women to fit into this constrained stereo-type of femininity to divorce and depression. She correlated the trend toward post-WWII younger age at marriage to social pressures to constrain women's choices and increase the number of children women would have.

We got the baby boom as a result of these social pressures, but the backlash from the constraints women experienced from these limitations in accept-able social roles drove much of the first wave of the women's movement in the 1960s and 1970s, with legislative remedies enacted to prevent overt discrimination in education, sports, and the workplace. What women are experiencing now is discrimination based on unconscious bias, where the female archetypes constrain women in the minds and actions of those they interact with in the workplace, schools, sporting events, etc., and women conform their behavior to the acceptable archetypal feminine traits such as caregiving and nurturing that prevents backlash against the witch/bitch labels that limit their power and influence.

When the landmark Title VII of the Civil Rights Act, Title IX of the Education Amendments of 1972, and other legislation prohibiting discrimination on the basis of gender were enacted, women did not suddenly experience an equal playing field with men. The workplace setting is still structured to favor men. In the late 1980s, when I was in medical school, I did not even consider surgical training because, among other factors such as my intellectual preference for diagnostic medicine, my husband and I wanted to start a family, and I was told point blank that would exclude me from acceptance into surgical training programs. We started our family right in the middle of my medical school and his graduate school, and together worked around some extremely challenging structural barriers in the educational setting and workforce that are barely better today.

The Civil Rights legislation provided opportunities for women to enter the workforce, but it did not provide structural change to the workplace itself. For many women, that has continued to mean that choosing to become a mother means choosing career trajectories with fewer leadership opportunities, lower pay, and, working less than full time when one's children are young, foregoing years of accumulated retirement benefits. In medicine, this means there are fewer women surgeons and specialists, fewer women CEOs, and fewer women policy leaders.

For those of us who have refused to accept the family and professional roles as an either/or pathway, it has meant devising strategies that permit us to serve in both roles. For my husband Tim and me, it meant surreptitious breast feedings in the Duke Medical Center parking lot, evenings of playing "Doggy, Doggy, Who's Got Your Bone?" in the Wake Forest Baptist call rooms with a three-year-old, living with my in-laws for a year during my medicine internship, and joining their medical practice when I finished training and had two young daughters. For Tim, it meant choosing a career path that allowed him the flexibility to pick up children from day care, gymnastics, dance, and soccer.

Being a mother and a physician is not a new path. My mother-in-law, Dr. Eldora Terrell, was among the first generation of female physicians who balanced these dual roles. She is the mother of six children, and practiced medicine throughout the time her children were growing up, with the exception of when my husband was born and she had three children in diapers at the same time (!). She took 18 months off from her full-time practice at that point. Like Tim and me, she and her husband, Dr. Eugene Terrell, used a divide-and-conquer strategy, and also relied on family members, in this case, her mother, to be home with the children when they were at work.

Eldora's career trajectory included being chief of staff of High Point Regional Hospital, medical director of a regional Medicaid clinic, and medical director of a nursing home. But even with experiences such as Eldora's and mine, many women who are pursuing a medical career still see family and professional advancement as being incompatible.

Dr. Leana Wen, in her wonderful book *Lifelines*, tells the story of her own incredible life journey as an immigrant who has become one of our most important public health leaders. Particularly relevant to me is her description of when she told her staff about her pregnancy in 2016, and how her special assistant about to start medical school at Columbia University reacted:

> That's why I was surprised when she became visibly emotional at my news. Kathleen would tell me later that my being a mother and a leader was important for her to see firsthand. Like so many young people, she envisioned having a family and a career, too, and she appreciated being there with me as I made this choice and learned to grow into a new identity.[345]

When she experienced motherhood firsthand Dr. Wen began to apply the lessons she was learning in her personal life to her work:

> Being a mother dominated my thoughts and consciousness in a way that I could have never imagined before I had Eli....Everything I did in my professional life was also suddenly shaped by my new perspective. During my maternity leave, Kristin would come to my house a couple of times a week and review key decisions. When she brought over the minutes from an overdose meeting, I saw the victims for the first time as somebody's child. When I chaired the next convening of the Child Fatality Review, I saw in every case of child death the face of the mother and her grief...My changing perspective made me acutely aware of workplace policies that were needed to better support pregnant women and parents. Before I had to navigate the day care drop-off, I didn't understand the impact of early morning meetings on my staff who had childcare needs.[346]

Incorporating her identity as a mother into her experiences as a physician and healthcare leader broadened Dr. Wen's perspective and leadership skills. Her experience illustrates the benefit of an integrated approached to motherhood and physician leader for adapting the workplace to a more gender-friendly environment. Studies demonstrating that female physicians spend more time listening to patients, are more conscientious and have better surgical outcomes and higher quality scores quantify why we need to have an enabling workplace environment for women physicians who choose to become parents. Stories like Dr. Wen's provide the qualifying stories of how the experience of being a mother can improve one's leadership capabilities.

On the flip side, I have also observed situations where women have not been able to distinguish between their parenting role at home and their management style at work, much to the detriment of their team and their perceived leadership potential. One female physician leader I have worked with in the past was called "the mother hen" behind her back. She treated every direct report like one of her children, to their loss and hers.

Her management style focused on nurturing and protecting "her" employees. In their interactions with other employees in the organization, she defended their behavior irrespective of the adequacy of their performance. She checked over their work like it was her children's homework. Her employees learned dependency and did not advance their own leadership skills as rapidly as their potential indicated was possible. They felt safe to the point of complacency at times.

Her turnover rate was higher than that of other managers, as employees found they needed to leave to advance their own careers. Eventually, this physician leader moved on to another organization to further her own career because "over-mothering" her employees had become a barrier to her own advancement as well as theirs.

A vexing problem in developing more gender-inclusive workplaces is the unresolvable and unending debate as to whether humans are "naturally" male or female, or whether the dichotomy is socially constructed. Those who argue the nature of human gender patterns are limited to the two categories of male and female by the sex-dimorphic biological processes applicable to all vertebrates base their perspective on the biological elements of sex including male and female chromosomes, hormones, and the endocrine system, and internal and external sexual and reproductive organs and central nervous system sex differentiation. Their opponents argue that gender is a social construct built on interpersonal interactions and culturally constructed as a mode of social organization, structuring status, and power dynamics in cultural institutions.[347]

It is factually true and verifiable that on average, males have greater physical strength and are taller, and females have the unique capacity for childbearing.

The *biological essentialists* assert that biological *sex* differences lead to behavioral, cognitive, and emotional differences between males and females that explains *gender* differences. The essentialist perspective is frequently used to justify cultural roles constraints, such as environmentally accommodating one gender in the workplace but not the other. Thus, surgical suites and C-suites accommodate men but not women, from medical instruments and executive furniture designed for taller people, to structural barriers to simultaneously accommodating both childbearing and work promotion.

In the contrasting position, *social constructionists*, who argue that gender is a multidimensional category of identity encompassing distinct patterns of social and cultural differences, provide evidence that gender-specific social expectations for behavior and temperament, sexuality, kinship and interpersonal roles, occupation, religious roles and other social patterns are not tied to an anatomical dichotomy, but to social gender dichotomy tracking at birth to categorize the newborn into one or the other of two social role complexes.[348]

Evidence supporting the cultural construct of gender non-biologically determined is provided by the 150 separately documented Native American societies where a third gender, *"berdache,"* exists and allows biologically female sexed persons to undertake a man's lifestyle and biologically male sexed individuals to adopt women's social roles (and sometimes dress) and do women's work. The berdache gender "is not a deviant role, nor a mixture of two genders nor less a jumping from one gender to its opposite. Nor is it an alternative role behavior for nontraditional individuals who are still considered men or women. Rather it comprises a separate gender within a multiple gender system."[349]

The contemporary Euro-American dialogue about gender and sex variation has tended to use mutually exclusive terms emphasizing either gender variation "hermaphrodite" or sexual variation "homosexual" or "transsexual" but has ultimately engendered a substantive conversation about gender diversity in the ever-expanding label of LGBTQIA (Lesbian, Gay, Bisexual, Transsexual, Queer, Intersex, Asexual). Even so, the rigid archetypal categories we have explored throughout this book still constrain choices for women in the professional workforce, when women are expected to provide most of the caregiving responsibilities in the home and oftentimes at work as well. In doing so, they often resort to the "mother" persona in their management style, getting trapped into career pathways that will not allow them to track to the most senior leadership roles.

Sometimes, women have been able to leverage their caregiver role to achieve positions of leadership. The modern nursing profession was established in the 19th century by women serving as heroic caregivers. In the United Kingdom, Florence Nightingale came to prominence as a manager and trainer of nurses during the Crimean War after she organized care for wounded soldiers in Constantinople. She professionalized nursing, established the first nursing school, and was a pioneer in statistics and the presentation of data. The media focused on Nightingale's heroic caregiving role in the Crimean War far more than her work in statistics, although her modern circular histogram is still regularly used in visualization of data.[350]

In the United States, Clara Barton founded the American Red Cross and served on the Union battlefield in the Civil War as a nurse, tending to hundreds of soldiers in Virginia, Maryland, and South Carolina. Other 19th-century women who served as military nurses during wartime include Dorothea Six, Mary Ann Bickerdyke, Harriet Tubman, and Louisa May Alcott. Like the frontline healthcare workers, mostly women, caring for patients with COVID-19, these women have been celebrated for their "devotion of their lives to others," a mothering role if there ever was one.[351] These women are not depicted as "running with the wolves" or "tomboys" or "goddesses." Rather, their leadership position is legitimized through its personification of the Caregiver.

For physicians who are women, the Doctor Mom persona sometimes juxtaposes the two roles to emphasize caregiving. Several Doctor Moms blog about their experiences. Dr. Nadia Sabri, who writes the Mindful MD Mom blog, is a pediatrician who asserts "being a doctor mom is a beautiful paradox of feeling like a badass one moment and a frazzled I-don't-know-what-the-heck-I-am-doing mess of a person. Being a female physician, the majority of us feel there is a societal and cultural pressure to be perfect all the time in every sphere of our life: as a professional, parent, and person."[352]

Dr. Stephanie Liu's blog Life of Dr. Mom focuses on working "to educate the modern mom with the most relevant up-to-date medical evidence to support families and the healthy development of their children." She defines herself on the blog as a community family medicine and acute care physician who is "wife to Graeme, an otolaryngologist head and neck surgeon and mommy to Madi, a sweet and spunky little girl."[353]

Emily Gottenborg, MD, declares that "you can't have it all" when describing what it is like to be Doctor Mom. She highlights five common challenges that physician mothers face:

1. Lack of access to paid parental leave.
2. Difficulty in performing the daily work of a physician while enduring the physical challenges associate with the peri-partum period.
3. Breastfeeding challenges.

4. Being passed over for career opportunities as colleagues perceive their plate to be too full for additional projects.
5. Microaggression responses directed toward their position as a mother.

She notes the impact of motherhood on physician mothers' ability to empathize with their patients. In other words, their skills as a physician are enhanced by their new caregiving trait of empathy.[354] Unsurprisingly, a brief search of Google will show Doctor Dad is not an equivalent category or professional identity inspiring multiple bloggers.

Several years ago, I attended a meeting of medical alumni at my medical school, Duke University. At lunchtime, I happened to sit at a table of eight where all the doctors were women. As the women introduced themselves to one another, every single one of them identified herself by her medical specialty, identified herself as a mother, and described her children. It was remarkable. I have sat at scores of similar luncheons through the years and since that meeting have noticed not a single male physician introduces himself by talking about the number of children he has. Sometimes at mixed-gendered tables the women will describe their specialty and child status, but men will not follow with describing themselves similarly.

This distinction is important. Women signal their caregiving roles. Their need to do this signaling is consistent with a 2005 study by Catalyst that showed that managers perceived that there are in fact distinct differences between women and men leaders. Women and men both perceived that more women leaders than men leaders were effective at "caretaker" behaviors such as supporting others and rewarding subordinates. However, they perceived that more men leaders than women leaders were effective at "take charge" behaviors such as delegating and problem-solving. Notably the study found these perceptions were not supported by research on actual leadership behavior, which finds that gender is not a reliable predictor of how a person will lead.[355]

In a separate study, the Catalyst group found that managers' perceptions from different cultures — Anglo (United Kingdom, United States), Germanic (the Netherlands, Germany,) Latin (France, Italy, Spain), and Nordic (Denmark, Norway, Sweden) — held stereotypic perceptions of women's and men's leadership that bore striking similarities across the cultures — stereotypic perceptions that discredited the effectiveness of women leaders' highly valued leadership attributes.

These stereotypes create a double-bind for women. Women are perceived as "atypical leaders" and as going against the norms of leadership or those of femininity. Caught between impossible choices, those who try to conform to traditional (masculine) leadership behaviors are "damned if they do, doomed if they don't." The cognitive shortcuts that perpetuate gendered stereotypes over-simplify reality and hinder the advancement of women into leadership positions. It is misleading to presume "taking-care" and "taking-charge" skills are mutually exclusive, but this false dichotomy between "feminine" and "masculine" culturally defined characteristics creates a double-bind for women by casting men as "natural" leaders who "take charge" and women as, well, "mothers," who "take care."

The Catalyst studies defined the double-bind dilemmas for women in three categories:

1. **Extreme Perceptions**: Women are perceived to have traits that are too soft, too tough, and never just right.
2. **High Competence Threshold**: Women leaders face higher standards and lower rewards than men leaders.
3. **Competent but Disliked**: Women leaders are perceived as competent or likable, but rarely both.[356]

It is no small wonder, then, that the women at the Duke Medical School meeting took such pains to describe themselves in their professional identities and as mothers. Their ability to define their personhood required both professional and family role identities. I have observed some lesbian and straight women colleagues who do not have children do this by talking about the relationships they have with nieces and nephews. And I frequently see older men do this in describing their grandchildren. But it is rare for most younger men to do this, as their personal identity can be externally perceived as adequately whole without the need for them to signal their family role. The non-familial archetypal male role of Hero does just fine in delineating their "take charge" role as leader. Women, in contrast, require more complex cues to signal who they are. The Mother archetype is the most powerful female archetype. No wonder she popped up at the Duke Medical School alumni luncheon table.

Not in many years have I heard what I used to hear frequently: that medical school is "wasted" on female candidates because they will leave the career to raise their children when the spot could have been provided to a man who would work more years and longer hours. I do occasionally still hear someone complain about the risk of hiring a younger woman, because "she will probably get pregnant and not work after that."

For some women, leaving their profession or working part-time when they are raising a family is the right choice, but medical training is expensive, and student debt loads now average more than $241,000 when training is completed. Consequently, many women completing their medical professional training do not believe part-time practice is an option, or they have done the complex calculus of deciding the financial risks of having a family versus longer and more extensive specialty training, fearing reduction in fertility as they slog through 10 years of training post college.

I do not believe that women who choose to stay home and raise their children while their spouse works outside the home are making a poor choice, provided it is what they want to do. I do believe women who choose to leave the professional workforce due to burnout from the challenges of practicing medicine and taking on most of the responsibilities of raising a family should more accurately be seen as victims of gender bias who failed to navigate work environments designed by and for men.

Angela Lowe Heider, MD, shared her experience as 22-year-old first-year medical student at UNC Chapel Hill admonishing Kim, a 30-something woman in the class with a small child discussing her plans for a part-time job in the future to allow her more time for family and home. Heider said to Kim, "Are you kidding? You are taking up a valuable spot in this class, wasting time and money! Do you know how much the taxpayers are contributing to your education?"

Over the course of the next 10 years, Heider trained as an obstetrician and gynecologist, married, had three children, and, ultimately, left the medicine to be a full-time stay-at-home parent just three years after entering private practice because of the overwhelming burnout she was experiencing. She shares her poignant story in *The Rise and Fall of Doctor Mom*, which she began writing the day she retired, asserting the "telling has been many things to me, not the least of which is a chance to heal."[357]

Heider documents the environment of abuse and burnout she experienced as a resident, but calls the experience, "in part, a story of my failure."[358] She speaks of some of her supervising physicians as "overburdened, hateful people" who often treated residents, nurses, and medical students "with utter contempt and deplorable disrespect."[359] She tells of being pregnant with her first son in the second year of her residency while working 90 hours a week, being admonished by her chief resident that she would have to make up all the days of call she missed for maternity leave.

In her exit interview with the department chair after she completed her residency, she was told her decision to have a child while in residency was not a good one. Out in private practice, she experienced postpartum depression with the birth of another child and a medical malpractice suit, and found that working part-time as an ob-gyn still obligated her to covering full-time malpractice insurance.

Documenting her experiences and that of six other female physicians who struggled to achieve balance between work and family, Heider called for change to medical residency programs that would allow women to balance medical practice with home life, including adequate maternity leave, job-sharing, flextime, part-time positions, onsite child care facilities, reductions in med-mal premiums for part-time providers, and increasing usage of hospitalists, laborists, and other shift-based physician work to permit broader flexibility in on-call responsibilities. Ultimately, Heider assesses that:

> We need to rethink the way we define success. While growing up, I do not remember ever being told motherhood would be an important component of my achievement. My parents concentrated on my professional goals. Being an involved mom and influential physician married to a busy surgeon seemed reasonable to me. I would like for my daughter to strive towards academic success and feel empowered in the pursuit of any profession. I want her to know she can do anything; she just cannot do everything. I want her to find her talents and develop them. I do not "only want her to be happy." She should find some way to contribute. She should have goals. If her future is to include children though, I want her to consider their needs. She will have to find some way to make her professional goals mesh with her personal life. Maybe she will marry someone who is willing to be a stay-at-home dad, or maybe extended families are the answer. Contributing to the upbringing of my grandchildren would be a welcomed honor. I want her to understand motherhood is an important endeavor, one to be proud of. I want to temper her idealism with a touch of reality. Maybe being a top-notch world-renown physician, or scientist, or musician, or whatever is not compatible with being a committed wife and mother. Maybe it is, but I will challenge her to consider not if, but how.[360]

Based on what we have documented in this book, the plight of women physicians is not much better in 2023 than it was 15 years ago when Heider published her book, although some of the structural changes she called for are more common today. Heider was able to make the choice to retire because her husband was a full-time surgeon. Not all women physicians have that luxury. She is quick to condemn the "entitled poor" in her book as part of what contributed to her burnout but does not necessarily see her own experience as entitled. She is nonetheless correct in her assessment that medicine as currently designed is not conducive to gender equality.

A study presented at the 2022 American College of Obstetricians and Gynecologists (ACOG) annual meeting showed one in four new mothers who are physicians report experiencing postpartum depression, a rate twice that of the general population. The researchers recruited 637 physicians and medical students who were pregnant to respond to a survey adapted from the U.S. Centers for Disease Control and Preventions' Infant Feeding Practices Study and the CDC's Pregnancy Risk Assessment Monitoring System.

With regard to results, 25% of participants reported postpartum depression with the highest rates seen among Hispanic/Latina respondents (31%), Black persons (30%), and non-Hispanic white persons (25%), and the lowest rate for those identifying as Asian (15%). Eighty percent of the respondents with postpartum depression attributed their condition to sleep deprivation, with 44% citing problems related to infant feeding, 41% citing lack of adequate maternity leave, and 33% attributing lack of support at their workplace.[361] The healthcare industry and society in general continue to be based on archetypal understandings of male and female societal roles, and those who stray from these constraints often must overcome many headwinds.

Much of my personal story, told in bits and snippets throughout this book, is based on my own strategies to overcome these headwinds because, in contrast to the advice Heider gave her daughter, I do not believe women must understand that they "can do anything but can't do everything." By understanding the constraints that archetypes seek to impose, we have taken the first step in breaking through these barriers to full personhood irrespective of gender. The next step is to learn how to identify these archetypal constraints in the context of our daily lived experiences. Finally, we must develop tactical skills that can be deployed to design solutions to these barriers. In the final chapter, I will tell a few more stories from my own experiences to flush out some of these tactics.

PART III

How Shall We Fix This?

If the fault for poor health, or the privilege and praise for good health, lies within individuals, their innate biology, and social groups with whom they individually and independently choose to affiliated, then, per the dominate status quo framing, social group differences in health are simply a reflection of innate biology, values, and choices.

If responsibility lies within societal systems in which some groups have power at another group's expense in ways that affect options for living a healthy life, then the social group differences in health constitute health inequities, that is, differences in health status that are unfair, avoidable, and in principle preventable.

Source: Nancy Kreiger, *Ecosocial Theory, Embodied Truths, and the People's Health*, Oxford University Press, 2022.

CHAPTER EIGHT

From Nouns to Verbs

There is one thing that unites cultural conservatives throughout the world, a critique that joins Protestant fundamentalists, Islamists, Hindu Nationalist, ultra-Orthodox Jews, and ultramontane Catholics. All view women's equality and self-possession as unnatural, a violation of the established order.[362]

— Michelle Goldberg, *The Means of Reproduction: Sex, Power, and the Future of the World.*

We are now going to move from nouns to verbs. Witches, bitches, grandmothers, queens, doctors, maidens are nouns. Specifically, a noun is a word used as the name or designation of a person. My argument has been that women are categorized in very specific ways, unconsciously via nouns that are archetypes, which Jung defined as a pervasive idea, image, or symbol that forms part of the collective unconscious, and which, interestingly, in comparative anatomy, is defined by the Oxford English Dictionary as an assumed ideal pattern of the fundamental structure of each great division of organized beings. But understanding the constraints and possibilities of these archetypes and their implications for healthcare leadership for women begs the question as to what we can do about it. That's why it's time to move from nouns to verbs, which are words used to indicate action.

I've spent seven chapters and many pages making the argument that systemic barriers exist for women in healthcare, as in other professions, to rise to top leadership roles, and that many of the barriers are cultural in nature, embedded in universal archetypes that limit acceptable behavior for women and, hence, their opportunities to advance. Human beings are subconsciously influenced by these tropes, irrespective of policies and regulations intended to enforce equal opportunities. As a result, female physicians are paid less for equal work and have had higher rates of burnout and dropout during the pandemic.

For women and their families, wage discrimination has lifetime impact. For society as a whole, inadequate integration of diverse leadership limits the strength and creativity of our healthcare institutions. For our patients, the statistically better-quality scores and longer time spent with patients observed on average in female physicians, and the statistically better outcome among female surgeons, is disincentivized by the current culture and payment systems. No one benefits from patriarchal gender restrictions on leadership teams.

In the *First Political Order*, Valerie M. Hudson, Donna Lee Bowen, and Perpetua Lynne Nielsen compare political systems across cultures to understand how patriarchies maintain male supremacy. Governments have kept women in positions of inferiority through many means: making early claims on them (childhood marriage), financial control (dowry or bride-price), multiple wives per man (polygamy), license violence (wife beating), sequestering them from outside influence (patriolocation), reducing sexual gratification (genital mutilation), and religious role assignment (nun).[363]

But I did not write this book as a highly footnoted whine session. I wrote it to provide insights that will allow us to develop solutions. Solutions require actions that I have categorized in a series of steps building upon each other that can serve as a toolkit. This part of the book is not so highly footnoted. It is based on my personal experiences and observations over the course of my career. In the personal examples I give, I have worked to make sure the people involved are anonymous, so details of time and place have been mixed a bit. But each of these examples is, in fact, from my own life, albeit disguised for the sake of my colleagues, patients, and friends. For those who are reading this and think they might recognize themselves — I'll never tell.

ACTION 1: RECOGNIZING

There are two young fish swimming along, and they happen to meet an older fish swimming the other way, who nods at them and says, "Morning boys. How's the water?" And the two young fish swim on for a bit, and then eventually one of them looks over at the other and says "What the hell is water?"[364]

Before one can change things, one has to be able to recognize what's going on. When we are immersed in a patriarchal culture, sometimes we are like the fish who don't recognize what water is. For example, in the version of the parable quoted above, the fish are all male, as if the default fish, just like the default human, is male. We have lived in a world our whole lives where the baseline archetypes identifying us as Maidens, Mothers, Goddesses, Witches, Bitches, Whores, and Crones have been the background characters in predetermined storylines in which we live our lives. Recognizing them in real time is sometimes more difficult than it might appear on the surface.

Just as pattern recognition is an important skill in the practice of medicine, it is important in interacting with others at work as well. As a primary care physician who has listened to my patients tell me thousands of stories through the years, I have learned to recognize in my patients that when I hear the same story from them over the years, and only the individual characters have changed, it means that this is their story and how they interpret their place in the world.

One patient of mine told me about a difficult relationship she had with her father when she was a teenager. She left home and met a boyfriend but felt betrayed when he left her. A few years later, she was working through her feelings about her recent divorce and feelings of betrayal after her newest relationship broke it off. I heard a third version of this story several years later when she left a job with an oppressive boss but felt betrayed when she was fired from her new job a few months after accepting it. It doesn't take a Jungian psychologist to see a pattern of a woman who perhaps was living a story in a Daughter archetype who runs away from an oppressive father but finds the rescuing Hero isn't all she had hoped he would be. The story she told me over and over through the years was her story of how she was betrayed.

I have watched women in healthcare leadership do things that subconsciously put them into a situation in which they may be perceived to be in one of the feminine archetype stories, much to their detriment in being perceived as a leader. A very strong chief medical officer I knew baked cookies and brought them to board meetings where all the other board members were male. I actually heard one of these board members say to her, while munching on a cookie, "Thanks, Mom!" Another excellent female physician leader I know was often criticized for "mothering" her team. They could do no wrong and their performance could not be questioned by anyone but her. She sometimes had difficulty keeping team members because they complained she was too controlling and did not allow them independence to grow professionally. Women who are perceived as mothers in their professional role are seldom seen as adequate to lead at the top of an organization. Sometimes they become the nurturing "helpmate" of a male CEO.

A few women have gotten into a daughter-like relationship with a male boss. The relationship can be comfortable because there are no sexual undertones and the man can impart wisdom and champion the woman in her career development. But true mentorships have to mature over time, and on more than one occasion I have seen the relationship become unhealthy if the structure remained unequal — women can come to resent "mansplaining" over time.

I learned to be wary of social events involving male members of leadership teams in which women were not invited, even if the events were not part a company program. The "no girls allowed" treehouses are all over the place, including annual golfing trips, skiing trips, fishing trips, sporting events, and cigar bars. When these events are ostensibly co-ed, I go, albeit without smoking a cigar. In situations where I cannot or should not go, I recognize them as a potential risk of power exclusion and can apply mitigation if necessary.

"Bro" culture needs to be challenged when it affects the business. At times I have deliberately played the Tomboy role to prevent exclusion. I tend to perceive real danger in gender exclusive situations. I enter anyway, when I want to, and challenge the situation when necessary. There is nothing wrong with men getting together without women to participate in activities they enjoy. But when they become the conduit for acquisition of "work capital," the ability to hone relationships with co-workers and develop networks, they can be problematic for women.

I once witnessed this happening when two male executives excluded the woman whom one of them reported to and the other had a parallel relationship with in the corporate structure when they traveled to visit potential clients. The road trips were by car, and they always returned in a cheerful mood, irrespective of their success with clients. They talked about golf scores and wine and sports teams.

The woman in this situation began to notice the two of them almost spoke with one voice in meetings, and she often had a sense that they had made decisions on these trips that should have involved the entire team. None of the women on the team participated in these road trips, and its impact subtly eroded comradery among all the team members — the majority were women — over time.

Unconscious bias is something we all are guilty of having, and recognition of the archetypal roles that underlie them in oneself, in others, and in social structures is crucial to overcoming the traps in which they can ensnare you as well as the opportunities they can present to change your storyline to meet your goals. The crucial skill to doing so is strengthening one's ability to recognize them.

For clinicians, pattern recognition is a crucial skill for diagnostic acumen. Likewise, pattern recognition in the determinants of gender bias is a skill that needs to be developed over time. Seeing and hearing are not the same things as observing and listening, and it is the discerning power of the latter two that are necessary skills for recognizing.

Observe and listen for repetitive stories, body language, and speech patterns. A group of healthcare professionals published an article in the *British Medical Journal* in January 2022 calling for more inclusive language in informal healthcare settings. Declaring, "we are women, not girls," they noted the use of the term "gas girls" to describe female anesthetists in the ICU is both infantilizing and misogynist and should be consciously eliminated from the day-to-day banter in the professional setting.[365]

These women had to recognize the language as being demeaning before they could actually address it. A cultural anthropologist named John-Henry Pffiferling created a coaching practice for physicians with disruptive behaviors. He taught me to look out for the use of verbal patterns he termed "DEXIFY." He noted this pattern is often used by male physicians when their behavior is challenged. First, they DENY whatever has been proposed as a problematic behavior, then they EXPLAIN what the behavior really was, and then they DEFINE how the behavior is to be accepted.

I have learned to recognize DEXIFYING speak and often find it associated with presumed authority. I used to warn my female colleagues to "beware of the tall white man who speaks in a deep voice in declarative sentences in board meetings." More recently, this has been labeled "mansplaining" and more people are developing the skill to recognize this pattern of power grabbing.

Recognition of the nuances of body language and spatial assertions is an important pattern recognition skill. We have all been made aware of the "manspread" in crowded public spaces, but there are more subtle physical traps in the work environment. Tables and chairs are often standardized for male proportions, such that women appear small or overwhelmed by furniture in group settings. Podiums for speeches and the microphones attached to them typically are standardized for men.

One particularly ambitious male executive with whom I worked in the past used his left handedness to make sure he always sat at the head of the table in board meetings. I have noticed women, irrespective of their rank in an organization, often will not sit near the head of the table in a board room.

I have observed men in executive positions putting their arm on a woman executive's shoulder or patting her back. I've never seen them do so with a male colleague. This type of touching should immediately set off alarm bells. It is not always sexual in nature. Sometimes, it cues the "father-daughter" archetype is being subconsciously acted out.

In general, the skill of pattern recognition should be trained to discern all the archetypal stories, whether mother, daughter, hero, witch, maiden, or otherwise. Unpacking one's emotions is important. Why did I feel tense? Did I feel included? Respected? Heard?

ACTION 2: EVALUATING

As we discussed in chapter two, Israeli-American psychologist Daniel Kahneman's 2011 book *Thinking, Fast and Slow* described the thesis he and his late colleague Amos Tversky developed over 30 years of research that demonstrated two separate modes of human thought : "System 1" that is fast, instinctive, and emotional, and "System 2" that is slower, more deliberative, and more logical.

When we are using System 1, the short cuts of the archetypes often cloud our ability to separate our options from a foredrawn storyline that is imbedded in the cultural stereotypes we have been born into. So, crucial to breaking through the limits of System 1 reliance on stereotypical storylines is to consciously practice moving from System 1 to System 2 thinking by evaluating with deliberation and patient, slow observation what is actually going on in a particular scenario.

From my perspective, System 1 may be emotional and instinctive, but System 2 is strongest when we are able to reflect on the emotions we may be feeling. For women, this may mean reflecting on some of the emotions just below the surface. Am I feeling like I am being treated like a damsel in distress? Am I not speaking out because I fear being labeled as a bitch? Why am I feeling excluded? Am I going into full caregiver mode, treating this colleague like I am his mother? Am I feeling resentful because I am being mansplained again? Do I feel like I'm being silenced by being interrupted, excluded from Old Boys Club activities, or physical distancing from loci of power?

Various forms of meditation, psychotherapy, and mindfulness disciplines are based on moving into a System 2 form of thinking that permits some distance from instinct and emotion in order to process them and deliberate more effectively in the insights they can provide. Pattern recognition tends to be part of the strength of System 1 thinking, so long as the patterns are accurate and the quick actions taken based on their recognition are correct responses to the current situation. But often they are not, so the ability to recognize the patterns and slow down can create the space needed to provide options are freedom in actions, that are less Pavlovian reflexes, and more nuanced and wholesome in quality.

The second component of evaluating is adding quantitative data to the thinking process. System 1, built on "the gut," often misses the power of data to both refute inappropriate assumptions and to provide significant alternative narratives from which to build new paradigms. This book has been full of references to data that demonstrate the negative consequences of gender stereotypes and its detrimental impact on our culture.

Thinking like a scientist can be a powerful antidote to prejudice. Recognizing the copious argument fallacies used in the day-to-day work environment can be a System 2 superpower: "He just didn't mansplain something to me, he actually used the classic 'straw man' ruse to do so." Count things and point them out. What is the ratio of male to female leaders in your organization? How often did the male members of the team interrupt the women in the room? Who spoke first? Who in the office is engaging in "caregiving" behavior? How often are outside speakers at educational seminars and conferences men rather than women?

Evaluating with System 2 thinking, quantitative data, and then weighing one's options toward what actions and behaviors to participate in can provide degrees of freedom through enhance awareness of options for action.

ACTION 3: CHOOSING

Once you recognize the archetypal story that is being played out in your workplace, you have the opportunity to make a choice. Recognition provides you with the gift of freedom. By flipping to a different archetype that better serves your own values, you have more control over the storyline.

Much of this book has been about recognizing the inappropriateness of the subconscious archetypes at play in our culture. But its purpose is not to provide a rant about something that cannot be altered. Rather it is about helping you recognize the factors at play so those factors can be re-designed.

One approach is to call out what is going on once you recognize it so others can see it too. This is sometimes adequate in and of itself. But a further step is to shift to a different archetype. Moving from the Mother role to the Queen role can be a deliberate decision, and includes consciously altering personal behaviors. Queens don't bring cookies to board meetings, but Moms sometimes do. Queens sit on thrones — which in a board meeting may mean the head of the table — and they wear regal (professional) clothes. Similarly, a woman who feels stuck in a Daughter role with an older male mentor may choose to switch to a Hero role, which may require pointing out to the mentor (father) the times he is rescuing her, preventing her from playing the game with the boys. When a woman is afraid of being perceived as a bitch for behaving assertively, she may choose to verbalize the risk out loud. It's a witchy move to do so, immediately garnishing power by exposing patriarchal tropes in their fullness.

Understanding one has choices is crucial. Having choices doesn't mean those choices will not have consequences, including adverse ones, but it does permit women to own their story and create the dialogue and characters they wish. Tomboys, witches, and non-binary thinkers of all types find freedom in choosing. Caregiver roles, family roles, non-family roles, shading and nuanced roles are all available, and the ability to create new types of stories that are not artificially bound by patriarchal constraints creates existential freedoms, and, I believe, will ultimately provide us with the tools to tear down the discriminatory walls that lead to all the poverty, violence, and abuse inherent in patriarchy.

ACTION 4: DECLARING

One of my favorite works of art is Fearless Girl, a statue of a little girl staring down the charging bull on Wall Street. I realize the statue has been controversial. Fearless Girl was commissioned by State Street Global Advisors, a large asset management company, and installed on March 7, 2017, in anticipation of International Women's Day the following day. The four-foot-high bronze sculpture was commissioned to advertise for an index fund that comprises gender-diverse companies that have a relatively high percentage of women among their senior leadership. A plaque was originally placed below the statue stating "Know the power of women in leadership. SHE makes a difference."

The sculptor of the charging bull, Arturo Di Modica, complained that the statue of the little girl altered the meaning of his charging bull from being a symbol of prosperity and strength to a villain. Kristen Visbal, the artist who sculpted Fearless Girl, responded in a tweet that "Men who don't like women taking up space are exactly why we need the Fearless Girl."[366]

I like the sculpture because it depicts a girl who is DECLARING her position, with a lifted chin and hands on her hip, facing down a charging bull. Visbal commented that "she's not defiant, she's brave, proud, and strong, not belligerent."[367] Fearless Girl is declaring her intentions with every aspect of her physical stance. The resulting image in powerful.

Women who learn to declare their point of view likewise are powerful. Effective communication and feedback are power stances. Using declarative sentences to name something is a form of power, and not all women use the power to name effectively. "Finding one's voice" is bandied about as something women need to learn to do. Although it is widely believed that women talk more than men, experimental evidence indicates this belief is untrue.[368] Male and female voices occupy different sound frequencies, with a typical male voice extending from 150 Hz to 6000 Hz and a typical female voice extending from 250 to 8000 Hz. The typical male voice is 85–180 Hz and a female voice is 165–255 Hz.

Humans are wired to associate lower frequency voices with authority. In a study of male CEOs, the size of the company that a CEO ran correlated with the frequency of his voice — a lower voice pitch was associated with running a larger company and correlated with a higher salary. Some sound systems are adjusted to make the male CEO sound great and puts people with higher frequency voices at an inherent disadvantage.

Women can equalize the acoustic playing field by speaking slightly louder than men, making sure sound systems are appropriately equalized for their voice pitch, and adjusting the microphone to their height.[369] Yale psychologist Victoria L Bescoll asked male and female employees to evaluate executive performances, and found that female executives who spoke frequently were given 14% lower ratings of competence, while chattier male peers were rewarded with 10% higher ratings.[370]

An app called GenderEQ monitors and evaluates meetings based on voice recognition, then analyzes the data to show the percentage of time taken up by male and female speakers. Such a tool can raise awareness in real time to make people conscious of their own behavior, whether that means speaking up more or checking their judgment when others do.[371] One study analyzed 31 separate two-part conversations, 10 of which were between two men, 10 between two women, and 11 between a man and a woman. The researchers identified seven interruptions overall in the two same-sex groups; in the male-female groups, the researchers found 48 total interruptions, and 46 of them were instigated by the man.

A study from George Washington University found that men interrupted 33% more often when they spoke with women than when they spoke with other men. A Northwestern Pritzker School of Law study found that this pattern of men interrupting women happens at the Supreme Court. With 15 years of oral arguments transcripts to see how often men interrupted female justices, whether from the bench themselves or advocates before the high court, 65.9% of all interruptions are directed at the three women who were on the court in 2015.

Women can counter this in several ways, including by saying they have a few more points to make and asking the other person to wait until they are done speaking, physically leaning in while speaking, maintaining eye contact, and using firmer language such as "will" instead of "might," "know" instead of "believe."[372]

In a board meeting recently, I noticed two men (a CFO and a board member), having a loud whispering side-bar conversation every time one of the women spoke during the meeting. When they attempted to do that while I was speaking, I simply stopped midsentence and stared at them silently until they shut up. When they started again, I repeated my strategy. Their disruptive and disrespectful behavior stopped without me having to say a word.

ACTION 5: HOLDING ACCOUNTABLE

Hope is not a strategy. We cannot assume that gender bias that harms women, their families, our businesses, and society will get better by itself. The hundreds of references in this book should be ample evidence of that. Rather, we must hold ourselves, our co-workers, and our society accountable for discriminatory permissiveness. Sometimes it is so inculcated in the culture that one isn't even aware of it, like the parable of two younger fish who had no idea what water was. When David Foster Wallace recounted this story at a Kenyon college speech, he elaborated:

> The point of the fish story is merely that the most obvious, important realities are often the ones that are hardest to see and talk about....The fact is that in the day-to-day trenches of adult existence, banal platitudes can have a life-or-death importance.... The capital-T Truth is about life BEFORE death. It is about the real value of a real education which has almost nothing to do with knowledge, and everything to do with simple awareness, awareness of what is so real and essential, so hidden in plain sight all around us, all the time, that we have to keep reminding ourselves over and over: This is water. This is water.[373]

This is water. We live in a patriarchal society where women are frequently discriminated against and don't consciously realize it. Data show those who are victims of the glass ceiling often deny it. This is water. Female Supreme Court justices are interrupted three times more often than their male colleagues. This is water. Male physicians refer to male surgeons 85% of the time. This is water:

> Reflecting upon their experiences of leadership emergence, male chairs saw leadership as their destiny, were motivated to be chairs to gain influence, were dismissive of risks associated with chairing a department, and were sponsored by senior male leaders to advance in leadership. Female chairs saw leadership as something they had long prepared for, were motivated to be chairs to make a difference, were cautious of risks associated with chairing a

department that could derail their careers, and relied on their own efforts to advance in leadership.[374]

Holding oneself accountable means owning one's actions toward one's own personal choices and those of others. It may mean pointing out when another woman has been interrupted by a man in conversation, or identifying structural barriers to advancement in the workplace. It may mean evaluating and redesigning compensation for physicians that rewards higher quality, longer conversations rather than RVUs, or using data to determine when equally qualified candidates are treated differently based on race, gender, ethnicity, age, or any other irrelevant personal variance. It means using data, developing policies, pointing out the water we all are swimming in.

ACTION 6: CHALLENGING

Holding others and oneself accountable requires challenging oneself to confront one's fears — particularly the fear many women feel about the b-word. Am I modifying my behavior because I fear being perceived as a bitch? Challenging social barriers is not easy.

When Ruth Bader Ginsburg entered Harvard Law School in 1956, there were only 9 women among 552 students. When the dean of the law school invited Ginsburg and her female colleagues to dinner, he asked each of them in turn, "Why are you here occupying a seat that could be held by a man?" Ginsberg answered him by stating she wanted to understand her husband's work — he was a second-year law student at Harvard at the time. She had to justify herself in terms of better serving a man. Ginsburg and the other women of her class at Harvard Law were treated as if they were "intruders" into a place not "natural" to them. Her response was designed to soften the challenge she and the other women were making to the "presumption that places of honor in society are primordial possessions of males, and that females must earn permission to intrude."[375]

In medicine, structures with command-and-control hierarchies have been shown to perform poorly relative to team-based structures. These structures tend to be patriarchal, as Boston surgeon Dr. Matthew McCarty describes them: "It was usually one guy — usually a man — who came in and kind of ruled everything and everybody bowed to that person's will....There are a lot of aggressive assholes. That's the industry norm."[376]

Challenging oneself to stand up to systemic barriers that impact patient outcomes and professional inequities requires courage, but women, including Ruth Bader Ginsberg, have often had to do so with nuanced behaviors. Pearl

Kendrick and Grace Eldering lead an all-female team that developed the first effective pertussis vaccine in the 1930s that saved countless children's lives from deadly whooping cough. They had to overcome the skepticism of much more prominent male physicians and deliberately modified their behavior to not threaten male hegemony:

> In their dealings with the public, though, neither Kendrick nor Eldering came across as bold or commanding. Instead, they were both unfailingly polite, gracious and a little formal. For women experienced in the gender politics of their era, modesty may have seemed obligatory. In college, Kendrick recalled, she'd gotten male science faculty to give her the instructions she needed by acting "as humble as I could be." Once she started working in labs, she said, keeping her head down and focusing on the work at hand "kept me from worrying if I was getting as much as my friend John, say, who was working beside me — though I knew very well I wasn't.[377]

ACTION 7: RE-DIRECTING

My mother, Anna Emerson, is a genius in the art of redirecting. I have seen her many times handle a toddler having a temper tantrum using witchcraft-like magic, by redirecting them in her gentle voice to look at something interesting out the window or listen to a sound of a cow or a bird. She has been known to do this with surly teenagers, too, by changing a conversation in midstream.

I have learned many things from my mother through the years, but one of the most useful tools has been the subtle art of re-directing. The tactical value of the head fake in basketball by leading with one's head pretending to move in one direction but then moving in the opposite has similar purpose: it permits one to move quickly off an unassailable trajectory to one more conducive to one's goals. In the world of gender politics, women can use these tools to re-direct conversation, policy, actions, to a more effective place.

I have pivoted conversations going down a gender-biased rabbit hole, such as one a few years ago at a mixed company dinner at which the man sitting to my left made several crude sexualized comments to the man seated to my right as if I wasn't present. I turned the remarks around with a quick and subtle quip that made him blush, but then quickly changed the topic to something related to the conference agenda we had heard earlier in the day. He instantly found himself debating the data with me and had very little time to realize I had stopped his sexist nonsense in its tracks.

Redirecting is a tactic that is effective when calling out the problem will make it worse in the moment. Combining it with a head fake, by later returning to the problematic conversation, is a way of biding time, controlling the time and emotional content of the problem at hand, and determining when it will be returned to. It is tactical, not strategic. It permits degrees of freedom with respect to when and how one wishes to handle issues with high levels of danger or emotional content.

ACTION 8: SELF-CARING

The various discussions over the years about whether women can or can't "have it all" or "do it all" have been so annoying to me. "Having it all" discussions are nearly always gender specific. Consider my Google search of "have it all" the morning I was writing this chapter. After getting past multiple pushes to the song "Have It All" by Jason Mraz or the Eagles lyrics of the same theme, one gets to Sarah Vine, in the British news service *Daily Mail*, excoriating Helena Morrissey, mother of nine and CEO of City in the UK, for having sold to women "a kind of machismo associated with the 'have-it-all' culture, one that refused to acknowledge the truth of what it took to juggle work and children."

Vine makes it clear that "The world has changed. Most families need two salaries to be able to put a roof over their heads. The idea that work for a woman is an exciting choice, not an obligation, belongs to another age. In short, women have thrown off their domestic chains only to find themselves shackled to a far more exhausting treadmill. And yet we are still the only ones who can have babies. Which means that if we choose to have children we'll be obliged to 'have it all,' aka work our socks off until we collapse or lose our marbles."[378]

The next article was Elisabeth Roider's "Women in Science Can and Should 'Have All,'" which decried her experience as a medical resident when, pregnant with her second child, she was told by her department's leaders that she "simply could not have it all."[379] The third was a link to a Facebook page that is a parody of patronizing self-help books for women called, *The Man Who Has It All*. The ironic articles are entitled "Genuine Question: Is explaining science to men a waste of time?" and "I'm interviewing a male academic about what it's like to be an academic at the same time as being a man. What should I ask him?" and "I'm writing an article called "'Tips for Middle-Aged Men on How to Look Stunning in Photos.' Suggestions?" And "My dream that one day boys will become anything they want to be: male mayors, men rugby players, male policewomen and even male prime ministers!"[380] These narratives are all about the need for women to choose or their right not to have to choose and "have it all": career and family life.

I think "How can I have it all?" is the wrong question. I think the right question is "How can I practice self-caring within the context of the choices I am making? For me, it has always included carving out time for exercise, including running and strength training, non-work stuff I make time for every day, which over the years has included everything from reading, and growing citrus trees indoors, to painting, learning how to play various musical instruments, Duolingo language lessons, and writing.

It has meant valuing simultaneously family time, personal time, and work time. And it has meant having a life partner who does an equal share of the work with respect to cooking (him), shuttling children to after school activities (both), household financial management (him), housekeeping (neither — that would be Cleston, our 60-year-old white male "maid" who has kept our house clean for 30 years).

For other women, there will be different things to prioritize, but one way or the other, self-caring means keeping oneself mentally and physically healthy. It prevents burnout, keeps one from unwittingly getting sucked into role-playing archetypal characters, and is important "design work" that needs to be accomplished before the deeper design work necessary in career development as an exercise in "difference making."

ACTION 9: IMAGINING

Archetypes in general are a form of constraint. If a woman only sees the possibilities for herself within the constrictions of certain pre-determined, proscribed gender-narrowed roles, then sometimes it is hard to fully develop all the possibilities from which true freedom can arise. Consequently, learning how to imagine is crucial.

As children, we are often frightened or excited by imaginary worlds of fairy tales. We think about magic and monsters under our beds and all sorts of possibilities. Gradually, reality becomes more defined and more confining, built on cultural norms of acceptable behaviors and roles, and better understanding of the laws of nature. But cultivating the art of imagining is how we broaden reality.

Goran Carstedt, an executive at Volvo in the 1980s, made the point that "The world simply can't be made sense of, facts can't be organized, unless you have a mental model to begin with. That theory does not have to be the right one, because you can alter it along the way as information comes in. But you can't begin to learn without some concept that gives you expectations or hypotheses."[381] Mental models can be labeled mindsets, schema, maps, cognitive lenses, metaphors.[382]

I have been arguing that for women, these mental models are sometimes a barrier because the maps that make it possible to register and assemble key bits of perceptual data into a coherent pattern become constraints to degrees of freedom. The process of matching situational clues with a well-learned mental framework, a "deeply-held, nonconscious category or pattern,"[383] limits while it defines. So, breaking down these constraining frames becomes a crucial skill for expanding boundaries. The process of using one's imagination can be helped through such techniques as these:

1. *Future planning*: Can I write out five different stories of my future?
2. *Reversing roles*: What if I were not the physician but the medical assistant? What if I were the chair of the board? What if I were a reporter interviewing me?
3. *Engendering empathy*: What are they feeling right now?
4. *Eliminating boundaries*: What if I could move my office to my home (this obviously happened for much of the world in 2020 as a result of the pandemic)?
5. *Realigning parts*: What if I moved this part over there and that part over here?
6. *Meditating:* Can I empty my monkey mind of distractions to allow some new ideas to take hold?

The trap many organizations get themselves into by only rewarding a "favored way of thinking" can be avoided by developing and accepting imagination. Divergent thinking occurs when one has time to sleep (and therefore dream) and play (and therefore create).

ACTION 10: DESIGNING

Design thinking is not something that has been part of traditional curricula for either medical professionals or managers. But the foundational requirements for design thinking can play a crucial role in a shift toward the more creative and collaborative ways of working that can build the framework necessary for more equitable leadership teams in healthcare. Design thinking is defined as:

> ...essentially a human-centered innovation process that emphasizes observation, collaboration, fast learning, visualization of ideas, rapid concept prototyping, and concurrent business analysis, which ultimately influences innovation and business strategy. The objective is to involve consumers, designers, and business people in an integrative process, which can be applied to product, service, or even business design. It is a tool to imaging future states and to bring products, services, and experiences to market. The term design thinking is generally referred to as applying a designer's

sensibility and methods to problem solving, no matter what the problem is. It is not a substitute for professional design or the art and craft of designing, but rather a methodology for innovation and enablement.[384]

A key tenet to design thinking includes developing a deep understanding based on field research through observation. Then one gets users involved early on to make it possible to get evaluation of a concept. Therefore, design thinking is collaboration with product users and multidisciplinary teams. Another tenet is to accelerate learning through visualization, hands-on experimentalism, and creating quick prototypes. Design thinking is focused on radical rather than incremental changes. Design can be powerful as a differentiator, integrator, and transformer of people, processes, and culture.

Applying design thinking to the wicked problem of gender bias can accelerate positive change. Women can use design thinking to expand their professional possibilities. Designing a particular look as it relates to clothing is typically the only way this type of thought process is directed toward women. But body language can be designed the way conversations can be designed, leadership pathways can be designed and board room architecture can be designed.

For example, when I served as a board chair at the American Medical Group Association, I noticed that nearly all agenda conversations began with men initiating the discussion. I designed the discussion process such that I did not ask open-ended questions at the beginning. Instead, I began with a particular fact or data point and asked a woman her opinion. Then I called on men and women equally. At that point, more open-ended questions typically elicited a robust discussion that involved everyone. If board members had not spoken up on the topic prior to moving to the next item, I specifically asked each one what their thoughts were.

I have noticed that at large healthcare conferences, when microphones are set up in the aisles for audience members to ask questions, most, and certainly the first, people to line up are male. At one recent conference I noticed the first 15 people in line were men, which was not the gender ratio in the audience. However, at the same conference, when a smart phone app was used to ask the questions of the speaker, the gender of the question appeared to have a more equal share of women and men asking questions.

Design thinking can move beyond material to social and cultural design. The four basics of effective graphic design can also apply to cultural design:

1. *Contrast*: If the elements are not the same, then make them very different.
2. *Repetition*: Repeating elements helps develop the organization and strengthens the unities.

3. *Alignment*: Every element should have some connection with another elements.
4. *Proximity*. Items relating to each other should be grouped close together.[385]

Paola Antonelli, curator of architecture and design at the Museum of Modern Art, said, "Good design is a renaissance attitude that combines technology, cognitive science, human need, and beauty to produce something that the world didn't know it was missing."[386] We can use good design thinking to produce something in the world that is definitely missing: equitable leadership for women and men.

Five rules of thumb for designing:

1. Design when there is a compelling reason.
2. Develop options before deciding on design.
3. Choose the right time to design.
4. Look for clues that things are out of alignment.
5. Stay alert to the future.[387]

ACTION 11: STORYTELLING

Since we gathered around campfires as small groups of people in prehistoric times, storytelling has been the basic tool humans have used to express our experiences in meaningful ways and to connect us to others. Roger C. Schank, a cognitive scientist, said "Humans are not ideally set up to understand logic; they are ideally set up to understand stories."[388] Our brains naturally make up stories from data we experience, and controlling the narrative of stories is a crucial component to controlling culture. Ursula K. Le Guin noted, "The story — from Rumpelstiltskin to *War and Peace* — is one of the basic tools invented by the human mind for the purpose of understanding. There have been great societies that did not use the wheel, but there have been no societies that did not tell stories."[389]

We can tell stories to explain who we are on our own terms rather than default to the archetypes that often define and limit women's journeys. As a primary care physician, I have spent my professional career listening to and attempting to understand my patients' stories. By doing this, I am able to understand how they can best be diagnosed and treated within the context of their own lives. I have learned that everyone has the ability to tell stories once they are allowed the space to do so, and by providing them that space, in my clinical practice, I am better able to help them with their healthcare needs.

Women can use their innate storytelling skills to expand their personal and professional options. Storytelling can provide a deep tapestry for weaving meaning into events that would otherwise be dismissed or slotted into rigid cultural archetypes.

When I was CEO of Cornerstone Healthcare, we developed a ritual of beginning every board meeting with a patient story. Sometimes they were stories of wonderful care our patients received, and sometimes they were stories of where we failed our patients. Sometimes a board member would relate what had happened to them personally, and sometimes a letter from a patient or perhaps from another team member about someone who did outstanding care was read. All these stories, whether positive or negative, helped center all of us around our central mission to provide patient-centered care, and our board meetings were elevated accordingly.

I am told that after I left Cornerstone Healthcare's leadership team, the new Wake Forest leadership team changed this practice to one that was more specifically about "a patient safety" event. This signaled a change in culture with the new leadership and I do not know if this more specific ritual was useful. To me, it misses the point by narrowing what type of story could or should be told.

Several years later I was told by the chairman of the board in another company in which I was involved in leadership to stop telling patient stories at board meetings. Rather, the board only wanted to hear financial and growth numbers. Although data is essentially part of the "story" a CEO needs to tell her board, I knew at that point the culture of the organization would not likely be capable of meeting its goals because the story that was important as it related to patient care would not be heard.

The Grandmother archetype emphasizes the wisdom of the female story teller. The myth of Persephone emphasizes the danger of women in being silenced from telling their stories. Don't let them. Stories provides us with the deep understanding of who we are and why that matters. We need to continue to listen to each other's stories and remain the author of our own stories.

ACTION 12: FIGHTING

We must fight. We must fight discrimination, achieve power over the adversaries of equality and equity, confront injustice with effective weapons. I am a member of the Society of Friends, (i.e., a Quaker) a traditionally pacifist religious group that does not agree with participating in killing or in waging war. From this perspective, Quakers believe there is something of God (Spirit) in everyone and therefore killing is wrong.

This pacifist perspective is not the same as denying the need to fight. Quakers have been advocates of women's rights since the 17th century, were crucial participants in the Underground Railroad, and early advocates of mental health treatment, prison reform, and freedom of speech. The group has always punched above its weight because knowing how to fight effectively is an important skillset for committed pacifists. From that point of view, I am an advocate of fighting, when appropriate.

Fighting is grounded in understanding the sources of power and confronting those who place barriers. Social justice is not achieved by passively avoiding conflict. The struggle to achieve an objective requires contending with forces that oppose it. Power is the medium through with conflicts are ultimately adjudicated. Power influences who gets what, when, and how.

Within organizations, there are multiple sources of power and influence:

1. Formal authority
2. Control of scarce resources
3. Use of organizational structure, rules, and regulations
4. Control of decision processes
5. Control of knowledge and information
6. Control of boundaries
7. Ability to cope with uncertainty
8. Control of technology
9. Interpersonal alliances, networks and control of "informal "organization"
10. Control of counter organizations
11. Symbolism and the management of meaning
12. Gender and the management of gender relations
13. Structural factors that define the state of action
14. The power one already has.[390]

Understanding these sources of power in organizations and cultures helps us understand how we can fight:

Formal Authority	Evaluate all positions of formal authority within the organization, from board member and CEO on down the hierarchy, and determine the gender mix of each. Measure unexplained variation that suggests statistical inequities and explore how positions of formal authority are determined.
Control of Scarce Resources	Organizations depend on the adequate flow of resources for their continued existence, including money, materials, technology, and people. The most liquid asset is money and is the tool for distributing resources. Establish who and how budgeting is determined, including compensation, benefits, FTEs, technology, capital prioritization. Develop a strategy for increasing power by creating dependencies through control of critical resources.

Use of Organizational Structure, Rules, and Regulations	Organizations are subject to statutes and regulations, and have formal legal structures and by-laws. Organizational policies must comply with federal and state laws, including all related to civil rights and discrimination. Although many organizations position their human resources department as their employee advocates, the role of the HR function is to protect the company, not the employee.
Control of Decision Processes	Determine how organizational decisions are made, both formally and informally. Determine whether decision making takes into account committees, whether management is equitable, whether unconscious bias is built into the process.
Control of Knowledge and Information	Request access to data. Recent studies indicate requiring transparency around salary data can eliminate gender-based salary discrimination.
Control of Boundaries	Control of boundaries is one way people are able to build up considerable power. Acquiring knowledge of critical interdependencies outside one's degree of control can make a difference. It is common for secretaries and special assistants to exercise impact on the way their boss views the reality of a given situation by determining who is given access to the manager. For women, not having access to the "old boys clubs" and other places of boundary access can be a problem that should be addressed.
Ability to Cope with Uncertainty	The ability to cope with uncertainty is often controlled through the routinization of processes. Women must fight when "routine" becomes exclusive.
Control of Technology	We have seen the exclusion of women from STEM education and technical careers. At the organizational level, lack of access to technologies often leads to exclusion from higher-paid positions of those capable of utilizing technologies. In healthcare, the highest paid specialties are highly dependent on technology, and men dominate these fields.
Interpersonal Alliances, Networks, and Informal Organizations	Women must learn to cultivate sponsors, mentors, coalitions of other women in networks, cultural and ethnic affiliations, and other alliance and coalitions necessary to build one's organizational power. The informal alliances from which woman are excluded must be exposed and called out.
Control of Counter-organizations	Trade unions are the most obvious example of counter-organizations. A strategy of exercising countervailing power can provide ways to influence organizations where one is not part of the established power structure, whether by jointing social movements, cooperatives, or lobby groups.
Symbolism and the Management of Meaning	Symbolism and management of meaning rests in one's ability to persuade others to enact realities that further one's own interests. This is where storytelling comes into play, as well as designing space, cultural symbols, décor, layouts, dress, style, branding, and logos.

Gender and the Management of Gender Relations	Gender biases are found in the language, rituals, myths, stories, and other modes of symbolism that shape the culture of an organization. Gender management can be a conscious strategy by calling out obvious examples, switching archetypes, opposing hierarchies with networks.
Structural Factors That Define the State of Action	The structural factors that define the stage of action are often defined by the economics, race, class relationships, and other deep-structural factors that shape the social epoch in which one lives. For Ruth Bader Ginsburg, speaking to the dean in law school within the context he could accept and understand at the time, was very different from what she was able to say and achieve 30 years later as a Supreme Court justice. For women now, there is substantial opportunity to redesign the organizational and societal landscape in ways that have not been possible in the past 500 years. There is also great risk of erosion of progress in the current political climate.
The Power One Already Has	Mindfully evaluating the power one already has is a route for gathering more power. Women who are conscious of their sources of personal power can exploit them to transform the world.

SUMMING UP

When we move from nouns (doctor, mother, bitch, witch) to verbs (recognizing, evaluating, choosing, declaring, holding accountable, challenging, redirecting, self-caring, imagining, designing, storytelling, and fighting) we render our power. With these 12 action words we have the ability to:

Repair the Broken Rung: We will resolve the structural barriers women face in climbing the career ladder, including inadequate information about competencies and skills sets required to advance, limited access to mentors, and inadequate policies and processes that ensure we have equal opportunity to participate in early promotions.

Warm up the chilly climate: We will identify the barriers to advancement and redesign our lives, workplaces, and communities to eliminate them.

Carpet the Concrete Floor: We will not consider boards and leadership teams with a minimum number of women or minority persons to be adequately signaling "legitimacy" with respect to equity and inclusion.

Thaw the Frozen Middle: We will measure the rate of promotion for women from middle management to higher positions and develop specific leadership tactics to identify barriers to advancement.

Break the Glass Ceiling: We will become leaders in the C-suite, on boards, and in government by revealing inequities, building paths to advancement, networking, and mentoring.

Avoid the Glass Cliff: We will demand appropriate resources when promoted into situations of crisis management.

Unlock the Glass Door: We will expose specific hiring practices in which jobs appear to be open to everyone but, in fact, are closed to women.

Disrupt the Glass Escalator: We will identify and expose the issues to intersectionality in terms of race, sexuality, and class that have fast-tracked heterosexual white men to advanced positions when entering primarily female-dominated professions, especially nursing and teaching, that have permitted them higher wages and faster career mobility.

Remove the Glass Wall: We will cast broad nets to fill positions internally, including job positions and job descriptions that are overly prescriptive.

Navigate the Labyrinth: We will evaluate gender bias comprehensively, exploring the complex set of obstacles that inhibit the development and advancement of female leaders, rather than focus on a few unsupported "solutions."

Plumb the Leaky Pipes: We will work from the entry point of education through early career to midcareer barriers and beyond to identify all the phenomena where women and girls disappear in the pipeline for certain types of high status and high paid careers dominated by men and resolve them.

Redesign the Mommy Track: We will provide opportunities for women who choose to become mothers to advance their careers without sacrificing their caregiving needs.

Scrub the Sticky Floors: We will develop policies that eliminate shuttering women into lower-paid roles, design maternity benefits and child-care friendly benefits into our workplaces, create leadership development programs for women throughout the organization, and discourage afterhours rituals, meetings, and work cultures.

As we move from **nouns** to **verbs** and perform these important actions, we should keep in mind the type of **adjectives** that will help define our success, descriptive words such as tenacity, courage, transparency, honorableness, kindness, thoughtfulness, and gumption. We've got this, ladies.

CHAPTER NINE

Real Women

I n two of my previous books, I interviewed individuals from whom I have learned and told their story to illustrate important aspects of the points I was trying to convey. I continue that tradition here, with the story of four remarkable healthcare leaders: Jennifer Bepple, Katherine Henry, Sharon McLaughlin, and Mary Jo Williamson.

Although I have shared significant portions of my personal story throughout this book, the stories of each of these other female healthcare leaders have resonant themes that will help us lean in closer to the gender-specific issues many of us have faced.

LIKING HARD THINGS

Dr. Jennifer Bepple grew up in a small town in Maryland, the daughter of a social worker and an addiction counselor who let her know that they believed she had the ability to do anything she wanted in life. Early on, she knew she wanted to be an Olympic gymnast or a doctor; she moved away from the gymnast dream once she got too tall.

Her move toward medicine when she was in middle school was influenced by the serious illness of her mother. When Bepple was in middle school, her mother was diagnosed with renal cell carcinoma. Bepple heard the words "a chance to cut is a chance to cure" from the surgeon who cared for her mother, and believed she could be a surgeon herself and cure people.

Bepple says she never considered herself the smartest person in the room, but certainly believed that she could be the hardest working, and that she would get where she wanted in life by working as hard as she needed to work. She attributes some of her work ethic to her early gymnastics training, where she was taught to push her body as far as it could go to perform the necessary routines.

She was always attracted to anything others had declared "too hard," like organic chemistry and calculus, and enjoyed the challenge of succeeding at the most difficult academic courses. "If somebody told me something was going to be hard, I was determined to like it," she says.

As an undergraduate at Penn State, she told the pre-med advisor that she wanted to be a surgeon and he said to her, "Oh, Jennie, you are much too nice to be a surgeon!" She assumed he knew something important that she didn't know and revised her plans to "I guess I'll be a pediatrician."

When she began rotating through her various clinical blocks at Eastern Virginia Medical School in Norfolk, however, she learned quickly that pediatrics was not the specialty that appealed to her. She did not like the emotions of feeling like there shouldn't have to be sick kids in the world. In contrast, she loved her surgery rotations and responded positively to the declaration by one mentor that "in medical school, you find you are either a cutter or you are not." She was a cutter. She liked when things were difficult. She liked being in the OR.

When she was on the surgery rotation, a surgery intern introduced her to the subspecialty of urology. Bepple was immediately attracted to the subspecialty. She didn't recognize what a big deal it was that she was female interested in this field, but she soon began getting the message from some advisors that it was. One emphasized that "at some point you are going to want a family."

In her fourth year of medical school, as she was planning a September wedding, her mother developed a metastasis from her renal cell carcinoma and went into cardiogenic shock during a surgical procedure. Based on the emotional impact of her mother's diagnosis, Bepple questioned whether urology was the right direction, but Ann Becker, a urology resident, helped her to see the possibilities of the specialty. She stayed in Norfolk for her urology residency, becoming the second female urological surgery resident in the program's history.

During her final year of urology residency, when she was chief resident, she became pregnant with twins. She had been told previously that if she got pregnant during her residency it would be "catastrophic for any program." Yet here she was, pregnant with twins.

When she found out one of the twins, her son, had a congenital heart defect that would require her to deliver at a hospital that had pediatric specialty care, she moved with her husband to Philadelphia to be near CHOP (Children's Hospital of Philadelphia) and where her parents were nearby to support them. Her obstetrician placed her on bed rest, but she arranged a research rotation on bed rest, had the twins by C-section, then returned to work as chief resident five weeks after their birth, relying heavily on her parents and husband for help with caregiving and support.

When she returned to work, she felt guilty about having not been able to support the residency team during her absence, all the while being questioned about why she was back. Someone even asked her, "Why are you back, don't you love your children?"

After her children were born, Bepple's career decisions were more directed by her family's ongoing needs, including the need to be near CHOP for her son's open-heart surgery when he was six months old and her daughter's need for therapy due to a rare genetic disorder that included some developmental delay.

She forewent a fellowship to enter private practice in Maryland, where she was near pediatric specialty care services. Her husband left his career in the Navy for a career in the civil service to help with the ongoing needs of the children; she also relied on her parents who were nearby.

Bepple limited her practice to four days a week so she could care for her children's ongoing medical needs on the fifth day, which meant she was ineligible for partnership in the private practice because she was not considered "full time." When she became pregnant with her third child, she discovered there was no maternity leave policy in the practice. When she was put on modified bed rest, she wheeled herself around the office in a chair, from patient to patient, to continue working, then took eight weeks off with unpaid leave because there was no payment policy at the practice.

Bepple noticed that many of the issues affecting her own life were also affecting the lives of her patients, including the inability for some to get to the office to receive care because they were taking care of sick children or were unable to take time off work. She began to think about how to improve access for her patients and became interested in the possibilities of telemedicine.

In 2018 and 2019, she developed a telemedicine platform for her urology practice, which had grown into a large multi-state practice. She rolled out a pilot for 50 patients that was successful. Serendipitously, she launched the first Digital Health Summit for the company in January 2020, just prior to the pandemic, allowing her practice to successfully transition to telemedicine when it was most needed.

Bepple began to see her career as being about more than going to the same office every day, and embraced the possibilities of digital health and telemedicine for redesigning a better healthcare system, built around access. She continued to ask "Where can we do better?" for patients with the new digital tools, and left her practice to receive a Master of Management in clinical informatics from Duke University. She is now retooling her career to accommodate her personal motto of HOPE (helping other people enthusiastically), a phrase she learned while volunteering at Camp HOPE with her son. As volunteers, they helped to rebuild homes and as a physician; she now hopes to rebuild the healthcare system.

She muses that in the past, she believed success was linear. "You checked the boxes off the list of things you were to do one by one." Then life happened and she began to follow a very nonlinear career path. She is ready to influence and improve healthcare at scale, with digital tools that accommodate the complex lives of her patients.

A qualitative, systematic review of gender bias in the surgery profession, synthesizing the perspectives of both female surgical trainees and surgeons, was conducted in 2021 to gauge the pervasive gender barriers against the progression of women in surgery. The review cited 14 articles describing unfavorable work environments, male-dominated culture, and societal pressures.

The findings asserted that females in surgery lacked support, faced harassment, and had unequal opportunities, which were often exacerbated by sex-blindness by their male counterparts. Mothers were especially affected, struggling to achieve a work-life balance while facing strong criticism.[391] Bepple's capacity to do hard things allowed her to successfully complete training in one of the most rigorous and currently male-dominated specialties, even as the mother of twins with special needs. She was able to do so with the support of mentors, family, and her own implacable attitude.

Urology continues to be one of the more gender-lopsided specialties in medicine, and a recent study revealed worrisome forecasts about the inadequate postgraduate pool to replace retiring surgeons and meet the demand from an aging population that must increasingly depend on a female workforce.[392]

Understanding the "hard things" that Bepple had to do in order to design for a competent workforce not dependent upon women or men needing to do "hard things" should be part of how we solve our supply issues in healthcare.

HOW TO DO IT YOURSELF

Katherine Flynn Henry, Esq.'s mother stated quite emphatically that day over 40 years ago, "Nope, she's doing it herself!" Katie Henry remembers the event from her early childhood in small-town Ohio, where her dad was an attorney and her mother taught school.

An adult had commented that Katie should "marry a rich man because she has such high-minded tastes," but Katie's mother emphasized to her that whatever she achieved, it was hers to accomplish. "Don't ever depend on a man, Katie."

Henry took her mother's advice to heart. Today, she is chief administrative officer of the Austin Regional Clinic, an independent physician-owned, multispecialty clinic in Austin, Texas, serving more than 540,000 patients across 33 locations throughout the greater Austin area. Her journey from rural Ohio to Austin, Texas, was built upon the lesson to find her own way.

As a child raised in the 1970s, she was told that as a female, her only three career options were to be a teacher, secretary, or nurse, or to define herself solely within her role as a mother. But her dream was to be an attorney like her father, and she assumed she would practice general law in a small town, like her father. Her favorite book, *To Kill a Mockingbird*, presented the heroic justice-fighting attorney Atticus Finch, and she saw no reason why she couldn't be that kind of attorney, too.

Henry took her mother's early wisdom to heart, and deliberately chose to go out of state to law school, graduating from Wake Forest University School of Law in North Carolina.

After law school, Henry remained in North Carolina, where she began her legal career, married, and started her family. She began her 20-year meteoric rise to the C-suite by practicing law as a plaintiff's attorney. She didn't like that, so she flipped to defense, specializing in defending physicians in medical malpractice cases. Learning something new with every case, she found working directly with physicians enjoyable, and ultimately became in-house legal and compliance counsel for Cornerstone Health Care, an independent multispecialty medical group.

Henry became part of the C-suite at Cornerstone during a dynamic time, when the company was pushing the envelope on healthcare innovation, but struggling with inadequate capital financing for its pathbreaking strategies. When Cornerstone spun off a population health management company, CHESS, Henry took on a dual role as legal and compliance officer for that company also. She remained in the leadership of both companies when they were acquired by Wake Forest Baptist Health, an academic medical center whose goal was to develop its own integrated delivery system.

The profoundly different cultures between Cornerstone and Wake Forest were stressful, however. She missed Cornerstone's culture, where in every meeting, decisions were guided by "How will this decision impact our patients?" In contrast, Wake Forest Baptist Health approached decisions by asking, "How does this fit into the budget?"

When leaders at Austin Regional Clinic came knocking on her door, Henry jumped at the opportunity to return to a dynamic independent multispecialty physician-led medical group, where she is the highest-ranking administrative leader.

Henry's real-life hero, in contrast to Atticus Finch, is Ruth Bader Ginsberg. She points out to younger women on her team that during her lifetime, prior to Ginsberg, women did not have the right to open a bank account or have a credit card without their husband's permission. She, herself, remembers from her first years as a lawyer, there was a dress code for female attorneys in court (but not men) that required her to wear "stockings" and "skirts." At her first deposition as a young attorney, the other attorney ("an old white man") declared when she entered the room, "Well, I didn't know they let paralegals do depositions, now!"

Henry has learned to call out language and behavior that is sexist. She has been in many situations where she and her husband, also an attorney, are together and he is assumed to be an attorney but not her. She recalls an administrator at Wake Forest advised her to make career choices "based upon what was in the best interest of her children." She immediately asked him whether he would ever advise a male colleague in that way.

She witnesses a lot of "he-repeating" — the phenomenon whereby a man will repeat what a female colleague has just said, as if it is his idea. She always calls it out when she witnesses it. She has learned that most men do not know they are doing this, and pointing it out improves their behavior. The worst case of "mansplaining" she remembers involved a man explaining to her how a pregnant woman felt.

As the first female executive at Austin Regional Clinic, she believes her gender difference has allowed her to teach her colleagues to see a broader perspective in their governance and decision-making. For example, during the COVID pandemic, male physician executives were going down the road of putting in place different rules regarding women and vaccinations versus men, due to women's "child-bearing potential." She simply stated, "Women have as much right to make decisions about their body as men do. We are absolutely not going to change that here."

At Austin Regional Clinic, 83% of the employees are female, although, prior to Henry's arrival, like much of the rest of the world, leadership positions were mostly filled by men. That is changing; 40% of current board members are female and, among Henry's 18 direct reports, 15 are women. That's not intentional, she says, but rather, "it seemed to happen organically."

Since Henry's arrival at Austin Regional Clinic, the organization has added four weeks of guaranteed pay for physicians after childbirth and has put into place a "mother's best friend" center with a number of free nanny days per year for all employees who need childcare unexpectedly.

Henry declares that she loves her job and loves interacting with physicians and patients. She is a strong believer in the superiority of the independent physician practice, for its cultural focus on patients and innovation. When she is having a bad day, all she has to do to cheer herself up is visit one of the clinical practices and see what her colleagues are doing to provide good patient care.

It is not surprising that Ruth Bader Ginsberg has served as Henry's role model. Henry's mother's admonishment that what she was to achieve would be hers to accomplish for and by herself, rather than depend upon "marrying a rich man" is exactly what Ginsberg was able to solidify for women. Ginsberg said her mother told her "two things constantly. One was to be a lady, and the other was to be independent."[393] Ginsberg championed women's right to financial autonomy by founding the ACLU Women's Right Project in 1972, years before she served on the Supreme Court. The project focused solely on gender and financial equality and paved the way for the Equal Credit Opportunity Act of 1974, that allowed women to access bank accounts, credit cards, and montages without a male co-signer. Her legal work led to remarkable changes in financial independence for women. Ginsberg successfully argued five of six cases before the Supreme Court that taught the court "a gender line helps to keep women not on a pedestal, but in a cage."[394]

Henry's deft management of male colleagues' thoughtless sexism and two mothers' lessons in the value of independence are a next generation legacy in healthcare leadership.

SECRETS OF A FEMALE PHYSICIAN ENTREPRENEUR

"I am a woman physician who experienced burnout, and my goal is to help inspire others with what I have learned. Physicians have the ability to change the world and make it a better place," says Sharon McLaughlin MD, FACS, in her manifesto announcing the founding of Female Physicians Entrepreneurs.

McLaughlin tells her personal story by remembering how she was a very anxious child, worrying every day about death and dying. She was diagnosed with non-Hodgkin's lymphoma at a young age and spent years in and out of hospitals for treatment. Not all children with non-Hodgkin's lymphoma survived, and she often returned to the healthcare setting after a time away to discover another child had died in the meantime. At age 13 she made a deal with God that if God let her live, she would dedicate herself to being a physician when she grew up.

She thinks of herself not as a great student, but as a persistent one. Once she decided what she was going to do, she worked until she got it done. She paid for her education herself; she worked as a nurse's aide while she was an undergraduate and completed her degree in biochemistry in three and a half years. Yet she admits that success from her persistence alone often left her feeling inadequate. "By the time I was in medical school, I had imposter syndrome. I don't know why I felt that way. It wasn't anything anyone else said or did, I just felt like I didn't belong there, like I wasn't good enough."

McLaughlin intended to go to medical school to be a pediatric oncologist, but then pivoted to surgery when she found out how much she loved it. She recalls many people at the time advising her to not go into surgery. She was told, "You'll get married and have a child and just quit."

She went into surgery anyway, spending five years in a general surgical training program where she felt that her gender was not an issue. She does remember sometimes feeling separated from the rest of her colleagues — all men — when a conversation continued as they all went through the male locker room into the surgery theatre; she was no longer a part of the conversation as she entered alone through the female locker room.

When she subsequently entered a two-year plastic surgery fellowship, however, she felt significant gender discrimination. She was often told she wasn't good enough, her surgical technique was nitpicked, and her program director excluded her from national conferences while she covered call for the male fellows who attended with him.

She was confused by the sudden criticism of her surgical technique considering she had successfully completed a five-year surgical residency without such negative feedback. The program director told her he did not want her to complete the program. Fortunately, the hospital leadership above the program director reviewed her file, noticed the extra call she took and other aspects indicating she was treated differently than her male colleagues, and overruled the program director.

The two years after she completed her training were life-changing. She worked long hours in a plastic surgery practice as a junior associate and was able to pay off all of her student loans. She met her husband and decided to open her own private practice where she could have more control over her own work hours and accommodate her husband's eight-to-five career path.

For 11 years, she managed and grew her own practice, gave birth to her daughter, and began adding other responsibilities such as helping with quality assurance at the hospital. When she was asked to take on more and more responsibility, she did so. Still, she remembers being in tears one day after agreeing to do some additional quality work at the hospital and asking herself how she could have just agreed to do one more thing when she was already so burned out.

She walked away from her practice when she realized the burnout that she was experiencing was not something she was willing to put up with anymore. She took on new roles in consulting, marketing, manufacturing, sales, and several other entrepreneurial pursuits that allowed her to spend more quality time with her daughter. She admits that at times she felt quite lost and as she has learned how to be a businesswoman and entrepreneur through the school of hard knocks, she hopes to provide insights and resources to make this journey easier for other women in medicine.

McLaughlin notes that mentorship and coaching resources that are now available where not available to her when she refused a default future based on burnout. She advises others to "think before you jump." She made choices after thinking deeply about what she wanted, including financial stability and availability for her daughter.

She has been with her current company for nine years and faced burnout again when feeling a reduction in autonomy after a corporate merger. She now uses the resources of a therapist and coach to work on herself. "I have learned I can't change the system but I can change myself," she says.

Yet she is working to change the system, nonetheless. She founded a business program for women to teach them how to grow and develop businesses. Female Physician Entrepreneurs, with more than 9,000 members, provides a supportive environment where women physicians learn more about building their business with monthly trainings, podcasts, summits, and guidebooks developed for career transition and business building.

Physicians continue to be at higher risk for burnout compared to workers in other sectors.[395] Both informal and formal mentorship have demonstrated positive effects in reducing the risk of burnout.[396] Recently, a coaching program developed specifically for female resident physicians at the University of Colorado demonstrated significantly reduced emotional exhaustion and imposter syndrome while increasing self-compassion over a six-month study period.[397]

Sharon McLaughlin is forging a new career and personal journey based on helping women in medicine eliminate the toll that burnout can have on their lives.

THE ACCIDENTAL EXECUTIVE

Mary Jo Williamson calls herself "an accidental healthcare executive." A native Midwesterner, she had hoped to move out of the region to advance her career in financial services and consulting, but after she married her husband, she found herself in his hometown of Rochester, Minnesota, where he was going to medical school. Somehow, the two of them never left Rochester.

He went on to train as a radiologist and then joined the faculty. Williamson began pounding on doors looking for various financial services jobs in Rochester, but found it to be essentially "a company town. It was all about healthcare at the Mayo Clinic." She landed a position at the Mayo Clinic in the contracting and payer relations team, which she attributes to "a man named Al Schilmoeller taking a chance on me." She honed her administrative and strategy skills by working with a small team taking a very forward-looking strategic approach to payer contracting.

Williamson worked in this team for 14 years until her boss came to her one day and said, "You have to get out of this department to grow your horizons!" Although she was on a track to be promoted to department head in this area, her boss recommended she make a lateral move into an operational role to broaden her skills.

Her career trajectory at Mayo accelerated from that point forward: administrator of the department of physical medicine and rehabilitation, director of provider relationship, vice chair of the Mayo Health System Administration, administrative director of the Mayo Clinic Care Network, chair of practice administration of the Mayo Clinic, chief administrative officer of the Mayo Clinic Rochester and Mayo Clinic Health System.

"I never thought I would be in that role," she demurs, "but I loved it!" She led her organization through an EPIC implementation, the COVID pandemic, and broad expansion of their practice network. With Mayo's rotating leadership expectations, she has moved to a new role in the organization, chief administrative officer of Mayo Collaborative Services, overseeing the broad external-facing strategies and services of the Mayo Clinic, including its national reference laboratory. She is also in the executive committee of the American Medical Group Association's Board of Trustees.

In telling her story, the "accidental healthcare executive" calls out sponsors along the way who advocated for her and pushed her to challenge the boundaries of her career expectations, and a husband who made some sacrifices in his early career journey to support her advancing career path, participating actively in raising their two children and at one point turning down a leadership opportunity in another community that could have derailed Williamson's career trajectory.

Studies indicate that one in three women attempt to break the glass ceiling and achieve a high-level position, but fewer than half succeed, often due to lack of mentorship or sponsorship.[398] Mentors in the workforce provide guidance and support, whereas sponsors are advocates who actively work to advance the careers of those they are sponsoring.

In general, women in organizations are under-sponsored compared to men, even if they may need it more.[399] An obstacle in breaking the glass ceiling is the "sticky middle": the phenomenon describing women's career progress halting in middle management positions. A *Harvard Business Review* study found that women with sponsors are 22% more likely to ask for stretch assignments to push them further than non-sponsored peers.[400]

The phenomenon, called "work-to-family conflict" (WFC), has been studied as an additional factor impacting the "glass ceiling" for many women. Babic and Hansez found that work-to-family conflict mediates the effects of the glass ceiling on job strain and job engagement and partially mediates the effect on job satisfaction and intention to quit.[401]

In other words, individuals take on more than one social role every day (i.e., parent, spouse, employee) and the contradictory demands arising from these multiple social roles can produce incompatibility between professional and family roles. Inter-role conflict in which the demands of time devoted to and strain created by a job can interfere with performing family-related responsibilities.[402]

For Mary Jo Williamson, her husband's decision to turn down a job early in his career that would have disrupted their balanced workshare in their family life permitted her to continue her own career advancement and break a glass ceiling along the way.

Pearls Are a Woman's Necktie

I grew up in rural North Carolina in the 1960s, the oldest of four children. I was a classic tomboy, spending most of my free time playing outside with my brother and cousins when I wasn't working in the garden, feeding the livestock, going to school and church, or watching favorite TV shows.

My first years in school were stressful for me, because temperamentally I was different from the other girls. As a result, I was picked on by the boys, and became disruptive in class. I dreaded report card days, when my all-A record was inevitably spoiled by that D-minus in conduct.

Although the bullying I experienced in school was quite severe, as I gradually became more confident of my own talents and self-worth, it actually made me fearless. Later, as a medical student and resident, behavior others would interpret as harassing or abusive just rolled right off my back.

Reading finally saved me from perpetual misery at school. I devoured books by the dozen and developed a love of reading that has remained an important part of my life. My parents knew they had their hands full with me, so they made sure I had lots of activities to keep me focused.

Starting at age six, I participated in scouting, choral music, piano lessons, oil painting, and plays. Though not typical then, this was very much like the activity-filled lives of many children today. I even had my own horse, named Daisy. Since none of my siblings liked to ride, some of my best memories are of my Dad and me riding our horses together.

The culture in which I grew up drew clear distinctions between the roles of girls and boys and I often felt uncomfortable with those traditionally assigned to women. I didn't want to learn to cook, sew, or homemaking and I didn't want to become a secretary, teacher, or nurse — the only careers I thought available to women. Although I had the highest grade point average in my class, I was told to learn to type. That way, "if I had to work," I could always get a job.

Prior to Title IX, there were few sports opportunities for girls. I was jealous of my brothers' participation on baseball and football teams. I wanted to be an athlete, but year after year I was cut from the basketball team, the only sport open to girls at the time. Despite many hours of practicing alone, my petite and clumsy self couldn't seem to master the game.

Luckily, I discovered running. In ninth grade I tried out for track and excelled, lettering in it. The following year, there were not enough girls trying out to form a team, so I ran on the boys' team. I ran the mile and the 880. Every boy I beat would promptly quit the team as a matter of pride rather than wait to be cut. As a result, I was middle of the pack at the first of the season but dead last by the end.

As a young person, I began to become a student of human nature. This was in part a result of experiencing so much death in the people I was close to, including family. First, my grandfather died of a cardiomyopathy at age 59. Not long after, my third grade schoolteacher died of metastatic breast cancer in the middle of the school year. My other grandfather died of coronary disease when I was in eighth grade, and one of my grandmothers died of colon cancer when I was 15. My last grandparent died of a stroke when I was 19.

My parents are only 20 and 22 years older than me. As I think back now, they had lost all four of their parents before they were 40. They were wrestling with all the issues of young adulthood while deeply grieving. In the midst of all that, they were able to create a family life that emphasized the moral imperative to make one's life meaningful in a loving and supportive environment.

The message I heard from my mother, whose own life choices had been theoretically limited by economic circumstances, was "you can do anything you want to do, Grace, so long as you set your mind to it." This existentialist message I have taken to heart.

Like Barack Obama, I graduated high school in 1979. This was the class that divided the baby boomer from generation X. I believe our values are boomer: focused on hard work, achievement, finding meaningfulness in our careers and life choices. But our circumstances are X-er: attending high school during the Watergate-driven cynical '70s, graduating college in the midst of the Reagan recession of 1983, entering our 50s after the 2007 crash.

From a leadership perspective, this historical margin creates the possibility of a group of individuals who are simultaneously idealistic and cynical, hardworking and somewhat self-centered. That juxtaposition allows a certain degree of conviction mixed with energy, perseverance, and caution that may be just what is necessary to lead us through our current national challenges.

In 1979, I won a Morehead scholarship to attend the University of North Carolina at Chapel Hill. At that point, the scholarship had been open to females for only three years. The scholarship allowed me to obtain an incredibly rich undergraduate education. During the summer months before college, I participated in an Outward Bound program in Colorado. I got to ride a plane for the first time and spent four weeks in the Rockies in a challenging physical and mental environment. Other summer experiences included working for a police department in California, a law firm in North Carolina, and, in 1982, during the Falklands War, working for the Liberal Whip's Office of the Parliament of Great Britain.

In college I ran on the women's track team for a year and participated in crew another year. Track turned me into a life-long runner. Choosing a major was difficult because I wanted to learn "everything." I ultimately majored in religion and English, with enough economics courses to nearly declare a third major.

More importantly, college is where I met the love of my life. Tim is the fifth of six children. Both his mother and father are physicians. Like me, he grew up in a large, close-knit family. We had both grown up on farms where we lived with grandparents in the same house. Our families were intensely committed to Democratic politics in an increasingly conservative state and equally involved in church — his were sixth-generation Quakers, mine were Southern Baptists.

College for me included student government, track, and crew. For Tim it included managing the kitchen at his fraternity, delivering pizzas for Dominos, working as a camp counselor, exploring the new field of computer science with punch cards, algorithms, and programming. We both majored in religion because it was the most intellectually comprehensive department in the university.

A week after we graduated in 1983, we married. In the midst of a recession, we had about $500 between us, no jobs, and liberal arts degrees in humanities. A year before, almost on a whim, I began thinking about medical school. The idea of taking a deep dive into the natural sciences, which I had not really studied since high school, with a career focused on helping people seemed appealing.

Tim's mother, Dr. Eldora Terrell was a role model. She showed me such a life was possible. In an era in which women's choices were supposedly fixed, she had six children, practiced internal medicine, founded a clinic for uninsured patients in the community, took a public stand for integration in the Civil Rights era, was active in her church, served as a medical director of a nursing home, a college board trustee, chief of staff of the hospital where she attended patients, and still managed to can green beans, make strawberry jelly, harvest asparagus, and ride horses to help with the cattle round-up on the weekends. Through her, I saw how the professional role of physician actually frees women from certain social constraints.

Ten days after graduating and three days after getting married I was in summer school studying physics. That wasn't the only course I had to take before applying to medical school. There were two physics courses, two organic chemistry courses, and some biology. Then I had to take the MCAT and do well in order to be accepted.

From 1983 to 1985 we lived in Richmond, Indiana, while Tim pursued a master's degree in Quaker history at Earlham School of Religion. We had a three-room cinderblock apartment in an undergraduate dormitory where I worked as head resident. My salary was $3,000 dollars a year. We ate for free in the campus cafeteria. I thought it was the coldest place in the universe.

At age 22, I found myself married to a creative, idealistic, and definitely unfocused man, working in a job where I was responsible for students only a few years younger than myself. They challenged me, insulted me, and generally pursued their own agendas. They didn't know that I had a recent "grand past" as a Morehead scholar, intern to Parliament, and UNC varsity athlete. To them, I was either the person who let them into their dorm room when they lost their key, the one from whom they hid their marijuana, or the person who was supposed to settle their roommate complaints.

For intellectual enrichment I took a "wives' course" on John Updike at the School of Religion. It was awful: faculty wives crocheting and talking about their children's preschool experiences.

Tim was trying to find himself and I was trying not to lose myself. I focused upon those science courses at the college that I needed for medical school. Fortunately, I could take these for free as part of my employment. In addition, I decided to expand my general knowledge base.

First, I found a Cliff's Notes pamphlet and looked at all the great books listed on the back page. Then I started from the As and read each work of literature, from *Absalom, Absalom* on down the alphabet. After that I read all the works of philosophy I could locate, including all of Hegel, all of Kant, all of Kierkegaard, and so on.

I told myself I was doing this before I went to medical school because then I wouldn't have time to read for pleasure. In retrospect, though, I was probably depressed. Training and running a triathlon finally got me out of my funk. I took the MCAT, interviewed, and applied for several medical schools. I was accepted at Duke and entered in 1985.

Tim and I traded places in the fall of 1985. Suddenly I was the medical student, with purpose and focus, and he was looking for a job. He worked as a bartender in the Duke faculty lounge for a bit, and finally landed a job counseling Native American high school students, helping them get into college through the North Carolina Commission of Indian Affairs. For the first two years we scraped by on his $13,500 a year salary. Then we decided we just had to have a baby.

Katy was born at the end of my third year of medical school. I took eight weeks off, then did my fourth year "in reverse," taking the sub-internships at the end of the fourth year rather than at the beginning.

The year Katy was born, Tim decided to return to school for a master's degree in the burgeoning new field of computer science. He took all of his classes on Tuesdays and Thursdays so he could be home with the baby on the other days. On Tuesdays and Thursdays, my sister, a freshman at UNC drove over to Durham to watch the baby, while Tim drove over to NC State University to take his classes.

After I graduated from medical school, I stayed at Duke Medical Center an extra year and did an internship in pathology, reasoning that without night call, I could be with the baby at home giving Tim time to finish his degree.

My year as a pathology intern still seems surreal. Like many working mothers, I felt the pangs of guilt every morning as I left my daughter at home. It didn't matter that her father and aunt were available as primary caregivers. Katy walked early, talked early, and was like a little Tasmanian devil full of energy. I hated missing any part of her development, although her irregular sleeping and eating patterns kept us all perpetually exhausted.

I spent my days doing surgical and autopsy pathology. The autopsies on fetuses and children were particularly difficult for me. I still remember how I felt entering the autopsy suite to view one particular case. The little girl was almost the same age as my Katy, her body in a nightgown, still clutching a teddy bear.

Like many internships of that era, the pathology department at Duke was not a particularly warm environment. Because the program directors knew I did not intend to remain in pathology as a specialty, they focused their mentoring energies elsewhere.

When some of the physicians learned of my plan to practice general internal medicine, I began to experience discrimination for the first time. Duke was not primary care friendly. One professor told me that I should leave and find some primary care program in a community setting, that as a "real" academic institution, there was no place for a generalist at Duke.

That year, while in the surgical suite, I accidentally severed the artery and nerve to my left index finger on a formalin-hardened surgical specimen. The injury required hand surgery. For eight weeks while the re-anastomosis healed, I was unable to cut surgical specimens. When I returned to work the day after my surgery, an upper level resident yelled at me for a good 30 minutes, making it clear that my injury was going to make life difficult for the other pathology interns. The department administrator was equally unsympathetic; his only concern that this might bring OSHA down on the department.

Once Tim finished his degree, we knew we needed to make a change. I was accepted into the primary care track in internal medicine at NC Baptist Hospital in Winston-Salem. I completed my pathology internship on June 29, 1990, and began my second internship July 1. That was the start of the second craziest year of my life.

We were living with Tim's parents in High Point, North Carolina, about 20 miles from Winston-Salem. Tim got a job in public health sciences in research computing at the medical school. Our household was not exactly mainstream America. We had four generations, including Tim's 94-year-old grandmother, my busy internist mother-in-law and father-in-law, Tim, me, and Katy, the quintessential "terrible two" year old. The four dogs in the house added to the chaos. Still, it was wonderful having the security of two salaries for the first time after eight years of marriage.

Like every other medical intern, I rotated through cardiology, heme-onc, general medicine, emergency medicine, and the other specialties with every second or third night call. I do not remember that time as being difficult or abusive. I was excited to finally learn my craft in a residency environment that was both rigorous and supportive.

I developed a very close relationship with Dr. Bryant Kendrick, a chaplain at the medical center who managed the internal medical primary care track. He became my real mentor, helping me process my continued "strangeness": we focused upon medical ethical issues, the excitement engendered by the Clinton era anticipated healthcare reform, and the spiritual wholeness of the doctor-patient experience.

After 14 months of living with Tim's parents, we had saved enough for a down payment to purchase our first house. It was on a wooded lot with a stream, a tree house, a swing set, and an elementary school and playground next door. We balanced our roles as young parents and professionals, began paying off our student loans, and spent our free time together hiking, parenting, exercising, and keeping up this new house.

In 1993, seven months pregnant with my second daughter, Robyn, I completed my residency and began private practice with my in-laws. I took my medical boards that September, before promptly going into labor. The next eight weeks were some of the sweetest of my life. I took maternity leave and was able to walk Katy to the neighborhood school for her first days of kindergarten. I also got to spend some very quiet and special time with my new little girl.

Although as grandparents, my in-laws were both interested in the welfare of their new granddaughter, as medical practice partners they were equally eager for my return to work. This was the period when primary care started to lose status and get slogged by the economic forces of managed care. Our once-a-week call meant covering seven internists, three nursing homes, and unassigned hospital cases.

These were also the days before hospitalists and before nurse triage. The paradigm was still for the internist to be the center of all activity in the middle of the medical universe, despite the degradation of both reimbursement and status. It was far more brutal in many respects than my residency, but also more rewarding.

The intensity of the experiences with patients in the office, the hospital, and the nursing home in that era has been unsurpassed. It was comprehensive, and I had been trained to be effective in a multitude of settings. In areas where I had not, the 40-year experience of my father-in-law and mother-in-law filled in the gaps left in my training. It helped me understand the real role of physicians: to listen, to act, to help, to heal.

About six months after I had joined my in-laws' private practice, administration at High Point Regional Hospital, where I admitted patients, began discussions about the creation of a PHO (physician hospital organization) as a response to anticipated changes in the healthcare environment from managed care.

The chief-of-staff, Dr. Al Hawks, gave a passionate speech about the need for collaboration and cooperation and a steering committee of seven was formed.

The three specialists and three primary care physicians nominated to form the steering committee were all established male medical staff members.

Almost as an afterthought, my father-in-law nominated me. Over the course of the next 18 months, we met every Thursday night, sometimes until one or two o'clock in the morning, to create what ultimately became Cornerstone Health Care.

Most of us were junior partners in our practices. Because we were young and less established in the community, we were more willing to be reckless. We figured out our governance and income distribution and began developing a culture based less on autonomy and more on collaboration. We also focused on investing in information, technology, and advanced models of care delivery.

Cornerstone Health Care was established October 1, 1995, from the merger of 16 practices in High Point, North Carolina. In 2000, I became CEO. During that time, I saw my daughters grow to young adults, my in-laws retire from medical practice, and my practice merge with two other Cornerstone internal medical practices to become the first NCQA-recognized level-three Physician Practice Connection Medical Home in our state.

Cornerstone grew from the original 16 practices in High Point, to 93 locations throughout the Piedmont Triad region of North Carolina, with over 300 providers practicing in 10 separate hospitals that were part of six separate health systems.

Our company's focus was to be the model for physician-led healthcare in America. We were committed to transform our model from a volume-based system to one that was value-based, leading our market in innovative approaches to a sustainable 21st century healthcare delivery system.

From 2013 through 2017 Cornerstone and I gained a lot of national prominence and, some would say, notoriety.

In 2013 Cornerstone Health Care developed innovative care models in primary care, cardiology, oncology, pulmonology, and dual-eligible populations, and moved all of our contracts to early value-based models. Within 18 months, we had lowered the cost of care by 20% and in 2015 won the prestigious AMGA Acclaim Award for its highest-performing medical groups.

We spun off our infrastructure into a company called CHESS, which was invested in by LabCorp, Wake Forest, and now, Atrium. That company, for which I was the first CEO, remains an under-recognized powerhouse in value-based care, managing over 150,000 lives in high-performing risk contracts in Medicare Advantage, NextGen ACO, and commercial contracts. I remain on the board of CHESS and am proud to see the vision we had for it a decade ago is coming to fruition as "the market catches up."

Under my leadership, Cornerstone made the move to value-based healthcare earlier than much of the rest of the market. Our rationale was built upon our confidence in our ability to provide higher-quality healthcare at a lower cost in a physician-led independent medical group.

We went all in, but the market did not. Payers talked a good game about wanting to move to value, but they were as ill-equipped to do so as the high-cost hospital systems. As the payers dragged their feet in providing value-based reimbursement, the move to value strained our finances and local hospitals quickly took advantage by hiring our physicians feeling the strain of our financial commitments. In 2016, Cornerstone lost its independence, becoming part of the Wake Forest Health System, which is itself, now part of the multi-state Atrium Health System.

By 2016, the other physicians at Cornerstone had had enough of me and I was mentally exhausted and quite heartbroken at the public animosity I experienced in the local medical community to which I had dedicated 23 years as a practicing physician and CEO of Cornerstone. I had a new ambiguous role at Wake Forest within the confines of CHESS, and I was certainly not culturally well-suited for the Wake Forest environment at that time.

Two women academic department heads at Wake took me out to dinner and told me about their own challenges, emphasizing that Wake was not a good environment for women leaders. Although now Dr. Julie Freischlag is the CEO of Wake and much of that culture has changed, at the time, the entire executive team at Wake consisted of white men. Two of them, Dr. Russ Howerton and Terry Williams, are very good friends of mine, but that did not make my ability to navigate the Wake environment any easier, an environment that felt as sexist and unwelcoming as any I had ever experienced.

In 2017, I could stand it no longer. I accepted a position as CEO of Envision Genomics at the Hudson Alpha Institute of Biotechnology in Huntsville, Alabama, a startup founded by the legendary team featured in the Pulitzer prize-winning article and subsequent book *One in a Billion* that made the first diagnosis of a rare disease in a child using genomic sequencing technology that resulted in a life-saving cure.

Our startup company had a revolutionary information technology that could use whole-genomic sequencing to diagnose heretofore rare and undiagnosed illnesses. Although I practiced primary care medicine every day, I, like most physicians, was not very knowledgeable about the capabilities of cutting-edge genomics. To get up to speed, I used my reading superpowers to read every textbook on genomics I could find and quickly got a professional certification in genomics from Stanford University through their online learning platform.

Upon arrival at Envision, I wrote a business plan built upon the unmet needs of patients with rare disease and went to the market to get out a minimally viable product. Compared to the resources of Cornerstone and Wake, Envision's resources were minimal. I learned the world of venture capital, start-ups, biotechnology, pitch decks, and fundraising.

Once again, I was in a company trying to do something ahead of the market. Payers would not reimburse our technology and potential health system partners were not interested in any technology, no matter how much it improved patient care, if they didn't make money using it. Over the course of the past few years, that has changed, but not soon enough to save Envision.

On September 19, 2018, I learned that Tom Main, a long-time friend, mentor, Envision board member, and investor, had died unexpectedly of a pulmonary embolus, just hours after we had communicated about the next round of funding for Envision. While I grieved Tom's death, I realized it was the death knell for Envision, too.

Although I spent the next six months desperately seeking alternative sources of funding and used a considerable amount of Tim's and my personal savings to do so, I was unsuccessful. We closed down Envision in early 2019. I spent the next several months working in a strategy position at Kailos Genetics, an innovative company focused on pharmacogenetics, as well as doing 5,000 pre-pandemic Teladoc visits, consulting for Oliver Wyman's healthcare practice, and, continuing to see some patients at the internal medicine practice I have been part of since 1993, now part of Atrium Health.

Out of the blue, a recruiter contacted me in July 2019 for a CEO position at a North Carolina-based company called Eventus WholeHealth. When I looked at the job description, I couldn't believe it — it read like my dream job.

Eventus is a company that provides an integrated model of care to medically vulnerable adults who reside in skilled nursing facilities, assisted living facilities, or are home bound. I started the position in November 2019. Since then, the integrated primary care, mental health, and podiatry care model has expanded to more than 1,200 facilities and private homes in five states.

The 650 providers and support staff have been on the front lines during the COVID pandemic, serving the sickest, most medically vulnerable patient population with patient-centered, evidence-based models of care.

I believe the Eventus model of care is not "ahead of its time" but, in fact, just in time, as our country takes on the challenge of providing whole-person care to the 70 million baby boomers beginning to enter their senior years. Eventus is positioned to be a transformative healthcare delivery platform just when our aging population needs it the most.

In 2021, I left Eventus and am looking for my next adventure. I believe all my previous experiences, from running multimillion-dollar businesses to startups; developing deep expertise in care model design, healthcare policy and economics; and continuing to practice (very) part time in the internal medicine practice I've been a part of since 1993, positions me to continue to improve our healthcare delivery system. Stay tuned...

It is said that women leaders do not articulate their accomplishments as assertively as men and that is one reason we aren't as likely to rise to the top leadership positions. Maybe that is true. Here are some things I haven't talked about here.

While I have been living the life I articulated above, I've written three books, served as vice-chair of the federal Physician-Focused Technical Advisory Committee (PTAC) commission, chair of the American Medical Group Association (AMGA), a board member of the American Association for Physician Leadership, an advisor to the innovative IKS company, founding member of the Oliver Wyman Health Innovation Center, given scores of talks, earned a Master's in Medical Management, and, above all, tried to lead with authenticity.

I've taught myself Spanish and I still run 25 miles or so a week, although very slowly these days. I've built four medical buildings and have kept a fern alive for 40 years. I have certainly failed at a lot of things. Just Google me if you want the dirty details.

Today both my daughters are married to wonderful men. Katy is an attorney and pregnant with my first granddaughter. Robyn is in medical school. I doubt when she graduates there will be many other women physicians who can say that she has both a mother and grandmother who are physicians. Tim is most certainly not "a 22-year-old unfocused young man" anymore. My gorgeous gray-haired husband of 38 years continues his own successful career in health information technology and remains the love of my life.

MY MESSAGE

The story I have written here is not the one I expected to write. It is deeply personal and one that speaks to many elements of my life that are not directly pertinent to my day-to-day role as a physician executive. I have not discussed in detail my 21 years of experience as chief executive officer or my more than 30 years as a practicing physician in terms of lessons learned that might help other women physicians considering a career in medical management.

Instead, I have decided to share my story within the context of my complex roles as daughter, mother, wife, and daughter-in-law because I believe it is these roles that help define how women are viewed as professionals and the special skills they bring to their leadership responsibilities.

We are at the beginning of what I expect will be the single fastest transformation of any industry in U.S. history. Physician leadership in healthcare during this transformation is crucial and the healthcare delivery system transformation will be an enormous opportunity for women. But the relative lack of women in leadership roles in healthcare currently needs to be understood and addressed.

I would suggest that one approach to addressing this discrepancy is through the language of archetypes as articulated by Carl Jung. Jung theorized that archetypes are symbolic figures hardwired into our unconsciousness. He focused upon the archetypes of hero, father, mother, temptress, witch, villain, wise old woman (or man), and innocent, ingrained in our collective unconsciousness as identified in myths across cultures and times.

Unlike men, most of the female archetypes are characterized by relationships that adhere to traditional social roles (mother, daughter, grandmother, sister). Although men are also represented in archetypes based upon traditional social roles (father, son, grandfather, brother), there are some strong male archetypes based on the relationship between man and society. These are the roles of hero and villain, both of which are external to the family. The hero is focused more upon saving the group, defending the weak and innocent, administering justice. The villain is his foil.

Our country's future success depends upon our ability to transform our healthcare delivery system to one that is equitable, affordable, and effective. That transformation will require leadership from many individuals who have neither prepared for nor expected to play these critical roles.

For women it is crucial that we understand that effective leaders learn the language of leadership and master it. Using Jung's paradigm, we need to appreciate how we are perceived in various situations in order to discern how a particular female gender archetype might impact our message. By listening to the language used by others, we can create the situational story in which our role is played. Then we can choose which voice to use in order to be most effective leaders.

The *grandmother voice* is the storytelling voice. It is particularly useful when giving a presentation, as the human mind is designed to retain information it hears from stories. For physicians, a story about a patient that teaches a lesson and evokes empathy can be a very powerful tool.

In the working world, the *mother voice* can be dangerous. It can be perceived as both loving and scolding and should be used with caution. On the other hand, the *sister voice* is powerful because it is collaborative. The connotations of sisterhood eliminate inappropriate sexual overtones and its implied equal status in the sibling relationship can positively impact team building.

Women tend to overuse the *daughter voice*. Female subordinates often find the daughter role to be a safe relationship with male bosses/mentors because it may diminish sexual tension. However, this is a problem when attempting to transition to a leadership role. Beware of language in which sexual allusion are used in descriptions of women.

The *temptress/prostitute* archetypes are universal and powerful, but not appropriate within the context of leadership. Likewise, the *domineering woman/bitch* role is dangerous. Some women avoid leadership roles because they fear being depicted within this context.

The most enigmatic role for women is that of *witch*. The witch role is powerful, but frightening because it is a role contextualized around female power that is outside of the standard male dominant cultural context. Powerful men may rely upon the language of the warrior/hero archetype as the context for their effective leadership, but being perceived as powerful using the witch archetype is generally a problem for women in leadership roles.

As women leaders, pay attention to the language you are speaking and the language in which others speak to you. Pay attention to the subtle messages of clothing, body language, and underlying archetypes in the language of colleagues. Choose the voice with which you speak and the language with which you organize your leadership roles. Think about those symbols that project power.

Leadership is an existential construct based upon social roles, language, and archetypal understandings that constitute the deep wisdom written into the human experience. We ARE tomboys, sisters, mothers, daughters, grandmothers, temptresses, bitches, and witches. To be leaders we must also be authentic. I do not believe authentic leadership for women is found within a neutered male heroic archetype. It rises out of our own experiences. Pearls are a woman's necktie.

I wrote the above message for the original *Lessons Learned: Stories from Women in Medical Management* published 10 years ago. When I reflect on those words about my life story since, I do not see anything I would change in the narrative to that point, nor my general beliefs about how women physician leaders can navigate some of the gender challenges that often bedevil us. I believe the Jungian archetypes are still pertinent and listening deeply to how one is spoken to in conversations can help one perceive gender biases.

The archetypes for me are life hacks, allowing me to judge quickly how to steer through some of the unconscious stereotypes inherent in the dialogue and alter my responses accordingly. My "pearls are a woman's necktie" is meant to distinguish gender-based equivalent signals of power and professionalism that can serve to equalize in appropriate business settings. But boy, a whole lot has happened in the world and to me since I wrote those words and used that metaphor, from the *#metoo* movement, great progress in LGBTQ+ rights that have challenged such gender binary categories altogether, to the defeat of Hillary Clinton by Donald Trump, with all the not-so-subliminal gender-hate speech the 2016 political campaign evoked. I will leave the reader to reflect on their own regarding the relevance of my original necktie metaphor within the context of the national dialogue, but I believe updating my own story has relevance, too.

Bottom line: Here's the lesson I've learned over the past 10 years: For women in leadership roles, there is always a fine line between bitch and badass in how one is perceived. Turns out that fine line is what my "strangeness" is really all about. At this point in my life, I'm good with that.

This chapter is reprinted from *Lessons Learned: Stories from Women Physician Leaders,* which profiles 33 exceptional women physician leaders and is edited by Deborah M. Shlian, MD, MBA. Published by the American Association for Physician Leadership, 2022. Additional reading: *Lessons Learned Stories from Women Leaders in STEM,* profiles 29 extraordinary women who have excelled in a range of STEM-related leadership roles and is edited by Deborah M. Shlian, MD, MBA. Published by the American Association for Physician Leadership, 2023.

Epilogue

I told you this would be a weird book, but I hope you found its layers of anecdotes, storytelling, analysis, and data a useful new approach to tackling the wicked problem of gender bias as it is currently construed in the healthcare landscape. Consisting of nearly a fifth of the entire U.S. economy, the healthcare delivery system is big enough and socially important enough that if we redesign healthcare to be diverse and equitable for our patients and our professionals, we will have adequate impact to change the world in far greater ways than just our own industry. Our momentum will deliver healthy people and a healthy planet. Let's get started.

REFERENCES

1. United Nations. Combating Discrimination Against Women. United Nationals Human Rights Office of the High Commissioner. www.ohchr.org.
2. Steward A. The Gender Pay Gap Is Real. To Close It, Pay Equity Needs to Be a Continuous Practice. Payscale.com blog. April 30, 2021.
3. Spiggle T. The Gender Pay Gap: Why It's Still Here. Forbes. May 25, 2021.
4. Fuhrman V. Where Are All the Women CEOs? *The Wall Street Journal.* February 6, 2020.
5. UN Women. Facts and Figures: Women's Leadership and Political Participation. unwomen.org.
6. Kane L, Koval ML. Medscape Female Physician Compensation Report 2021: The Recovery Begins. Medscape. April 16, 2021. www.medscape.com/slideshow/2021-compensation-overview-6013761.
7. Stone T. Closing the Gender Gap in Healthcare Leadership. OliverWyman blog. https://www.oliverwyman.com/our-expertise/insights/2020/mar/needed-more-women-with-power/collection-of-articles/closing-the-gender-gap-in-healthcare-leadership.html.
8. World Health Organization. Closing the Leadership Gap: Gender Equity and Leadership in the Global Health and Care Workforce. Policy Action Paper. June 7, 2021. https://who.int/publications/item/9789240025905.
9. Van Daalen KR, Bajnoczki C, Chowdhury M, Sada S, Khorsant P, Socha A, et.al. Symptoms of a Broken System: The Gender Gaps in COVID-19 Decision-making. *BMJ Glob Health.* 2020;5(10): e003549.
10. Women in Global Health. COVID-19 Global Health Security Depends on Women: Rebalancing the Unequal Social Contract for Women. Women In Global Health. September 2020. http://covid5050.org/Global-Health-Security-Depends-on-Women-WGH.pdf.
11. Chamorro-Premuzic T, Wittenburg-Cox A. Will the Pandemic Reshape Notions of Female Leadership? *Harv Bus Rev.* June 26, 2020. https://hbr.org/2020/06/will-the-pandemic-reshape-notions-of-female-leadership.
12. Dada S, Ashworth HC, Bewa MJ, Dhatt R. Words Matter: Political and Gender Analysis of Speeches Made by Heads of Government During the COVID-19 Pandemic. *BMJ Glob Health.* 2021;6(1):e003910.
13. Global Health 50/50. The Sex, Gender and COVID-19 Project: The COVID-19 Sex-Disaggregated Data Tracker. Global Health 50/50. https://globalhealth5050.org/the-sex-gender-and-covid-19-project.
14. Berlin G, Lapointe M, Murphy M, Viscardi M. Nursing in 2021: Retaining the Healthcare Workforce When We Need It Most. May 11, 2021, McKinsey & Company. 2021. www.mckinsey.com/industries/healthcare-systems-and-services/our-insights/nursing-in-2021-retaining-the-healthcare-workforce-when-we-need-it-most.
15. Frink E, Zhao Z, Fang Y, et.al. Experiences of Work-Family Conflict and Mental Health Symptoms by Gender Among Physician Parents During the COVID-19 Pandemic. *JAMA Netw Open.* 2021;4(11): e2134315.

16. U.S. Equal Employment Opportunity Commission. The Equal Pay Act of 1963. www. eeoc.gov/statutes/equal-pay-act-1963

17. U.S. Equal Employment Opportunity Commission. Title VII Civil Rights Act of 1964. www. eeoc.gov/statues/title-vii-civil-rights-act-1964.

18. United Nations. Combating Discrimination Against Women. United Nationals Human Rights Office of the High Commissioner. www.ohchr.org.

19. Ciminelli G, Schwellnus C, Stadler B. Sticky Floors or Glass Ceilings? The Role of Human Capital, Working Time Flexibility and Discrimination in the Gender Wage Gap. OECD Economics Department Working Paper No. 1668. /www.oecd-ilibrary. org/economics/sticky-floors-or-glass-ceilings-the-role-of-human-capital-working-time-flexibility-and-discrimination-in-the-gender-wage-gap_02ef3235-en;jsession-id=M42McZ1xwnem-DhqugdCq0h9.ip-10-240-5-26.

20. Williams C. The Glass Escalator: Hidden Advantages for Men in the 'Female' Professions. *Social Problems.* 39;(3):253–267. Doi:10.1525/sp.1992.39.3.03x0034h. JSTOR 3096961

21. Goudreau J. A New Obstacle for Professional Women: The Glass Escalator. *Forbes.* May 21, 2021.

22. Dandar VM, Lautenberger DM, Garrison G. Exploring Faculty Salary Equity at U.S. Medical Schools by Gender and Race/Ethnicity. Washington, DC: Association of American Medical Colleges, October 2021. www.aamc.org/data-reports/workforce/report/exploring-faculty-salary-equity-us-medical-schools-gender-and-race/ethnicity.

23. Gottlieb AS, Jagsi R. Closing the Gender Pay Gap in Medicine. *NEJM.* 2021;385:2501–2504.

24. Acuna AJ, Sato EH, Jella TK, Samuel LT, Jeong SH, et al. How Long Will It Take to Reach Gender Parity in Orthopedic Surgery in the United States? An Analysis of the National Provider Identifier Registry. *Clin Orthop Relate Res.* 2021;479(6):1179–1189.

25. Fields J. Achieving Gender Parity Could Take Over 100 Years. Women in Business & Industry. Society and Politics blog. April 27, 2021. wib-i.com/achieving-gender-parity-could-take-over-100-years

26. Pladson K. Pandemic Has Reversed Progress on Gender Equity. DW Business blog. March 31, 2021. https://www.dw.com/en/wef-coronavirus-has-reversed-progress-on-gender-equality/a-57048120

27. DW. Female World Leaders Highlight Pandemic's Impact on Women. DW Equality blog. March 9, 2021. https://www.dw.com/en/eu-us-and-new-zealand-leaders-highlight-pandemics-impact-on-women/a-56811249

28. Ibarra H, Ely RJ, Kolb DM. Women Rising: The Unseen Barriers. *Harv Bus Rev.* September 2013. hbr.org/2013/09/women-rising-the-unseen-barriers.

29. Slavina V. Why Women Must Ask (The Right Way): Negotiations Advice from Stanford's Margaret A. Neale. The Muse.com. May 27, 2013.

30. Steele CM. *Whistling Vivaldi.* New York: W.W. Norton & Company;2010:14–15.

31. Steele CM. *Whistling Vivaldi.* New York: W.W. Norton & Company;2010:15.

32. Jung C. The Archetypes and the Collective Unconscious. *Collected Works*, Vol. 9, Part 1. Princeton, NJ: Princeton University Press;1959.

33. Oxford English Dictionary. www.oed.com.

34. Wikipedia. Jungian Archetypes. https://en.wikipedia.org/wiki/Jungian_archetypes

35. Cattoi T, Odorisio DM. Depth Psychology and Mysticism. Cham, Switzerland: Palgrave Macmillan;2018:72.

36. Wikipedia. Carl Jung. Wikipedia. https://en.wikipedia.org/wiki/Carl_Jung

37. Reed T. Demon-Lovers and Their Victims in British Fiction. Lexington: University Press of Kentucky;2009.

38. Wehr DS. Religious and Social Dimensions of the Archetype. In *Feminist Archetypal Theory: Interdisciplinary Re-Visions of Jungian Thought*. E Lauter and CS Rupprecht, eds. Knoxville: University of Tennessee Press;1985:34.

39. Ibarra H, Ely RJ, Kolb DM. Women Rising: The Unseen Barriers. *Harv Bus Rev*. September 2013. hbr.org/2013/09/women-rising-the-unseen-barriers.

40. Ibarra H, Ely RJ, Kolb DM. Women Rising: The Unseen Barriers. *Harv Bus Rev*. September 2013. hbr.org/2013/09/women-rising-the-unseen-barriers.

41. Gunja MZ, Seervai S, Zephryn L, Williams RD. Health and Health Care for Women of Reproductive Age. The Commonwealth Fund. Issue Brief. April 5, 2022. https://www.commonwealthfund.org/publications/issue-briefs/2022/apr/health-and-health-care-women-reproductive-age

42. Scheinman T. The Historical Roots of Racial Disparities in American Health Care. *Smithsonian*, April/May 2022:22.

43. Lerner G. *The Creation of Patriarchy*. New York: Oxford University Press;1986:229.

44. Benson B. Cognitive Bias Cheat Sheet, Simplified. Medium.com. January 8, 2017. https://medium.com/thinking-is-hard/4-conundrums-of-intelligence-2ab78d90740f

45. Jung CG. *Synchronicity: An Acausal Connecting Principle*. Princeton, NJ: Princeton University Press;1960.

46. Van Zyl M. The 7 Female Archetypes and What They Tell Us About Being A Woman. Blog. August 5, 2022. https://drmelanevanzyl.com/the-7-female-archetypes-and-what-they-tell-us-about-being-a-woman-2/

47. Khalif M. What Are the 13 Archetypes? WikiLivre. March 19, 2021. https://wikilivre.org/culture/what-are-the-13-archetypes

48. Pearson CS. *The Hero Within: Six Archetypes We Live By*. New York: Harper & Row:1989.

49. Bear-Tibbs TM. Female Fantasists: Re-visions the Archetypal Warrior. Masters Thesis 2243. 1991. Eastern Illinois University. https://thekeep.eiu.edu/theses/2243.

50. Raglan FRS. The Hero: A Study in Tradition, Myth, and Drama. Westport, Conn: Greenwood Press; 1975.

51. Pratt A. Spinning Among Fields: Jung, Frye, Levi-Strauss and Feminist Archetypal Theory. In *Feminist Archetypal Theory: Interdisciplinary Re-Visions of Jungian Thought*. Lauter E and Ruprecht CS, eds. Knoxville: University of Tennessee Press;1985: 93-136.

52. L'Engle M. *A Wrinkle in Time*. New York: Dell Publishing;1962.

53. Le Guin UK. *The Books of Earthsea: The Complete Illustrated Editions.* New York: Saga Press;2018.

54. Pearson CS. *The Hero Within: Six Archetypes We Live By.* New York: Harper & Row:1989:1-2.

55. Raglan FRS. The Hero: A Study in Tradition, Myth, and Drama. Westport, Conn: Greenwood Press; 1975;191.

56. Faines AK. An Explanation of the 7 Feminine Archetypes. Women Love Power blog. 2021. https://www.womenlovepower.com/2016/03/an-explanation-of-the-7-basic-feminine-archetypes

57. Radu S. (October 25, 2017) How #MeToo Has Awoken Women Around the World. *US News & World Report.* January 6, 2018.

58. Zillman C. (October 16, 2017) A New Poll on Sexual Harassment Suggests Why 'Me Too' Went So Insanely Viral. *Fortune.* January 13, 2018.

59. Mal S. Despite #MeToo, U.S. Workers Fear Speaking Out About Sexual Harassment. Reuters. November 10, 2017.

60. Rubin AJ. "Revolt" in France Against Sexual Harassment Hits Cultural Resistance. *The New York Times* November 19, 2017.

61. Rich M. She Broke Japan's Silence on Rape. The New York Times. December 29, 2017.

62. Launer J. Sexual Harassment of Women in Medicine: A Problem for Men to Address. Postgrad Med J. 2018;94(1108):120–130.

63. Kroll L (ed). Guidelines for Establishing Sexual Harassment Prevention and Grievance Procedures. *JAMA.* 1992;268(2):273.

64. Reshma J. Sexual Harassment in Medicine — #MeToo. *NEJM.* 2018;378:209–211.

65. Reshma J, Griffith KA, Jones R, Perumalswami CR, et al. Sexual Harassment and Discrimination Experiences of Academic Medical Faculty. *JAMA.* 2016;315(10):2120–2121. Doi:10.1001/jama.2016.2188.

66. Ovid. *Metamorphosis.* C Martin, trans. New York: W.W. Norton; 2004:212.

67. King-Slutzky J. After Philomela: A History of Women Whose Tongues Have Been Ripped Out. The Hairpin blog. March 10, 2014. www.thehairpin.com/2014/03/after-philomela-a-history-of-women-whose-tongues-have-been-ripped-out

68. Cheney C. Emergency Medicine Residents Subjected to Discrimination, Abuse, and Harassment. HealthLeaders. August 23, 2021. www.healthleadersmedia.com/clinical-care/emergency-medicine-residents-subjected-discrimination-abuse-and-harassment.

69. Paul M. Women Surgical Residents Suffer More Mistreatment Leading to Burnout and Suicidal Thoughts. Northwestern Now. October 28, 2019. news.northwestern.edu/stories/2019/10/women-surgical-residents-suffer-more-mistreatment-leading-to-burnout-and-suicidal-thoughts/

70. Arnold LF, Zargham SR, Gordon CE, McKinley WI Bruendermanth, EH, et al. Sexual Harassment During Residency Training: A Cross-Sectional Analysis. *Am Surg.* 2020;86(1):65–72.

71. Sudol NT, Guaderrama NM, Hornberger P, Weiss J, et al. Prevalence of Nature of Sexist and Racial/Ethnic Microaggressions Against Surgeons and Anesthesiologists. *JAMA Surg.* 2021;156(5):e210265.

72. Guzie T, Guzie NM. Masculine and Feminine Archetypes: A Complement to the Psychological Types. Journal of Psychological Type. 1984;7:3–11. www. Capt.org/ jpt/pdFiles/Guzie_T_and_Guzie_N_Vol_7_3_11.pdf.

73. Sanfey HA, Saalwachter-Schulman ER, Nyhof-Young JM, Eidelson B, Mann BD. Influences on Medical Student Career Choice: Gender or Generations? *Arch Surg.* 2006;141(11):1086–1094.

74. Rangel EL, Smink DS, Castillo-Angeles M, et al. Pregnancy and Motherhood During Surgical Training" *JAMA Surg.* 2018;153(7): 644–652.doi:10.1001/ jamasurg.2018.0153.

75. Khoushhal Z, Hussain MA, Greco E, Mamdani M, Verma S, et al, Prevalence and Causes of Attrition Among Surgical Residents: A Systematic Review and Meta-analysis. *JAMA Surg.* 2017;152(3):265–272.doi:10.1001/jamasurg.2016.4086.

76. Smith PM, Nordness MF, Polcz ME. The American Board of Surgery Should Reconsider Its Parental Leave Policy. *JAMA Surg.* 2022;157(1):7–8.

77. Rangel EL, Smink DS, Castillo-Angeles M, et al. Pregnancy and Motherhood During Surgical Training. *JAMA Surg.* 2018;153(7):644-652.doi:10.1001/ jamasurg.2018.0153.

78. Diwan MA. Conflict Between State Legal Norms and Norms Underlying Popular Beliefs: Witchcraft in Africa as a Case Study. 14 *Duke Journal of Comparative & International Law.* 2004;14(2):351-388. https://scholarship.law.duke.edu/djcil/ vol14/iss2/5

79. Yaseen A. Witch Hunts in Modern South Africa: An Under-Represented Facet of Gender-Based Violence. MRC-UNISA Crime, Violence and Injury Lead Program. June 2009. web.archive.org/web/20120425074549/http://www.mrc.ac.za/ witchhunts.pdf.

80. Jamjoom M, Abedine S. Saudi Woman Beheaded for 'Witchcraft and Sorcery'. CNN. com. December 14, 2011.

81. Moreno M. UN Council Adopts Historic Resolution Condemning Harmful Practices Related to Accusations of Witchcraft and Ritual Attacks. The Wild Hunt. July 28, 2021. https://wildhunt.org/2021/07/un-council-adopts-historic-resolution-condemning-harmful-practices-related-to-accusations-of-witchcraft-and-ritual-attacks.html.

82. Mace R. Why Are Women Accused of Witchcraft? *Scientific American.* January 11, 2018. www.scientificamerican.com/article/why-are-women-accused-of-witchcraft

83. Miller M. From Circe to Clinton: Why Powerful Women Are Cast as Witches. *The Guardian.* April 7, 2018.

84. Michigan GOP Chair Calls Top Democratic Women 'Witch'. nbcnews.com. March 26, 2021.

85. Anderson AR. The Salem Witch Trials and the Political Chaos That Caused Them: How the Glorious Revolution Kindled the Fire of Colonial Unrest. Masters Thesis. Western Illinois University. 2019. www.wiu.edu/cas/history/wihr/pdfs/Spring%20 2019%20Anderson%20final%20draft.pdf

86. George AS, McConville FE, Vries S, Nigenda G, Sarfraz S, McIsaac M. Violence Against Female Health Workers Is Tip of Iceberg of Gender Power Imbalances. *BMJ.* 2020;371:m3546. https://doi.org/10.1136/bmj.m3546)

87. Reshma J, Griffith KA, Jones R, Perumalswami CR, et al. Sexual Harassment and Discrimination Experiences of Academic Medical Faculty. *JAMA*. 2016;315(10):2120–2121. Doi:10.1001/jama.2016.2188.

88. Snavely C, Romeo M, Ciardiello A, Mojica M. The Pandemic of Workplace Violence: The Gendered Experience of Emergency Medicine Trainees. AEM Education and Training. 2021;1:5(3):e10630. doi:10.1002/aet2.10630.

89. Anonymous. Knowledge and Powers, Isabel Perez Molina. Duoda, Women Research Center. University of Barcelona. http://www.ub.edu/duoda/diferencia/html/en/imprimible7.html

90. Karlsen CF. *The Devil in the Shape of a Woman: Witchcraft in Colonial New England*. New York: W.W. Norton and Company;1998.

91. Kantar. The Reykjavik Index for Leadership: Measuring Perceptions of Equality for Men and Women in Leadership. www.kantar.com/campaigns/reykjavik-index.

92. Ro C. Why Do We Still Distrust Women Leaders? BBC.com. January 8, 2021. www.bbc.com/worklife/article/20210108-why-do-we-sti—distrust-women-leaders

93. Lintern S. Female Doctors Earn £40,000 Less Than Male Colleagues Due to 'Two-Tier-GP Pay Gap.' Independent. January 10, 2020. www.independent.co.uk/news/health/nhs-gender-pay-gap-doctor-ippr-study-a9276981.html.

94. American Association of University Women. Barriers and Bias: The Status of Women in Leadership. 2016. www.aauw.org/resources/research/barrier-bias.

95. Madsen SR, Andrade MS. Unconscious Gender Bias: Implications for Women's Leadership Development. *Journal of Leadership Studies*. 2018;12(1):62–67.

96. Westergaard D, Moseley P, Brunak S. Population-wide Analysis of Difference in Disease Progression Patterns in Men and Women. *Natural Communications*. 2019;10;666.

97. Samulowitz A, Gremyr I, Eriksson E, Hensing G. "Brave Men" and "Emotional Women": A Theory-Guided Literature Review on Gender Bias in Health Care and Gendered Norms Towards Patients with Chronic Pain. *Pain Res Manag*. 2018:6358624. https://doi.org/10.1155/2018/6358624.

98. Hansen M, Schoonover A, Skarica B, Harrod T, Bahr N, Guise J. Implicit Gender Bias Among US Resident Physicians. *BMC Med Educ*. 2019;19(1):396. https://doi.org/10.1186/s12909-019-1818-1.

99. Templeton K, Nilsen KM, Walling A. Issues Faced by Senior Women Physicians: A National Survey. *J Womens Health*. 2020;29(7):980–988. https://doi.org/10.1089/jwh.2019.7910

100. Mandurian C, Lenos E, Sarkar U, Rodriguez C, Jagsi R, What's Holding Women in Medicine Back from Leadership. *Harv Bus Rev*. Nov 7, 2019.

101. Lai C. The Way of the Dream: Part Two — Archetypes. Medium.com. August 14, 2019.

102. Collins Dictionary of Medicine. Robert M Youngson. 2004, 2005.

103. Wolff T. *Structural Forms of the Feminine Psyche*. P Watzlawik trans. Zurich: C.G. Jung Institute; 1956.

104. Glazebrook A. The Making of a Prostitute: Apollodorus's Portrait of Neaira. Arethusa. 2005;38(2):161. doi:10/1353/are.2005.0009.

105. Ulanov AB. *The Feminine in Jungian Psychology and Christian Theology*, ISBN 08101-0608-6, p. 195.
106. Daly M. *Beyond God the Father: Toward a Philosophy of Women's Liberation.* Boston: Beacon; 1973:8.
107. Weir DS. Religious and Social Dimensions of the Archetype. In *Feminist Archetypal Theory: Interdisciplinary Re-Visions of Jungian Thought.* E Lauter and CS Rupprecht, eds. Knoxville: University of Tennessee Press;1985:44.
108. Morgan G. *Images of Organization.* Thousand Oaks, CA: Sage Publications;1997: 153–213.
109. Morgan G. *Images of Organization.* Thousand Oaks, CA: Sage Publications;1997:227.
110. Banaji MR, Greenwald AG. *Blind Spot.* New York: Bantam Books;2016:19.
111. Smith, JA, Ross WD (tr.) *The Works of Aristotle* (Oxford: Clarendon Press;1912), "De Generatione Animalsiuim," II, 3, 729a, 26–31.
112. Isabella Baumfree (c. 1797-1883) renamed herself Sojourner Truth after experiencing a vision. She was born a slave in New York State and was sold as a nine-year old child for $100 and a flock of sheep. She was raped by her slave master and later forced into a marriage with an older slave and bore five children. She rescued her own child from slavery, and later left New York and supported herself as an itinerate preacher deriving her authority directly from God in her avocation of abolition, women's rights, and the protection of the poor. The "ain't I a woman" quote is from a speech given in Akron, Ohio at the Woman's Rights Convention on May 29, 1851 as accounted by Frances Gage, a white abolitionist and president of the Convention in the *National Anti-Slavery Standard* 12 years later.
113. Detsky AS. Learning the Art and Science of Diagnosis. *JAMA.* 2022;327(18):1759–1760. doi:10.1001/jama/2022.4650.
114. Thinknetic. *Cognitive Biases in a Nutshell.* Columbia, SC: Thinknetic;2022.
115. Jost JT, Rudman LA, Blair IV, Carney DR, Dasgupta N, Glaser J, Hardin CD. The Existence of Implicit Bias Is Beyond Reasonable Doubt: A Refutation of Ideological and Methodological Objections and Executive Summary of Ten Studies That No Manager Should Ignore. Research in Organizational Behavior. 2009;39–69.
116. Banaji MR, Greenwald AG. *Blind Spot,* New York: Bantam Books;2016:217.
117. Banaji MR, Greenwald AG. *Blind Spot,* New York: Bantam Books;2016:4.
118. Stottilien. Queen, Mother, Wise Women and Lover: Rediscovering the Archetypes of the Mature Feminine. Stottilien blog. February 1, 2013. https://stottilien.com/2013/02/01/queen-mother-wise-woman-and-lover-rediscovering-the-archetypes-of-the-mature-feminine.
119. Banaji MR, Greenwald AG. *Blind Spot,* New York: Bantam Books;2016:206–209.
120. Lerner G. *The Creation of Feminist Consciousness, From the Middle Ages to Eighteen-seventy.* New York: Oxford University Press;1993:3–4.
121. Ganguli I, Sheridan B, Gray J, Chernew M, Rosenthal MC, Neprash H. Physician Work Hours and the Gender Pay Gap -Evidence form Primary Care. *NEJM.* 2020;383:1349–1357.
122. Berthold HK, Gouni-Berthold I, Bestehorn KP, Bohm M, Krone W. Physician Gender Is Associated with the Quality of Type 2 Diabetes Care. *J Intern Med.* 2008;264(4):340–350.

123. Wallis C, Ravi B, Coburn N, Nam RK, Detsky AL, Satkunasivam R. Comparison of Postoperative Outcomes Among Patients Treated by Male and Female Surgeons: A Population Based Matched Cohort Study. *BMJ.* 2017;359. doi: https://doi.org/10.1136/bmj.j4366.

124. Tsugawa Y, Jena AB, Figueroa JF, Orav EJ, Blumenthal DM, Jha AK. Comparison of Hospital Mortality and Readmission Rates for Medicare Patients Treated by Male vs Female Physicians. *JAMA Intern Med.* 2017;177(2):206–213. https://doi.org/10.1001/jamainternmed.2016.7875.

125. Newman C, Templeton K, Chin EL. *Perm J.* 2020;24:20.024. https://doi.org/10.7812/TPP/20.024.

126. Dossa F, Zeltzer D, Sutradhar R. Simpson AN, Baxter NN. Sex Differences in the Pattern of Patient Referrals to Male and Female Surgeons. *JAMA Surg.* 2022;157(2):95–103. doi:10.1001/jamasurg.2021.5784.

127. Jung CG. *The Archetypes and the Collective Unconscious.* (Collected Works of C.G. Jung, Vol 9, Part 1). Read H, Fordham M, Adler G, McGuire W, eds. Princeton, NJ: Princeton University Press;2014.

128. Gillette D, Moore RL. *King, Warrior, Magician, Lover: Rediscovering the Archetypes of the Mature Masculine.* San Francisco: HarperCollins Publishers;1990.

129. Carol S. Pearson. www.carolspearson.com

130. Criado-Perez C. *Invisible Women: Data Bias in a World Designed for Men.* New York: Abrams Press;2019:XVI.

131. McKinsey Global Institute. The Power of Parity: How Advancing Women's Equality Can Add $12 To Global Growth. McKinsey Global Institute;2015.

132. Criado-Perez C. *Invisible Women: Data Bias in a World Designed for Men.* New York: Abrams Press;2019:71.

133. Anderson NS. Maiden, Mother, Keeper, Crone — The New Archetype for the 21st Century Woman. Nicole Sallak Anderson personal blog. September 7, 2018. https://nsallakanderson.medium.com.

134. Thomason SP. The Living Spirit of the Crone: Turning Aging Inside Out. Minneapolis, MN: Augsburg Fortess;2006:vii.

135. Ott JS. The Crone Archetype: Women Reclaim Their Authentic Self by Resonating with Crone Images. Master's thesis. St. Catherine University. 2011. https://sophia.stkate.edu/ma_hhs/17.

136. Kaplan DB, Berkman B. *The Oxford Handbook of Social Work in Health and Aging.* New York: Oxford University Press;2016:433.

137. De Vere T. I'm a Witch to be Feared All Year Round. Taryn De Vere personal blog. October 15, 2018. https://taryndevere.medium.com/im-a-witch-to-be-feared-all-year-round-1a203025c217

138. Tamayo YA. "Rhymes with Rich": Power, Law, and the Bitch. February 14, 2009. https://ssrn.com/abstract=1468989.

139. Anderson KV. "Rhymes with "Rich": "Bitch" as a Tool of Containment in Contemporary American Politics. *Rhetoric & Public Affairs.* 1999:2(4):600–601.

140. Carlson M. The Public Eye: Muzzle the B Word. *Time.* January 16, 1995.

141. Lakoff G. *Women, Fire, and Dangerous Things: What Categories Reveal about the Mind*. Chicago: University of Chicago Press;1990.

142. Lakoff G. *Women, Fire, and Dangerous Things: What Categories Reveal about the Mind*. Chicago: University of Chicago Press;1990:5.

143. Lakoff G. *Women, Fire, and Dangerous Things: What Categories Reveal about the Mind*. Chicago: University of Chicago Press;1990:98.

144. Lakoff G. *Women, Fire, and Dangerous Things: What Categories Reveal about the Mind*. Chicago: University of Chicago Press;1990:371.

145. Lakoff G. *Women, Fire, and Dangerous Things: What Categories Reveal about the Mind*. Chicago: University of Chicago Press;1990:6.

146. Two examples are Dawn Sears, MD@GutGirlMD and Valerie A. Firzhugh MD @ DrFNAtweet. The original quote is attributed to comedian Jeremy McClellan: "Men naturally gravitate toward higher-paying jobs, like doctors, lawyers, and other professionals. Women naturally gravitate toward lower-paying jobs, like female doctors, female lawyers, and other female professions."

147. @RMahmaoud181

148. Criado-Perez C. *Invisible Women: Data Bias in a World Designed for Men*. New York: Abrams Press;2019:195.

149. Chopra J, Abiakam N, Kim H, Metcalf C, Worsley P, Cheong Y, The Influence of Gender and Ethnicity on Facemasks and Respiratory Protective Equipment Fit: A Systematic Review and Meta-Analysis. *BMJ Global Health*. 2021;6(11):e005537. https://gh.bmj.com/content/6/11/e005537.

150. Ronnberg A, ed. *The Book of Symbols: Reflections on Archetypal Images*. Cologne, German: TASCHEN, The Archive for Research in Archetypal Symbolism;2021:302.

151. Ronnberg A, ed. *The Book of Symbols: Reflections on Archetypal Images*. Cologne, German: TASCHEN, The Archive for Research in Archetypal Symbolism;2021:702.

152. Jung CG. Psychology and Religion. In *Psychology and Religion: West and East, Collected Works of C.G. Jung*, Vol 11J. H Read, G Adler, RFC Hull, eds. Princeton, NJ: Princeton University Press;1958:131.

153. Ericksen K, Schrock D, Dowd-Arrow, B. Dignam P. Bitchifying Hillary: Trump Supporters' Vilification of Clinton During the 2016 Presidential Election. *Social Currents*. 2020; 7(6):526–542. https://doi.org/10.1177/2329496520941022.

154. Anderson KV. "Rhymes with "Rich": "Bitch" as a Tool of Containment in Contemporary American Politics. *Rhetoric & Public Affairs*. 1999:2(4): 599-623 https://www.jstor.org/stable/41939546

155. Hunt T. The Day Outspoken Barbara Bush Regressed Speaking Her Mind. Associated Press. April 18, 2018. apnews.com.

156. Pearson CS. *The Hero Within: Six Archetypes We Live By*. New York:HarperElixer; 1998:19.

157. KnoxPride. Deconstructing the Gender Binary. knoxpride.com. July 14, 2021.

158. Goodwyn E. Approaching Archetypes: Reconsidering Innateness. *J Analytical Psychology*. 2010;55(4):502–521 http://dx.doi.org/10.1111/j.1468-5922.2010.01862.x

159. Oxford English Dictionary. www.oed.com.

160. Porter T. *Breaking Out of the "Man Box."* New York: Skyhorse Publishing;2021.

161. Schwartz SH, Rubel T. 2005. Sex Differences in Value Priorities: Cross-cultural and Multimethod Studies. *J Personality and Social Psychology.* 2005;89:1010–1028.

162. Abate MA. *Tomboys: A Literary and Cultural History.* Philadelphia: Temple University Press;2008:6.

163. Gilman CP. *Women and Economics: A Study of the Economic Relation between Men and Women.* Boston: Small, Maynard & Company1898:56. http://books.google.com/books?id+94EEAAAAYAAJ&oe=UTF-8

164. Lee J. *Play in Education.* New York: Macmillan;1915:392–393.

165. Davis LS. *Tomboy: The Surprising History and Future of Girls Who Date to be Different.* New York: Hachette Books;2020:44.

166. Davis LS. *Tomboy: The Surprising History and Future of Girls Who Date to be Different.* New York: Hachette Books;2020:46.

167. Barclay D. "TOMBOY" PHASE CALLED NATURAL; Pamphlet Says that 'Rowdy' Period for Girls 7 to 10 Is Common Occurrence. *The New York Times.* September 20, 1950. https://www.nytimes.com/1950/09/20/archives/tomboy-phase-called-natural-pamphlet-says-that-rowdy-period-for.html

168. Powerpuff Girls Characters. Cartoon network.com.

169. Hutchinson K, McCracken C. The Powerpuff Girls: Who, What, Where, How, Why...Who Cares? 2009. powerpuffgirls.fandom.com.

170. Lemish D, Russo Johnson CR. *The Landscape of Children's Television in the US & Canada.* The Center for Scholars & Storytellers/UCLA and Ryerson. April 2019. https://static1.squarespace.com/static/5c0da585da02bc56793a0b31/t/5cb8ce1b15fcc0e19f3e16b9/1555615269351/The+Landscape+of+Children%27s+TV.pdf f

171. Phillips G, Over R. Differences Between Heterosexual, Bisexual, and Lesbian Women in Recalled Childhood Experiences. *Arch Sex Behav.* 1995;24(1):1–-20. doi:10.1007/BF01541985

172. Letters editors @sciam.com. *Scientific American.* December 2021, p. 6.

173. Davis LS. *Tomboy: The Surprising History and Future of Girls Who Date to be Different.* New York: Hachette Books;2020:4.

174. Davis LS. *Tomboy: The Surprising History and Future of Girls Who Date to be Different.* New York: Hachette Books;2020:99.

175. Davis LS. *Tomboy: The Surprising History and Future of Girls Who Date to be Different.* New York: Hachette Books;2020:255.

176. Perera, SB. The Descent of Inanna: Myth and Therapy. In *Feminist Archetypal Theory: Interdisciplinary Re-Visions of Jungian Thought,* E Lauter, CS Ruprecht, eds. Knoxville: University of Tennessee Press;1985.

177. Thomas JL. *The Heart of the Story: My Improbable Journey as a Cardiologist,* Washington DC: The American Association of Physician Leadership;2022:61.

178. Abate MA. *Tomboys: A Literary and Cultural History,* Philadelphia: Temple University Press;2008:6.

179. Abate MA. *Tomboys: A Literary and Cultural History,* Philadelphia: Temple University Press;2008:51.

180. Abate MA. *Tomboys: A Literary and Cultural History,* Philadelphia: Temple University Press;2008:55.

181. Jung CG. A Psychological Approach to the Dogma of the Trinity. In *Collected Works of C.G. Jung Vol. 11*. Princeton NJ: Princeton University Press;1969:107–200.

182. Allen PG. *Grandmothers of the Light: A Medicine Woman's Sourcebook*. Boston: Beacon Press;1991:3–24.

183. Jung CG, Kerenyi C. *Essays on a Science of Mythology: The Myth of the Divine Child and the Mysteries of Eleusis*. New York: Pantheon Books;1949:167.

184. Pratt AV. (1985). Spinning Among Fields: Jung, Frye, Levi-Strauss and Feminist Archetypal Theory. In *Feminist Archetypal Theory: Interdisciplinary Re-Visions of Jungian Thought*, E Lauter, CS Ruprecht, eds. Knoxville: University of Tennessee Press;1985.

185. Allen PG. *Grandmothers of the Light: A Medicine Woman's Sourcebook*. Boston: Beacon Press;1991:66.

186. Pearson CS. *The Hero Within: Six Archetypes We Live By*. New York: HarperElixer; 1998:236.

187. Gilligan C. *In a Different Voice: Psychological Theory and Women's Development*, Cambridge, MA: Harvard University Press;1982.

188. Pearson CS. *Awakening the Heroes Within: Twelve Archetypes to Help Us Find Ourselves and Transform Our World*. New York: HarperElixer;1991:267.

189. Johnson D, Johnson R. *Schooling Sexualities*. Buckingham, UK: Open University Press;1998:101.

190. Abate MA. *Tomboys: A Literary and Cultural History*, Philadelphia: Temple University Press;2008:xxx.

191. Stone M. *When God Was a Woman*, Orlando, FL: Harcourt, Inc.;1976:xix–xx.

192. Stone M. *When God Was a Woman*, Orlando, FL: Harcourt, Inc.;1976:227–228.

193. Pomeroy SB. *Goddesses, Whores, Wives and Slaves: Women in Classical Antiquity*. New York: Schocken Books;1995:68.

194. Pomeroy SB. *Goddesses, Whores, Wives and Slaves: Women in Classical Antiquity*. New York: Schocken Books;1995:15.

195. Guerilla Girls. *Bitches, Bimbos, and Ballbreakers: The Guerilla Girls' Illustrated Guide to Female Stereotypes*. New York: Penguin Books;2003:7.

196. Thomas JL. *The Heart of the Story: My Improbable Journey as a Cardiologist*, Washington DC: The American Association of Physician Leadership;2022:117.

197. Solnit R. *Men Explain Things to Men and Other Essays*. London: Granta;2014:4.

198. Wiki. Silence Is Golden. Deleted Songs, The Little Mermaid Song, Villain Song. Silence is Golden.disney.fandom.com

199. Gilligan C. *In a Different Voice*. Cambridge, MA: Harvard University Press;1982.

200. Kim C. The Gendered Landscape of Self-Silencing. *Applied Psychology Opus*. https://wp.nyu.edu/steinhardt-appsych_opus/the-gendered-landscape-of-self-silencing.

201. Pina-Watson B, Castillo LG, Jung E, Ojeda L, Castillo-Reyes R. The Marianismo Beliefs Scale: Validation with Mexican American Adolescent Girls and Boys. *J Latina/o Psychology*. 2014;2(2): 113-130. doi:10.1037/lat0000017.

202. Witte TH, Sherman MF. Silencing the Self and Feminist Identity Development. *Psychological Reports*. 2002; 90(1):1075-1083. doi:10.2466/pr0.2002.90.3c.1075.

203. Nadim N, Fladmore A. Silencing Women? Gender and Online Harassment. *Social Science Computer Review*. 2021;39(2):245–258. doi:10.1177/0894439319865518 journals.sagepub.com/home/ssc.

204. Quintana S. The Cultural Silencing of Women. Blog. October 3, 2018. https://medium.com/publishous/the-cultural-silencing-of-women-94f27fbb7ef1

205. Reardon J. How to Stop the Silencing of Women in the Workplace. World Economic Forum. February 24, 2015. www.weforum.org/agenda/2015/02/how-to-stop-the-silencing-of-women-in-the-workplace.

206. Sandberg S, Grant A. Speaking While Female. *The New York Times*. January 12, 2015.

207. Smartt N. Sexual Harassment in the Workplace in a #MeToo World. *Forbes*. January 16, 1018.

208. Zillman C. A New Poll on Sexual Harassment Suggests Why 'Me Too' Went So Insanely Viral. *Fortune*. October 17, 2017.

209. Jagsi R. Women in Medicine Say #MeToo, Report 'Appalling 'Experiences. Institute for Healthcare Policy and Innovation. December 13, 2017. https://ihpi.umich.edu/news/women-medicine-say-metoo-report-%E2%80%98appalling%E2%80%99-experiences.

210. Jagsi R. Sexual Harassment in Medicine – #MeToo. *NEJM*. 2018;378:209–211.

211. Bargh JA, Raymond P, Pryor JB, Strake F. Attractiveness of the Underling: An Automatic Power — Sex Association and Its Consequences for Sexual Harassment and Aggression. *J Pers. Soc. Psychol.* 1995;68(5):768–781. https://doi.org/10.1037/0022-3514.68.5.768.

212. Bargh JA, Raymond P. The Naïve Misuse of Power: Nonconscious Sources of Sexual Harassment. *J. Soc. Issues.* 1995;51:85–96.

213. Manne K. *Entitled: How Male Privilege Hurts Women*. New York: Crown;2020:7.

214. Manne K. *Entitled: How Male Privilege Hurts Women*. New York: Crown;2020:8.

215. The Facts on Gender-Based Workplace Violence. www.workplacesrespond.org.

216. Zafar M. 16 Shocking Facts About Violence Against Women and Girls. December 7, 2020. https://reliefweb.int/report/world/16-shocking-facts-about-violence-against-women-and-girls.

217. Rose J. *On Violence and On Violence Against Women*. New York: Farrar, Straus and Giroux;2021:365.

218. Rose J. *On Violence and On Violence Against Women*. New York: Farrar, Straus and Giroux;2021:37–38.

219. Pearson CS. *Persephone Risking: Awakening the Heroine Within*. New York: HarperOne;2018:x.

220. Pearson CS. *Persephone Risking: Awakening the Heroine Within*. New York: HarperOne;2018:xvi.

221. de Waal F. *Different: Gender through the Eyes of a Primatologist*. New York: W.W. Norton and Company;2022:13

222. Martin RD. No Substitute for Sex: 'Gender' and 'Sex' Have Very Different Meanings. *Psychology Today*. August 20, 2019. www.psychologytoday.com/us/blog/how-we-do-it/201908/no-substitute-sex

223. Whiting B, Edwards, CP. A Cross-Cultural Analysis of Sex Differences in the Behavior of Children Aged Three Through 11. *J Soc Psych.* 1973;91(2):171–188. https://psycnet.apa.org/doi/10.1080/00224545.1973.9923040.

224. Whiting B, Edwards, CP. A Cross-Cultural Analysis of Sex Differences in the Behavior of Children Aged Three Through 11. *J Soc Psych.* 1973;91(2):171–188. https://psycnet.apa.org/doi/10.1080/00224545.1973.9923040.

225. de Waal F. *Different: Gender through the Eyes of a Primatologist.* New York: W.W. Norton and Company;2022:317.

226. Planned Parenthood. What's Intersex? www.plannedparenthood.org/learn/gender-identity/sex-gender-identity/whats-intersex

227. Terrell G. *Reframing Contemporary Physician Leadership: We Started as Heroes.* Washington, DC: American Association for Physician Leadership;2022:195–196.

228. Thomas JL. *The Heart of the Story: My Improbable Journey as a Cardiologist.* Washington DC: The American Association for Physician Leadership;2022:64.

229. Tiffany K. How "Karen" Became a Coronavirus Villain. *The Atlantic.* May 6, 2020.

230. Freeman H. The "Karen" Meme Is Everywhere — And It Has Become Mired in Sexism. *The Guardian.* April 13, 2020.

231. Weiner J. Opinion: The Seductive Appeal of Pandemic Shaming. *The New York Times.* April 14, 2020.

232. Figes K. "Who Are You Calling a Bitch? *The Guardian.* January 26, 2007.

233. Joreen. The BITCH Manifesto. 1968. www.jofreeman.com/joreen/bitch.htm.

234. Taylor K. Who's Afraid of the Big Bad Bitch? *An Injustice.* November 26, 2019. https://aninjusticemag.com/whos-afraid-of-the-big-bad-bitch-699d47ba12b8.

235. Zhou L. Use of the Word "Bitch" Surged After Women's Suffrage. Vox.com. August 19, 2020. www.vox.com/21365241/19th-amendment-womens-suffrage-backlash.

236. Zingo MT. *Sex/Gender Outsiders, Hate Speech, and Freedom of Expression: Can They Say That About Me?* Westport, CT:Praeger;1998:1.

237. Whitlock RK. (1995), The Use of Hate as a Stratagem for Achieving Political and Social Goals. In Hate Speech, RK Willock and D. Slayden, eds. Thousand Oaks, CA:Sage;1995:36.

238. Lederer LJ, Delgado R. *The Price We Pay: The Case Against Racist Speech, Hate Propaganda, and Pornography.* New York, NY: Hill and Wang;1995:19.

239. Matsuda MJ, Lawrence CR, Delgado R, Crenshaw KW. *Words That Wound: Critical Race Theory, Assaultive Speech, and the First Amendment.* Boulder, CO: Westview Press;1993.

240. Nielson LB. Subtle, Pervasive, Harmful: Racist and Sexist Remarks in Public as Hate Speech. *J of Social Issues.* 2002;58:265–280.

241. Asbury ME. What's up, Bitch? The Judgment of Hate Speech Towards Women by College Students. Master's Thesis, University of Tennessee, Knoxville, August 2006. https://trace.tennessee.edu/utk_gradthes/4478.

242. Asbury ME. What's up, Bitch? The Judgment of Hate Speech Towards Women by College Students. Master's Thesis, University of Tennessee, Knoxville, August 2006: 26.

243. Kay K, Shipman C. The Confidence Gap. *The Atlantic*. May 2014. www.theatlantic.com/magazine/archive/2014/05/the-confidence-gap/359815.
244. Fitta J. Reclaiming the Power of the Word Bitch. swaay.com. September 2020. https://swaay.com/reclaiming-power-bitch
245. Gammage E. Florence Given Responds to Chidera Eggerue's Claims That She Copied Her Book. Fizzy Mag. 2021. https://fizzymag.com/articles/florence-given-responds-to-chidera-eggerue-s-claims-that-she-copied-her-book
246. Lempert C. You Say I'm a Bitch Like It's a Bad Thing. Carol Lempert blog. https://carollempert.com/you-say-im-a-bitch-like-its-a-bad-thing.
247. Ensemble. Bossy, Leader, Bitch. Ensemble Coworking blog. March 21, 2019. www.ensemblecoworking.com/post/2019/03/21/bossy-leader-bitch.
248. Anonymous. This doctor was called a bitch at work. Here's what she did next. KevinMD.com. March 21, 2020.
249. Kitty. One Reason Women Make Less Money? They're Afraid of Being Raped and Killed. bitchesgetriches.com. April 26, 2018.
250. National Academy of Sciences. *Sexual Harassment of Women: Climate, Culture, and Consequences in Academic Sciences, Engineering, and Medicine*. Washington, DC: The National Academies Press;2018. http://sites.nationalacademies.org/shstudy/index.htm.
251. Dunn J, Jamieson KH. The "B" Word in Traditional News and on the Web. *Nieman Reports*. Summer 2008. https://niemanreports.org/articles/the-b-word-in-traditional-news-and-on-the-web.
252. Schiff S. *Cleopatra: A Life*. New York: Little, Brown, & Co.;2010:248.
253. Castor H. *Joan of Arc: A History*. New York: HarperCollins;2015:187.
254. Fraser A. *The Warrior Queens: The Legends and the Lives of the Women Who Have Led Their Nations in War*. New York: Anchor Books;1988:10–12.
255. Dio C. Roman History, Epitome of Book LXII. In *Loeb Classical Library Edition, Vol 111*. 1925. http://penelope.uchicago.edu/Thayer/e/roman/texts/cassius_dio/62*.html.
256. Jaffe E. The New Subtle Sexism Toward Women in the Workplace. Fast Company. June 2, 2014. www.fastcompany.com/3031101/the-new-subtle-sexism-toward-women-in-the-workplace
257. Heilman ME, Okimoto TG. Why Are Women Penalized for Success at Male Tasks?: The Implied Communality Deficit. *J Appl Psychol*.2007;92(1):81–92. doi:10.1037/0021-9010.92.1.81.
258. Bowles HR, Babcock L, Lai L. Social Incentives for Gender Differences in the Propensity to Initiate Negotiations: Sometimes It Does Hurt To Ask. Organizational Behavior and Human Decision Processes. 2007;103(1):84–103. https://doi.org/10.1016/j.obhdp.2006.09.001.
259. Brescoll VL, Uhlmann EL. Can an Angry Women Get Ahead? Status Conferral, Gender, and Expression of Emotion in the Workplace. *Psychol Sci*. 2008;19(3):268–275.doi:10.1111/j.1467-9280.02079.x.
260. Cooper M. For Women Leaders, Likability and Success Hardly Go Hand-in-Hand. *Harvard Business Review*. April 30, 2013. https://hbr.org/2013/04/for-women-leaders-likability-a

261. Byers D. Turbulence at The Times. Politico. April 23, 2013. www.politico.com/story/2013/04/new-york-times-turbulence-090544.

262. Auletta K. Changing Times: Jill Abramson Takes Charge of the Gray Lady. *The New Yorker*. October 17, 2011.

263. Khazan O. Jill Abramson and the "Narrow Band' of Acceptable Female Behavior. *The Atlantic*. May 14, 2014. www.theatlantic.com/business/archive/2014/05/jill-abramson-and-the-narrow-band-of-acceptable-female-behavior/370916

264. Elsesser KM, Lever J. Does Gender Bias Against Female Leaders Persist? Quantitative and Qualitative Data from a Large-Scale Survey. *Human Relations*. 2011;64(12):1555-1578.

265. Koenig AM, Mitchell AA, Eagly AH, Ristikari T. Are Leader Stereotypes Masculine? A Meta-Analysis of Three Research Paradigms. *Psychological Bulletin*. 2011;137(4):616–642.

266. Khazan O. Are People Becoming More Open to Female Leaders? *The Atlantic*. May 2, 2014. https://www.theatlantic.com/business/archive/2014/05/the-myth-of-the-ineffective-female-leader/361559/

267. Prooker B. It's Time for Women To Break Up with Politeness. *Elle*. April 14, 2021. www.elle.com/culture/a35854625/no-more-politeness-2021.

268. Burchill J. Why I Was Labelled a Bitch: Joan Collins Remembers the Old Hollywood Days. *Spectator*. December 4, 2021. https://spectator.com.au/2021/12/the-life-of-the-party.

269. Roter DL, Hall JA, Aoki Y. Physician Gender Effects in Medical Communication: A Mata-analytic Review. *JAMA*. 2002;288(6):756–764.doi:10.1001/jama.288.6.756.

270. Kay K, Shipman C. The Confidence Code: The Science and Art of Self-Assurance — What Women Should Know. New York: Harper Collins; 2014.

271. Guillen L, Mayo M, Karelaia N. Appearing Self-Confident and Getting Credit for It: Why It May Be Easier for Men Than Women To Gain Influence at Work. *Human Resource Management*. 2018;57(4):839–854.

272. Guillen L. Is the Confidence Gap Between Men and Women a Myth? *Harvard Business Review*. March 26, 2018. https://hbr.org/2018/03/is-the-confidence-gap-between-men-and-women-a-myth.

273. Mill JS. *On Liberty*. In *The Collected Works of John Stuart Mill*, ed. John M. Robson. Toronto: University of Toronto Press;1963.

274. Appiah KA. *The Ethics of Identity*. Princeton, NJ: Princeton University Press;2005:71.

275. Appiah KA. *The Ethics of Identity*. Princeton, NJ: Princeton University Press;2005:194-195.

276. *The Complete Poems of Emily Dickinson*, 1583.

277. Rein V. *Patriarchy Stress Disorder: The Invisible Inner Barrier to Women's Happiness and Fulfillment*, Columbia, SC: Lioncrest Publishing;2019:265.

278. Bohn K. The Way New Women CEOs Are Announced May Shorten Their Tenure: Penn State Researchers Say The Endorsements May Trigger Stereotyping in Their New Role. Penn State News. June 16, 2021. www.psu.edu/news/research/story/way-new-women-ceos-are-announced-may-shorten-their-tenure/

279. Comprix J, Lopatta K, Tideman SA. The Role of Gender in the Aggressive Questioning of CEOs During Earnings Conference Calls. *The Accounting Review*. March 17, 2022. c709ac6f0a88f6a3a4e0cabf81bb5b978804ca33.pdf

280. Rogo-Gupta LJ, Haunschild C, Altamirano J. et.al. Physician Gender Is Associated with Press Ganey Patient Satisfaction Score in Outpatient Gynecology. *Women's Health Issues*. 2018;28:281–285. doi:10.1016/j.whi.2018.01.001.

281. Rowe SG, Steward MT, Van Horne S, et. al. Mistreatment Experiences, Protective Workplace Systems, and Occupational Distress in Physicians. *JAMA Network Open*. 2022;5(5):e2210768. doi:10.1001/jamanetworkopen.2022.10768.

282. Miller MK, Rauch JA, Kaplan T. (2016) Gender Differences in Movie Superheroes' Roles, Appearances, and Violence. *Ada: A Journal of Gender, New Media, and Technology*. Issue 10. doi:10.7264/N3HX19ZK

283. Miller J. Wiki Wars: Wikipedia's Inner Battles. BBC News. August 5, 2014. www.bbc.com/news/technology-28426674.

284. Sandler BR. The Chilly Climate. July 13, 2005. www.cic.uiuc.edu/groups/WISEPanel/archive/BestPractice/Best1Guidebook/chilly.

285. Peake B. WP: THREATENING2MEN: Misogynist Infopolitics and the Hegemony of the Asshole Consensus on English Wikipedia. *Ada: A Journal of Gender, New Media, and Technology*. 2015; Issue 7.

286. Carlana M. Implicit Stereotypes: Evidence from Teachers' Gender Bias. *The Quarterly Journal of Economics*. 2019;134(3):1163–1224. https://doi.org.10.1093/qje/qjz008.

287. Luigi G, Ferdinando M, Sapienza P, Zingales L. Culture, Gender, and Math. *Science*. 2008;320(5880):1164–1165.

288. Arabia J. Women in STEM Statistics to Inspire Future Leaders. Think Big Blog. Big Rentz. February 23, 2021. www.bigrentz.com/blog/women-in-stem-statistics.

289. Women in Science, Technology, Engineering, and Mathematics (STEM): Quick Take. *Catalyst*;2022. www.catalyst.org/research/women-in-science-technology-engineering-and-mathematics-stem.

290. Else H. Nearly Half of US Female Scientists Leave Full-Time Science After First Child. *Nature*. February 19, 2019. www.nature.com/articles/d41586-019-00611-1

291. Odei BC, Seldon C, Fernandez M, Rooney MK, et. al. Representation of Women in the Leadership Structure of the US Health Care System. *JAMA Netw Open*. 2021;4(11): e2136358. doi: 10/1001/jamenetworkopen.2021.36358.

292. Estes CP. *Women Who Run with the Wolves: Myths and Stories of the Wild Woman Archetype*. New York: Ballentine;1992:50.

293. Beard M *SPQR: A History of Ancient Rome*. New York: Liveright Publishing ;2015.

294. Beard M. *Women & Power: A Manifesto*. New York: Liveright Publishing Co.; 2017:86–87.

295. Beard M. *Women & Power: A Manifesto*. New York: Liveright Publishing Co.;2017:82.

296. Trevathan W. *Human Birth: An Evolutionary Perspective*. New York: Aldine de Gruyter;1987:108.

297. Shlian L. *Sex, Time and Power: How Women's Sexuality Shaped Human Evolution*. New York: Penguin Books;2003.

298. Graeber D, Wengrow D. *The Dawn of Everything: A New History of Humanity*, New York: Farrar, Strauss, and Giroux;2021:237.

299. Owen LR. Gender, Crafts, and the Reconstruction of Tool Use. *Helinium*. 1994; 34:186–200.

300. Graeber D, Wengrow D. *The Dawn of Everything: A New History of Humanity*, New York: Farrar, Strauss, and Giroux;2021:214-220.

301. Graeber D, Wengrow D. *The Dawn of Everything: A New History of Humanity*, New York: Farrar, Strauss, and Giroux;2021:221.

302. Robertson R. *The Enlightenment: The Pursuit of Happiness, 1680-1790*. New York: Harper Collins;2021:442.

303. Pomeroy SB. *Goddesses, Whores, Wives, and Slaves: Women in Classical Antiquity*. New York: Shocken Books;1995.

304. Law T. Women Are Now the Majority of the U.S. Workforce—But Working Women Still Face Serious Challenges. *Time*. January 16, 2020. https://time.com/5766787/women-workforce.

305. Connley C. Women's Labor Force Participation Rate Hit a 33-Year Low in January, According To New Analysis. CNBC. February 9, 2021. https://www.cnbc.com/2021/02/08/womens-labor-force-participation-rate-hit-33-year-low-in-january-2021.html.

306. Retailer Media Outlook 2022 Emerging Channel Spotlight. PWC Australia. www.pwc.com/workforcehopesandfears.

307. Kreimer S. Nurse Salaries Rise Amid Widening Gender Pay Gap and 'Precipitous Increase' In RNs Looking for the Exit. Fierce Healthcare. May 23, 2022. www.fiercehealthcare.com/providers/nurse-salaries-rise-amid-widiening-gender-pay-gap-and-preciptous-increase-rns-looking.

308. Avellar S, Smock P. Has the Price of Motherhood Declined Over Time? A Cross-Cohort Comparison of the Motherhood Wage Penalty. *Journal of Marriage and Family*. 2003;65(3):597–607.

309. Rutledge, MS Zulkarnain A, King SE. How Much Does Social Security Offset the Motherhood Penalty? Center for Retirement Research at Boston College. *Issue in Brief*. July 2021;21-11. https://crr.bc.edu/wp-content/uploads/2021/06/IB_21-11.pdf.

310. Gates M. *The Moment of Lift: How Empowering Women Changes the World*. New York: Flatiron Books;2019:116–117.

311. Campbell J. *Margaret Thatcher Volume 1: The Grocer's Daughter*. London: Jonathan Cape;2000:100.

312. Sandbrook D. Viewpoint: What If Margaret Thatcher Had Never Been? *BBC News Magazine*. June 8, 2013.

313. Thatcher M. Speech to Finchley Conservatives (Admits to Being an 'Iron Lady'). Margaret Thatcher Foundation. January 31, 1976. www.margaretthatcher.org/document/102947.

314. Oxford English Dictionary. OED.com

315. Moss V. How Margaret Thatcher Turned Her Handbag Into a Weapon. *Vogue*. November 27, 2020. www.vogue.co.uk/fashion/article/margaret-thatcher-handbag

316. Shaw B. Transcript: Interview with Margaret Thatcher. *World News.* June 30, 1997. http://edition.cnn.com/WORLD/9706/30/thatcher.transcript/.

317. Churchill Archives Centre. Margaret Thatcher: A Biography. The Thatcher Papers. Churchill College Archives Centre. https://archives.chu.cam.ac.uk/collections/thatcher-papers/thatcher-biography.

318. Churchill Archives Centre. Picture This #5—Baroness Thatcher's Handbag. www.cam.ac.uk/research/news/picture-this-5-baroness-thatchers-handbag-churchill-archive-centre.

319. Cochran A. Thatcher 'Tough as Nails' with a Warm Side, Colin Powell Says. CBS News. April 8, 2013.

320. Queen Elizabeth I's Speech to the Troops at Tilbury. www.rmg.co.uk/stories/topics/queen-elizabeth-speech-troops-tilbury.

321. Axelrod A. *Elizabeth I, CEO: Strategic Lessons from the Leader who Built an Empire.* Paramus, NJ: Prentice Hall Press;2000:242.

322. Borman T. Elizabeth I's Monarchy: Rule of a 'Weak and Feeble' Woman? The National Archives blog. November 1, 2016. https://blog.nationalarchives.gov.uk/elizabeth-monarchy-rule-weak-feeble-woman.

323. Massie RK. *Catherine the Great, Portrait of a Woman.* New York: Random House;2011:460.

324. Meehan-Waters B. Catherine the Great and the Problem of Female Rule. *The Russian Review.* 1995;34(3):293–307.

325. Ivleva V. Catherine II as Female Ruler: The Power of Enlightened Womanhood. *e-Journal of Eighteenth-Century Russian Studies.* 2015;3:20-46. https://iopn.library.illinois.edu/journals/vivliofika/article/view/584.

326. Puhak S. The Medieval Queens Whose Daring, Murderous Reigns Were Quickly Forgotten. *Smithsonian.* January-February 2022:86-97, 114.

327. Barnhart JN, Dafoe A, Saunders EN, Trager RF. The Suffragist Peace. *International Organization*;202074(4):633–670.

328. Goldstein JS. *War and Gender: How Gender Shapes the War System and Vice Versa.* New York: Cambridge University Press;2001.

329. Benenson JF, Webb CE, Wrangham RW. Self-Protection as an Adaptive Female Strategy. Behv Brain Sci. 2021;45:e128. doi: 10.1017/S0140525X21002417.

330. Edsall TB. The Gender Gap Is Taking Us to Unexpected Places. *The New York Times.* January 12, 2022.

331. Botelho EL, Powell KR. *The CEO Next Door.* New York: Currency;2018:11.

332. Lean In. Women in the Workplace 2021. Lean In. https://leanin.org/women-in-the-workplace/2021

333. McKinsey. A CEO's Guide to Gender Equality. *McKinsey Quarterly Executive Briefing.* November 1, 2015.

334. Kane L. Medscape Physician Compensation Report 2022: Incomes Gain, Pay Gaps Remain. Medscape. April 15, 2022. https://www.medscape.com/slideshow/2022-compensation-overview-6015043?icd=ssl_login_success_221103

335. Hess A. Mommy Is Going Away for a While. *New York Times.* January 14, 2022. www.nytimes.com/2022/01/14/movies/bad-moms-lost-daughter.html

336. Eunice Kennedy Shriver National Institute of Child Health and Human Development, NIH, DHHS. (2006). The NICHD Study of Early Child Care and Youth Development (SECCYD). Findings for Children up to Age 4 ½ Years (05-4318). Washington, DC: U.S. Government Printing Office;2006.

337. Lake R. How Long Is the Average Maternity Leave? The Balance. March 31, 2020. www.thebalancemoney.com/how-long-is-the-average-maternity-leave-4590252.

338. Frank E, Zhao Z, Fang Y. Experiences of Work-Family Conflict and Mental Health Symptoms by Gender Among Physician Parents During the COVID-19 Pandemic. *JAMA Netw Open.* 2021;4(11):e2134315. doi:10.1001/jamanetworkopen.2021.34315.

339. Narisetti R. Joann S. Lublin on Lessons for Working Mothers, Their Families, and Their Employers. McKinsey & Company. March 31, 2021www.mckinsey.com/featured-insights/mckinsey-on-books/author-talks-joann-lublin-on-lessons-for-working-mothers-their-families-and-their-employers.

340. Dandar VM, Lautenberger DM, Garrison G. Exploring Faculty Equity at U.S. Medical Schools by Gender and Race/Ethnicity. Association of American Medical Colleges. October 2021. www.aamc.org/data-reports/workforce/report/exploring-faculty-salary-equity-us-medical-schools-gender-and-race/ethnicity.

341. Gottlieb AS, Jagsi R. Closing the Gender Pay Gap in Medicine. *NEJM.* 2021;385(27):2501–2504. doi: 10.1056/NEJMp2114955.

342. Friedan B. *The Feminine Mystique,* 5ᵗʰ ed. New York: WW Norton and Company; 2013:xxii.

343. Friedan B. *The Feminine Mystique,* 5ᵗʰ ed. New York: WW Norton and Company; 2013:464.

344. Friedan B. *The Feminine Mystique,* 5ᵗʰ ed. New York: WW Norton and Company; 2013:465.

345. Wen L. *Lifelines: A Doctor's Journey in the Fight for Public Health.* New York: Henry Holt and Company, Metropolitan Books;2021:218.

346. Wen L. *Lifelines: A Doctor's Journey in the Fight for Public Health.* New York: Henry Holt and Company, Metropolitan Books;2021:220-221.

347. Paul EL. *Taking Sides: Clashing Views on Controversial Issues in Sex and Gender,* 2nd ed. Guilford, CT: McGraw-Hill/Dushkin;2002:xii–xxi.

348. Roscoe W. How to Become a Berdache: Toward a Unified Analysis of Gender Diversity. In *Third Sex, Third Gender: Beyond Sexual Dimorphism in Culture and History,* G. Herdt, ed. New York: Zone Books;1993:329–372.

349. Roscoe W. How to Become a Berdache: Toward a Unified Analysis of Gender Diversity. In *Third Sex, Third Gender: Beyond Sexual Dimorphism in Culture and History.* New York: Zone Books;1993:13.

350. Wikipedia. Florence Nightingale. https://en.wikipedia.org/wiki/Florence_Nightingale.

351. Bolick K. Clara Barton Epitomized the Heroism of Nurses. *Smithsonian.* December 2021:9–11.

352. Sabri N. The Truth and Challenges of Being a Doctor Mom. KevinMD.com. April 25, 2019. www.kevinmd.com/2019/04/the-truth-and-challenges-of-being-a-doctor-mom.html

353. Liu S. Life of Dr. Mom. Lifeofdrmom.com. December 29, 2021.

354. Gottenborg E. You Can't Have It All: On Being a Doctor Mom. University of Colorado School of Medicine News. April 2019. https://medschool.cuanschutz.edu/deans-office/cu-med-today/featuresarchives/doctor-moms-can't-have-it-all.

355. Catalyst. The Double-Bind Dilemma for Women In Leadership: Damned if You Do, Doomed if You Don't. Catalyst. July 15, 2007. www.catalyst.org/research/the-double-bind-dilemma-for-women-in-leadership-damned-if-you-do-doomed-if-you-dont/

356. Catalyst. The Double-Bind Dilemma for Women In Leadership: Damned if You Do, Doomed if You Don't. Catalyst. July 15, 2007:7. www.catalyst.org/research/the-double-bind-dilemma-for-women-in-leadership-damned-if-you-do-doomed-if-you-dont.

357. Heider AL. *The Rise and Fall of Dr. Mom*, Bloomington IN: Author House;2006:3.

358. Heider AL. *The Rise and Fall of Dr. Mom*, Bloomington IN: Author House;2006:13.

359. Heider AL. *The Rise and Fall of Dr. Mom*, Bloomington IN: Author House;2006:14.

360. Heider AL. *The Rise and Fall of Dr. Mom*, Bloomington IN: Author House;2006:149-150.

361. Wild D. US Docs at Double the Risk of Postpartum Depression. Medscape. Medscape.com, May 9, 2022. www.medscape.com/viewarticle/973632.

362. Goldberg M. The Means of Reproduction: Sex, Power, and the Future of the World. New York: Penguin Books; 2009.

363. Wills G. Women's Burden. *The American Scholar*. Spring 2022:31. https://theamericanscholar.org/womens-burden.

364. Wallace DF. This Is Water (Full Transcript and Audio). David Foster Wallace blog. https://fs.blog/david-foster-wallace-this-is-water.

365. Politis M, Runswick E, Costache C, Rampersad L, et al. Slang Use in the ICU: We Are Women, Not Girls. *BMJ*. 2022:376 doi: https://doi.org/10.1136/bmj.o174

366. Smith A. NYC Mayor to 'Charging Bull' Artist: 'Fearless Girl Is Staying Put.' CNN Money. April 12, 2017. https://money.cnn.com/2017/04/12/news/charging-bull-fearless-girl/index.html.

367. Dobnik V. Will New York Invite the 'Fearless Girl' Statue to Stay on Wall Street? *USA Today*. March 27, 2017.

368. Cutler A, Scott DR. Speaker Sex and Perceived Apportionment of Talk. *Applied Psycholinguistics*. 1990;11(3): 253–272.

369. Allen J. Gender Bias in Lecture Acoustics. Hospital Medical Director. Medical Education blog. November 12, 2019. https://hospitalmedicaldirector.com/gender-bias-in-lecture-acoustics.

370. Brescoll VL. Who Takes the Floor and Why: Gender, Power, and Volubility in Organizations. *Administrative Science Quarterly*. 2012;56(4). https://doi.org/10.1177/0001839212439994.

371. Miller M. This App Uses AI to Track Mansplaining in Your Meetings. Fast Company. March 8, 2017. www.fastcompany.com/3068794/this-app-uses-ai-to-track-mansplaining-during-your-meetings#:~:text=For%20that%2C%20it%20designed%20an,by%20male%20and%20female%20speakers. March 8, 2017.

372. Advisory Board. How Often Are Women Interrupted By Men? Here's What the Research Says. *Advisory Board Daily Briefing*. July 7, 2017. www.advisory.com/daily-briefing/2017/07/07/men-interrupting-women.

373. Krajeski J. This Is Water. *The New Yorker*. September 19, 2008.

374. Hobgood C, Dauker C. Gender Differences in Experiences of Leadership Emergence Among Emergency Medicine Department Chairs. *JAMA Network Open*. 2022;5(3):e221860. doi:10.1001/jamanetworkopen.2022.1860.

375. Wills G. Women's Burden. *The American Scholar*. Spring 2022:27. https://theamericanscholar.org/womens-burden.

376. McChrystal S. *Team of Teams: New Rules of Engagement for a Complex World*. New York: Penguin;2015: 112.

377. Conniff R. The Undaunted: How a Team of Fearless American Women Overcame Medical Skepticism to Stop a Deadly Infectious Disease and Save Countless Lives. *Smithsonian*. March 2022:22-31.

378. Vine S. "Have It All" Mea Culpa Is Too, Little, Too Late for Girls Today. Daily Mail. March 19, 2022. www.dailymail.co.uk/debate/article-10631475/SARAH-VINE-mea-culpa-little-late-girls-today.html.

379. Roider E. Women in Science Can and Should 'Have It All.' Cell Mentor. October 8, 2021. https://crosstalk.cell.com/blog/women-in-science-can-and-should-have-it-all.

380. Man Who Has It All. Blog. https://www.patreon.com/manwhohasitall

381. Hampden-Turner C. *Creating Corporate Culture: From Discord to Harmony*. Reading, MA: Addison-Wesley;1992:167.

382. Bolman LG, Deal TE. *Reframing Organizations: Artistry, Choice, and Leadership*, San Francisco, CA: John Wiley and Sons;2008:10.

383. Dane E, Pratt MG Exploring Intuition and Its Role in Managerial Decision Making. *Academy of Management Review*. 2007;32(1):33–54.

384. Lockwood T. *Design Thinking: Integrating Innovation, Customer Experience, and Brand Value*. New York: Allworth Press;2010:xi.

385. Pink DH. *A Whole New Mind*. New York: Penguin;2006:97.

386. Pink DH. *A Whole New Mind*. New York: Penguin;2006:72.

387. Stanford N. *Guide to Organizational Design: Creating High-Performing and Adaptable Enterprises*. New York: Bloomberg Press;2007:14–17.

388. Pink DH. *A Whole New Mind*. New York: Penguin;2006:102.

389. Pink DH. *A Whole New Mind*. New York: Penguin;2006:105.

390. Morgan G. *Images of Organization*. San Francisco:Berrett-Koehler;1998:171.

391. Lim W H, Wong Ch, Cong CS. The Unspoken Reality of Gender Bias in Surgery: A Qualitative Systematic Review. PLoS One. 2021;16(2): e0246420.ncbi.nim.nih.gov

392. Nam CS, Daignault-Newton S, Herrel LA, et.al. The Future Is Female: Urology Workforce Projections from 2020 to 2060. *Urology*. 2021;50:30–34.

393. ACLU.org. Tribute: The Legacy of Ruth Bader Ginsburg and WRP Staff.

394. Stacy F. Op-ed: 'RGB' Would Certainly Encourage Women To Take Control of Their Finances. cnbc.com. March 20, 2021.

395. Shanafelt TD, West CP, Sinksy C, et.al. Changes in Burn Out and Satisfaction with Work-Life Integration in Physicians and the General US Working Population Between 2011 and 2017. *Mayo Clinic Proc*. 2019;94(9):1681–1694.

396. Cavanaught K, Cline D, Belfer B, Chang S, Thomas E, Picard T, Holladay CL. The Positive Impact of Mentoring Burnout: Organizational Research and Best Practices. *Journal of Interprofessional Education and Practice.* 2022;28: 100521.

397. Fainstad T, Mann A, Suresh K, Shah P, et al. Effect of a Novel Online Group-Coaching Program to Reduce Burnout in Female Resident Physicians. *JAMA Network Open.* 2022;5(5): e2210752.

398. Cohen TE. One in Three Women Attempt to Break the Glass Ceiling, But Fewer than Half Succeed. Triplepundit.com

399. Center for Creative Leadership. Women Need a Network of Champions. ccl.org.

400. Marx J. Tackling the Glass Ceiling. professionalwomanmag.com

401. Babic A, Hansez I. The Glass Ceiling for Women Managers: Antecedents and Consequences for Work-Family Interact and Well-Being at Work." *Frontiers in Psychology.* 2021;12:618250.

402. Netemeyer RG. Booles JS, McMurrian R. Development and Validation of Work-Family Conflict and Family-Work Conflict Scales. *Journal of Applied Psychology.* 1996;81:400–410.

CPSIA information can be obtained
at www.ICGtesting.com
Printed in the USA
LVHW010737160523
747042LV00015B/1578